The Life of Isabel Crawford

The Life of
ISABEL CRAWFORD

More Than I Asked For

MARILYN FÄRDIG WHITELEY

Foreword by Paul R. Dekar

☙PICKWICK *Publications* · Eugene, Oregon

THE LIFE OF ISABEL CRAWFORD
More Than I Asked For

Copyright © 2015 by Marilyn Färdig Whiteley. All rights reserved. Except for brief quotations in critical publications or reviews, no part of this book may be reproduced in any manner without prior written permission from the publisher. Write: Permissions, Wipf and Stock Publishers, 199 W. 8th Ave., Suite 3, Eugene, OR 97401.

Pickwick Publications
An Imprint of Wipf and Stock Publishers
199 W. 8th Ave., Suite 3
Eugene, OR 97401

www.wipfandstock.com

ISBN 13: 978-1-4982-0222-0

Cataloging-in-Publication data:

Whiteley, Marilyn Färdig, 1936–.

    The life of Isabel Crawford : more than I asked for / Marilyn Färdig Whiteley ; foreword by Paul R. Dekar.

    xiv + 212 p. ; 23 cm. Includes bibliographical references and index.

    ISBN 13: 978-1-4982-0222-0

    1. Crawford, Isabel, 1865–1961. 2. Women missionaries—Oklahoma—Biography. I. Dekar, Paul R. II. Title.

E99.K5 W47 2015

Manufactured in the U.S.A.

Permission to use quotations and photographs has been granted by the American Baptist Historical Society, Atlanta, Georgia. Permission to use photographs has been granted by Barbara Cross McKinnon, Guelph, Ontario.

To the memory of my parents,
Marion Ross Färdig and Francis Färdig,
whose ideals and whose reminiscences about Bacone College
taught me more than I realized.

When Spurgeon became a Baptist his mother said "Well Charles we did pray that you would become a Christian but we never prayed that you would become a Baptist," and Sturgeon replied "That is always the way with the Lord, Mother. He always gives us more than we ask." I've got more than I asked for but I'll go.

—Isabel Crawford, Journal 1897–98

Contents

List of Illustrations | ix
Foreword by Paul R. Dekar | xi
Preface | xiii

    Introduction | 1
1. The Early Years | 10
2. On the Prairies | 22
3. Training for Mission | 38
4. Elk Creek | 54
5. Saddle Mountain | 68
6. The "Jesus Eat" | 85
7. Transition: New Work | 100
8. New York Reservations | 119
9. Coast to Coast | 135
10. Interlude Abroad | 144
11. Looking toward the Future | 154
12. Transition: Retirement | 168
13. At Home in Ontario | 189
    Epilogue | 197

Bibliography | 199
Index | 205

Illustrations

John Crawford and Sarah Louise Hackett Crawford | 12
Crawford house in Woodstock, Ontario | 15
Emily Crawford Cline, Frances Crawford Firstbrook, Hugh Crawford, and Isabel Crawford | 29
Nep, the Crawford family dog | 32
Isabel Crawford on horseback | 34
Isabel Crawford during her years at the Baptist Missionary Training School | 42
The Baptist Missionary Training School as pictured on the diploma of Isabel Crawford | 49
Gathering for the dedication of the Saddle Mountain Baptist Church, 1903 | 83
Saddle Mountain Baptist Church | 84
Lucius Aitsan and Isabel Crawford | 86
Lucius Aitsan | 97
Plate painted by Isabel Crawford | 103
Clifton Springs Sanitarium newspaper advertisement, 1906 | 104
Isabel Crawford in Kiowa costume signing the Twenty-third Psalm | 106
Isabel Crawford and Jack Crawford at Camp Adams | 107
Isabel Crawford in costume at a girls' camp at Northfield, Massachusetts, 1909 | 109
Isabel Crawford (marked with X) at the Grand Canyon, 1912 | 114
Isabel Crawford painting the church at Red House, New York, 1920 | 133
Chautauqua Home Reading Course graduation photograph of Isabel Crawford, 1922 | 138
Isabel Crawford with her doll Pal | 147

Perry Jackson with his wife and child | 163
Isabel Crawford's retirement photo | 170
Isabel Crawford with Mrs. Lone Wolf | 171
Isabel Crawford at the Kansas City Baptist Theological Seminary | 173
Isabel Crawford with a friend at the Mayo Clinic | 177
Isabel Crawford at her Florida apartment | 178
Elmcroft, Grimsby Beach, Ontario | 189
Bookcase in Elmcroft, with Isabel Crawford's journals | 191
Home on Nelles Boulevard, Grimsby, Ontario | 193
Isabel Crawford in her room in Grimsby, Ontario | 195

Foreword

Isabel Crawford spent thirteen years as a Christian evangelist and teacher in Oklahoma. Those she served remember her by her Indian name, Geeahhoangomay: she gave us the Jesus way. Crawford refused to accept the disparaging of First Peoples characteristic of her time and was relieved of her posting after she allowed Lucius Aitsan to lead a communion service. Subsequently, he was ordained as a minister and became one of the most influential Kiowa Christians, only to die in the 1918 flu epidemic.

In his introduction to a reprint edition of Crawford's *Kiowa. A Woman Missionary in Indian Territory* (Lincoln, 1998), historian Clyde Ellis observed that Crawford displayed a level of cultural sensitivity rare for the era. Isabel Crawford once wrote, "We are not here to boss the Indians, but to do what they let us ... no person has a right to domineer over them." (xv)

Almost completely deaf, Crawford overcame personal adversity to empower Kiowa of Oklahoma, where she taught practical skills, including farming, that enabled Indians to support themselves as their former ways of life gave way to more settled living arrangements. She also worked among Indians in the Finger Lakes area of New York and in the Pacific Northwest.

In her later years of retirement, Crawford returned to her native Canada, living in Grimsby, Ontario, near Hamilton where I taught at McMaster University. I learned that her father had taught at one of the antecedent institutions, the Canadian Literary Institute in Woodstock. Lois Tupper, my colleague at the Divinity School and the first woman tenured at a Canadian theological school, spoke of her friendship with Crawford, who had continued to champion the rights of Indians in retirement.

The original area that Crawford served in Oklahoma is now pastureland near the Wichita Range. Pulitzer Prize-winning author N. Scott Momaday captures the beauty and magic of the area in his book *The Way to Rainy Mountain* (Albuquerque 1969): "I have walked in a mountain meadow bright with Indian paintbrush, lupine, and wild buckwheat, and I have seen high in the branches of a lodgepole pine the male pine grosbeak, round and rose-colored, its dark, striped wings nearly invisible in the soft, mottled light. And the uppermost branches of the tree seemed very slowly to ride across the blue sky" (23).

In such a setting, as Dr. Whiteley describes in her introduction to this well-researched, well-written, and timely book, in 1961, a group of people gathered to witness the burial of someone who had come home to rest in the graveyard of the Saddle Mountain Baptist Church. A woman in her seventies had accompanied the casket from Canada. The service was conducted in two languages, Kiowa and English. The gravestone marks the event: "Isabel Crawford, 1864–1961, 'I dwell among my own people.'"

Paul R. Dekar
Niswonger Professor Emeritus of Evangelism and Mission
Memphis Theological Seminary

Preface

IN 2003, I HAPPILY accepted the invitation of Susan Hill Lindley to write a number of biographical sketches for the *Westminster Handbook to Women in American Religious History*. But on the list that she and Eleanor J. Stebner presented me, there was a mystery: Isabel Alice Hartley Crawford. They directed me to an entry in a biographical dictionary, and the mystery was solved. Then my problem was to limit myself to the specified 150 words.

I was intrigued by Crawford and wanted to learn more. Finally, when I had completed other projects, I began to read works by and about this articulate woman. As I shared my discoveries in academic papers and with friends, I was encouraged to write Crawford's biography. Although she published three biographical writings, none presented the full story of her life. And yet, not only did she keep journals for approximately fifty years, but she took care that they would be preserved. She wanted her life story to be understood and made known.

As I worked, I recognized personal connections that heightened my interest in Crawford's story. My mother's father had homesteaded in Kiowa County during the time Crawford worked there. My parents met while teaching at Bacone College, sponsored, like Crawford's mission, by the American Baptist Church. There, in 1931, my father directed a pageant of Indian history; my mother was also closely connected with it. One episode, titled "Early Missionaries to Western Oklahoma," told of the Kiowa chief Lone Wolf's appeal to the Baptists to send missionaries. My parents had known something of the story! And when my mother was nearing her death, she asked me to look among her papers for an Indian version of the Twenty-third Psalm; she wanted it read at her funeral. Only much later, as I read Crawford's journals, did I realize that this was written by Crawford herself, putting into English what she signed when she presented the psalm in Plains Indian sign language.

I had much help as I went about my task. The Isabel Crawford papers are a prized holding of the American Baptist Archives, and when I began work, they were located in Rochester, New York. When the archives moved to Atlanta, my research trips had to become very efficient, but the staff was extremely helpful. My husband and I now think of Jan Ballard, Betsy Dunbar, and Deborah Van Broekhoven as friends.

Other archives, too, proved useful, and I thank Gavin W. Kleespies of the Cambridge (Massachusetts) Historical Society; Adam McCulloch and Gordon Heath at the Canadian Baptist Archives in Hamilton, Ontario; and volunteers at the Grimsby (Ontario) Historical Society. In Grimsby, I read the excellent family history done by Doris Cline Ward, grandniece of Isabel Crawford, and one highlight of my research occurred when my husband and I were privileged to visit her in Asheville, North Carolina. I appreciate her skill, her enthusiasm, and her generosity. Then through Ward I learned of her cousin, Barbara Cross McKinnon. To my surprise, she lives in Guelph, Ontario, where I live; to my amazement, she has further notebooks of Isabel Crawford, including an unpublished manuscript written when Crawford was ninety. These she generously shared with me, and there is no way I can adequately express my gratitude.

All through the journey I was sustained by the support of friends who encouraged me with their interest and reinforced my determination to share Crawford's story. I fear omitting some if I tried to name them, but to all I give my heartfelt thanks. I especially appreciate the support of Paul Dekar and the skillful copyediting of our daughter-in-law, P. Rose Primeau, who helped save me from myself. Of course I take responsibility for whatever errors remain.

In my academic work as in my daily living, I have been wonderfully supported my husband, Hugh, but in this endeavor he took on new roles. He not only provided his usual steady and strong encouragement, but he also worked out the logistics of our travel. Furthermore, this retired professor of water resource engineering turned into an outstanding historical researcher. It is only due to him that I have been able to write the life story of Isabel Crawford, and I am profoundly grateful.

Introduction

IN LATE NOVEMBER, THE grasses are golden brown on the prairies near the Kiowa cemetery at Saddle Mountain, Oklahoma, and on the hills beyond. To the south, on the mountain that gives the area its name, autumn foliage lends a note of color. It was here, at this season in 1961, that a group of people gathered to witness the burial of someone who had come from Canada to rest there, and the memorial service was conducted in two languages, Kiowa and English. A gravestone marks the event:

Isabel Crawford

1864–1961

I dwell among mine own people

Yet unlike those buried around her, Isabel Crawford was not a Kiowa Indian, and though she had lived and worked at Saddle Mountain, she had left there fifty-five years earlier, returning only occasionally for brief visits. A token of her distance from the place appears in a mistake on the marker itself, for Crawford was born not in 1864, but in 1865. But the tombstone bears the inscription carved into it at her request: Isabel Crawford saw the Kiowas of Saddle Mountain as her "own people," and here she wished to rest.

Isabel Crawford was born in Ontario, Canada, the daughter of a Scots-Irish father and an Irish mother. They had met and married in England and left there several years before Isabel's birth because Britain offered poor prospects for a Baptist preacher. Isabel grew up in Ontario; in her teens she moved with her parents first to Manitoba and then to North Dakota. When she was eighteen, she became seriously ill, and the quinine intended to restore her to health robbed her of much of her hearing. Nevertheless, she attended the Baptist Missionary Training School in Chicago, and following her graduation in 1893, Isabel accepted an assignment from the Women's Baptist Home Mission Society to work among the "Blanket Indians" at

Elk Creek in the Oklahoma Territory.[1] After two-and-a-half years there, she accepted an invitation to move thirty miles east to Saddle Mountain, where there was a larger Kiowa community but no missionary. There she succeeded in making converts, and without calling for outside assistance, they built a neat frame church that celebrated its official opening on Easter of 1903. Soon, however, this success was shadowed by controversy. Feeling that her authority had been undermined, Crawford resigned her post and left Saddle Mountain in December of 1906.

Crawford's conflict was with the denominational society, the American Baptist Home Mission Society, and it did not cause her to stop working for the women's association. She spent the next twenty-three years under its employ, traveling to speak on behalf of missions in local churches and at regional meetings, and working with the Senecas in western New York. Through all these years, however, she spoke regularly about the time she had spent in Oklahoma. She frequently appeared in Kiowa dress and usually ended her presentations with the Twenty-third Psalm in Plains Indian sign language.

In 1915, Crawford published a book, *Kiowa: Story of a Blanket Indian Mission*. She retired in 1930, and two years later she published a second book, *A Jolly Journal*. It included sections on her childhood and on the years that she lived with her parents in North Dakota, but its final section related more of her experiences among the Kiowas. Through her speaking and writing, Crawford entered firmly into the memory of the American Baptists. Even at the age of eighty-six, when Crawford was confined to a wheelchair and had limited eyesight, she published another book, *Joyful Journey: Highlights on the High Way*. In it she recounted still more memories of her years among the Kiowa.

Isabel Crawford also visited the Kiowas whenever she could. As she approached retirement, she felt a strong desire to return to Saddle Mountain, to assist on the mission in any way possible and to remain there for the rest of her days. However, the animosity felt toward her by executive members of the American Baptist Home Mission Society had not abated over the

---

1. Journal 1893–94, letter from Mary Burdette, June 23, 1893, opposite page 1. The writings of Isabel Crawford are found in the Isabel Crawford Collection of the denominational archives of the American Baptist Historical Society (ABHS). The collection includes Crawford's journals and diaries from 1891 through 1948 as well as one unlabeled journal from 1954. In addition, the collection contains a number of notebooks, generally three-ring binders. Any footnote that does not include another specific reference is from the Isabel Crawford Collection of the ABHS. Each note gives the name of the book (e.g., Journal 1902), followed by whatever specific location is provided; sometimes the date of the entry is available, sometimes the page number(s), and sometimes both.

years, and that group exerted pressure on what was now called the Woman's American Baptist Home Mission Society to forbid Crawford's return to the site of her earlier work.[2] Bitterly she complained that for the second time, "God's plan" for her life was "completely wrecked."[3]

She was barred from fulfilling that desire, but her retirement quarters first in Florida and then in Ontario gave witness to her continuing interest in that segment of her past: in each she devoted significant space to her collection of Indian artifacts. Crawford's role as a missionary to the Kiowas remained central to her identity; though the decision about her burial and grave marker was made decades before her death, she continued during the rest of her days to think of the Saddle Mountain Christians as her own people.

How then are we to understand the life of Isabel Crawford? It might be seen as a narrative of early success followed by years of struggle and even failure, with Crawford clinging tenaciously to the memory of her long-ago triumph. Yet Isabel Crawford's life is more complex than that, and she wanted to be understood. She not only published three autobiographical writings: she kept journals covering more than fifty years of her life, spent much time editing them, and made plans for their care.

Crawford started writing in a journal in 1891, while she was a student at the Baptist Missionary Training School in Chicago. Students were instructed to keep journals to prepare them for the years to come when they would be required to send back regular reports of their missionary activities. Crawford's early entries described her experiences as she went out every Thursday afternoon on the "visit of mercy" that was part of her missionary training.[4] Soon, however, Crawford began to write of other experiences beyond her field work. When she left Chicago, the book went with her, and over the years she added volume after volume to her collection. While Crawford often wrote daily, she sometimes neglected writing for shorter or longer periods of time. Occasionally she simply left a hole in the record, but often she attempted to rectify the omission. When she did this, she often wrote with such immediacy that it is difficult to tell when the entries were penned.

Crawford added clippings, photos, letters, and greeting cards. Some of these she pasted in as she wrote. Others result from her later editing, when

---

2. The two geographically-based American Baptist women's home mission societies merged in 1909 and took the name of the eastern group, the Woman's American Baptist Home Mission Society.

3. Crawford to Westfall, June 23, 1927, Crawford, Correspondence, Katherine S. Westfall Files. See chapter 11.

4. Journal 1891–93, 2.

she might add an obituary, for example, to an account she had written earlier. The latter part of many of the journals became scrapbooks, their pages covered with poems, jokes, long articles, and short tidbits of information. She also compiled separate notebooks on a variety of subjects: albums of photos and postcards from various parts of the United States; Indian legends carefully copied by hand; correspondence regarding her books *Kiowa* and *A Jolly Journal*; collections on various subjects such as "War," "Baptists," and "Temperance"; and a book of "Pet Poetry." Some of these include Crawford's own observations while others do not, but all give evidence of her varied interests and concerns.

Crawford's journals served as source books for the missionary reports she was required to file, as well as for her three books. They helped her recall colorful details of her labors among the Kiowa and later among the Indians of western New York. While she was traveling and speaking on behalf of the woman's mission society, she recorded the details of her often demanding itineraries. Thus when she wrote reports, she was able to include vivid descriptions of her work over the past three months or year, and she could also look over her records and proclaim wearily, "I spoke 50 times last Oct. & slept in 28 different beds."[5]

While Crawford inscribed in her journals things she knew would be useful to share, she also committed to them thoughts and incidents that she would never publish. Early in 1907, in the first months after she left Saddle Mountain, she reread her journals and proclaimed them "full of horrid experiences that would better remain out of print."[6] Only in the privacy of her journal could she acknowledge her anger and her tears.[7] She also reported opposition more freely in her journal than in her correspondence and reports; these things did not become part of her public record.

At other times, her journals are noteworthy, not for what she wrote, but for what she omitted. The journals include information about her earlier history as do two separate brief biographies.[8] Nowhere, however, did Crawford mention that she was once engaged to be married. Yet according to G. W. Huntley, who wrote a recommendation for Crawford when she applied for admission to the Baptist Missionary Training School, it was "generally understood" that she was engaged to William Waldo when she left North

5. Journal 1908–10, pasted in at 196–97.
6. Journal 1906–8, February 4, 41.
7. For example, "Next day when Lucius returned from the station with only the women & no 'Jesus man' my heart rebelled & I went upstairs and had a good big cry" (Journal 1903–5, 127–28).
8. The Isabel Crawford collection of Journals and Diaries in the ABHS archives includes both an unsigned "Autobiography" and a "Life Story."

INTRODUCTION 5

Dakota.⁹ This Crawford probably omitted because since she and Waldo did *not* marry, it did not form an important part of her life story.

A more significant silence concerns her financial affairs and ownership of property. In 1895, she filed on land in Oklahoma, but even in her journals she made but scant reference to her "farm," and she did not mention it at all in her public writing. Similarly she noted only obliquely that she bought a lot in Florida and later sold it, and she did not mention at all that for years she owned the house in Oklahoma where her brother and his family lived. Yet when she died, she left an estate of $60,000. Using family sources, Doris Cline Ward, a grand-niece of Isabel Crawford and a skilled genealogical researcher, has written that while Crawford was in Oklahoma "working for a pittance of salary that was all the Missionary Society could afford, oil was discovered on Indian land. She bought a few pennies worth of shares, and laid the foundation for financial security in her old age."¹⁰

No one but Crawford can know for certain the reason for these silences, but Cline's reference to "a pittance of salary that was all the Missionary Society could afford" may offer a clue. Salaries were small and missionaries were self-sacrificing: this was the common—and accurate—perception. It seems likely that even to Crawford it may have appeared a bit unseemly, a bit worldly, to possess independent resources. Thus she recorded only the barest facts about her holdings, and her silences, as well as her words, became part of the record that she left for others to interpret.

Crawford did not consider her narrative to be fixed and inviolable, and she frequently reported working on her journals. Many insertions above the line or in the margin, often made in pencil or by a thicker or thinner pen nib, provide ample evidence of her editorial work. As she made corrections and additions, Crawford was preparing to share her records. Bound into the beginning of her 1947–48 journal is a handwritten note: "This journal is a continuation of the others in Chicago after the others were sent."¹¹ The place where she had trained for mission work and from which she had been sent out to Oklahoma seemed the right place for their safekeeping.

Yet the story is not quite so simple. In 1952, when Crawford traveled to Oklahoma for the sixtieth anniversary celebration of Rainy Mountain mission, she took with her seven volumes to leave with Tully Morrison, member of the Saddle Mountain congregation and librarian of the church.¹²

---

9. Application, Crawford, Biographical Files.
10. Ward, *Ancestry of Emily (Crawford) Cline*, Isabel Crawford section, 67.
11. Journal 1947–48, bound into the beginning of the book.
12. Wright, "Notes on Saddle Mountain Mission," 318.

Through these, Morrison learned about Crawford's life.[13] And in 1958, retired business man and avid historian Hugh D. Corwin published an article, "Saddle Mountain Mission and Church," in the *Chronicles of Oklahoma*. His sources included "letters from Miss Isabel Crawford and her personal Diary and a scrapbook of clippings kept by her during ten years as a missionary at Saddle Mountain."[14] These were apparently at least part of the material Crawford had placed at Saddle Mountain six years earlier. No surviving records indicate what items Crawford sent to Chicago, what she took to Oklahoma, and whether she retrieved some of her initial deposit. Her desire is clear, however: she wanted to share her story.

When Crawford wrote *Kiowa*, she was determined that she would "*never—never—never write one syllable that will bring unkind criticism on anybody!*" She went on to promise, "The Book shall end in victory so above the clash of dischord [sic] that no dischord [sic] shall be distinguishable."[15] She was true to her word. She never wrote of the controversy that caused her to leave: not in *Kiowa*, not in her later books, and not in any of her published reports. However in her private journals and in her 1896–1906 diary, she recorded the full, bitter story. When sufficient time had passed, she made this record available for posterity.

Of course it was not only her experience as a missionary that she presented to potential readers: through what she collected, copied, and pasted, and even more through what she wrote, Crawford inscribed herself in these writings. In her *Joyful Journey*, she described herself as possessing "a cast-iron constitution, a Scotch backbone, and a fully developed Irish

---

13. In 1961, speaking at Crawford's burial service, Morrison referred to the "seven volumes of material" through which he had learned the details of her life (Ward, *Ancestry of Emily (Crawford) Cline*, Isabel Crawford section, 67). Although the "seven volumes" cannot be identified, the mention of a diary is of particular interest. Most of Crawford's accounts are called journals, but three bear the name of diary. The entries in the 1896–97 diary place it neatly between the 1894–96 journal and the 1897–98 journal; similarly, the 1905 diary entries are for the time between the 1903–5 journal and the 1905–6 journal. The 1896–1906 diary is an anomaly, covering the entire period that Crawford was at Saddle Mountain. This is the same period that Crawford wrote about in her book, *Kiowa*, though *Kiowa* includes material that is not in the diary, so the diary is not simply a source book, let alone a rough draft, of the published work. There is no internal indication as to when Crawford compiled it. Since Corwin stated that he used Crawford's "personal Diary," this 1896–1906 diary appears to be that source.

14. Corwin, "Saddle Mountain Mission," 113. In the same year, Corwin also published *The Kiowa Indians: Their History & Life Stories*; it included a chapter on the Saddle Mountain mission. In his introduction to the volume, he listed Miss Isabel Crawford among those "who contributed letters and items" (ibid., *Kiowa Indians*, 6).

15. Journal 1906–8, February 4, 1907, 42.

funny-bone."[16] This was the "self" that she presented to the public, and many times in her journals she illustrated these traits. She also presented herself as called by God. The day after Crawford arrived at the Missionary Training School in Chicago, Mary Burdette, corresponding secretary of the Women's Baptist Home Mission Society, said to her, "I hope the Lord has called you and that you will bring great honor to His name."[17] Although Crawford had never before heard anyone say that *women* could be called to service, she quickly came to recognize that this accurately reflected her experience, and throughout her remaining years, she understood her life in this way.

Crawford's writings show her as a woman with wide-ranging interests and insatiable curiosity. She attended circuses, Wild West shows, and movies, and once she took some friends to a flea circus. She called upon hymn writer Fanny Crosby and cowboy artist Charles Russell. She went to see Jumbo the elephant a few days before his untimely death, and years later she visited his stuffed remains in a museum. On her one trip abroad she rode a camel in Egypt, flew as a passenger across the English Channel, and attempted to kiss the Blarney Stone. She delighted in both art and nature, and the extensive lists of books she read attest to the variety of her interests.

These broad interests point to an apparent contradiction in Crawford's nature, for theologically she was a conservative within her own denomination. Crawford counted herself a Fundamentalist, and in her journals she expressed disapproval of those Baptists who were deserting the traditional faith and becoming modernists. Yet she did not cut herself off from popular culture. She reveled in those aspects of it that she judged moral or harmless, and only avoided and criticized that which transgressed propriety.

Crawford's "Scotch backbone," her certainty of her call, and her wide and lively interests all give testimony to her strong and independent spirit. This independent spirit helps to explain how Crawford had the strength—even the audacity—to publish three autobiographical works and to place her extensive collection of private journals where they might be read by others. To be sure, for her published writings, she had the precedent of missionary autobiography. These works were intended to stimulate their readers' support for the missionary cause, and this noble purpose could overcome the reticence a writer—especially a woman—might feel about telling her story. As Terrence L. Craig has written, missionaries "were in the habit of self-description and self-justification, and in biography and autobiography found compatible vehicles for what they had to say. They knew they were interesting people, engaged in often fascinating and challenging work, and

---

16. Crawford, *Joyful Journey*, 41.
17. Ibid., 42.

as such could present a personalized face to mission work in lives that combined both strains."[18]

But Crawford went beyond publishing her story: she allowed her journals to be opened to the world. Isabel considered herself a witness to God's saving work and also to the less-than-godly actions of some of the church's leaders, and she allowed both aspects to be known. As for the vast amount of information in the journals not directly related to her mission work, Crawford herself was intrigued by a wide range of things, and she could easily assume others would share her interests.

It was this independent spirit that allowed Crawford to set out on her own to establish a mission at Saddle Mountain and to enjoy remarkable success there. It enabled her to travel from coast to coast as a popular public speaker and to endure great difficulties during her work in western New York—all the while with seriously impaired hearing. And this spirit kept her exploring after her retirement, in body as long as she was able, and in mind even when her physical limitations curtailed her activities.

Her independent spirit could sometimes push her beyond common gender roles. Not only did she found her own mission at Saddle Mountain, but when the mission society sent someone to help her, the assistant performed supportive functions much like the wife of a male missionary. And when Crawford recognized a threat to her mission, she became much more assertive than was seemly for a woman of her era. At Saddle Mountain, she fought to ensure that the church would received its full 160 acre allotment, and on a reservation in New York, Crawford even presided one time at the celebration of the Lord's supper when circumstances seemed to require it.[19] But here, too, there is an incongruity, for Crawford was an outspoken proponent of traditional roles for women, both in public and in the church. She was "disgusted" with the eight women ministers who participated in the Congress of Women at the Columbian Exposition in 1893, and she remained firm in her opinion against the ordination of women.[20] Regarding her mission work, she maintained that she was "a woman trying to do a woman's work in a womanly way."[21]

18. Craig, *Missionary Lives*, 56.

19. Journal 1915–16, June 11, 1916, 81–82.

20. Journal 1891–93, 130–31. Her view was slightly modified in a manuscript titled "Forever Moving" that she wrote in 1955. There she explained, "Although I am not a believer in the ordination of women I am a believer in others having the right to decide the matter for themselves and being ordained if the church so votes" (Barbara Cross McKinnon collection, 70).

21. Diary 1896–97, September 13, 1896, 135.

Yet there is another side to this independence of spirit, the shadow side of a strength, for when Isabel felt she was right, she did not hesitate maintain her position—strongly—against any and all opposition. This is what brought her into conflict more than once with the officials of her denomination; this is what so raised the rancor of one that he wrote to the current pastor at Saddle Mountain in 1929, twenty-three years after Crawford's departure, "You think you could get along with Miss Crawford. Then you could do something that no one else has EVER been able to do—man or woman."[22]

What emerges from the pages of Isabel Crawford's writing is the picture of a strong, even feisty, woman with a distinct sense of God's call. She attempted to follow that call and to labor faithfully for God. Only in her earliest work, in Oklahoma, was she conspicuously successful, but she remained just as faithful and just as energetic throughout the rest of her career and the remainder of her life. Yet she felt validated mainly by her one obvious success, and this feeling was reinforced as she retold her story countless times in order to raise people's enthusiasm toward missions and as she continued to receive adulation as the "heroine of Saddle Mountain."[23] Though she disliked the title,[24] the experience remained central to her identity, and so it was at Saddle Mountain that her body came to dwell among her own people.

---

22. Kinney to Perry Jackson, October 12, 1929, Crawford, Correspondence, Katherine S. Westfall Files.

23. Burdette, *Heroine of Saddle Mountain*.

24. Crawford, *Joyful Journey*, 159.

1

The Early Years

WRITING OF HER ARRIVAL of the Baptist Missionary Training School in 1891, Isabel Crawford claimed that she entered possessing "a Scotch backbone, and a fully developed Irish funny-bone."[1] These she attributed to her Scots-Irish father and her Irish mother.

Isabel's father, John Crawford, was born in 1819 near Castledawson, County Londonderry, Ireland. According to family tradition, his forebears had emigrated from Scotland to Ireland early in the sixteenth century, well before later waves of Scottish immigration to the island.[2] John's father, Hugh Crawford, had a large estate near Castledawson, and the family of Hugh's wife, Frances Brown, had been involved in the local linen industry for several generations.

The Crawfords were strict Presbyterians: Isabel wrote that her grandfather "never allowed [her father] to pick a flower or *whistle* on the Sabbath day." John joined the church at an early age, "and settled down to be a good boy."[3] Hugh and Frances had five daughters who survived infancy, but John was their only son.

John was a good boy but an independent spirit. In studying the Bible, he realized that "he had never been converted, nor had he been baptized the

---

1. Crawford, *Joyful Journey*, 41.

2. Ward, *Ancestry of Emily (Crawford) Cline*. Through her extensive genealogical research, Doris Cline Ward, granddaughter of Emily Crawford Cline and thus grandniece of Emily's sister Isabel, has added considerably to the family information provided by Isabel Crawford.

3. Crawford to Taylor, February 16, 1950, Notebook untitled [Miscellaneous 1950–53].

right way." So, at the age of fourteen or fifteen, he went seven miles on his pony to Tobermore to see Alexander Carson, an influential Baptist minister and scholar.[4] John Crawford was converted and baptized, but when he told his father of his actions, Hugh Crawford ordered John out of the house and disinherited him. Carson took the boy into his own home and tutored him, grooming John for study at Edinburgh University and then at Stepney Academy, where he prepared for the ministry.

Sometime during the next years, the hardworking new pastor met a young woman from Ireland. She was Sarah Louise Hackett. Born in 1821, Sarah was the second of eighteen children of Thomas Hackett and Mary Anne Fogarty. Isabel stated that Sarah was of Norman descent, and that she was from Dublin.[5] Her family belonged to the Church of Ireland. Sarah's comfortable childhood home was cared for by twenty-one servants; she was educated by private tutors and spoke several languages.[6] She was able "to quote from Shakespeare, Milton and other famous authors by the yard," and Isabel once speculated that her mother knew every one of Shakespeare's plays "by heart."[7] Sarah also learned the womanly arts of fine needlework.

Sarah moved to England and made her home with her cousin William Frederick Fogarty, a physician, who lived on Percy Circus in Clerkenwell, Borough of Islington, London.[8] On June 25, 1853, she married John Crawford in the Vernon Baptist chapel in Clerkenwell. Like her husband, Sarah, too, exhibited an independent spirit by embarking on a life far different from that which she had previously known. The couple lived in London and John Crawford served as a pastor to the poor in Lewisham, across the Thames. In April 1854, Sarah gave birth to their first child, Emily Augusta.

The Toleration Act of 1689 allowed freedom of worship to nonconformists who dissented from the Church of England. Nevertheless, Baptists and members of other nonconformist groups found themselves disadvantaged by

4. Garrett, *Baptist Theology*, 200–203.

5. Journal 1913–14, 104; Notebook Ireland XII, 48; and Journal 1926–27, 95. Doris Cline Ward lists Sarah Hackett's place of birth as Drogheda, County Louth, farther north than Dublin (Ward, *Ancestry of Emily [Crawford] Cline*, Sarah Hackett Crawford section).

6. Crawford, *Jolly Journal*, 18; Journal 1926–27, 95.

7. Crawford, *Jolly Journal*, 18; Journal 1941–42, 71.

8. Notebook England I, May 26, 1925. Doris Cline Ward noted that the marriage certificate of Sarah Hackett and John Crawford listed Sarah's father as "deceased" and speculated that it may have been after his death that Sarah was invited into the home (Ward, *Ancestry of Emily [Crawford] Cline*, Sarah Hackett Crawford section). She was certainly there by 1851 because she was listed as a resident at that address on the 1851 census. Ward identified Fogarty as Sarah's cousin while Isabel Crawford called him Sarah's uncle.

the restrictions that remained. John Crawford felt the brunt of these limitations, and Isabel wrote that her father built a chapel on wheels "when threatened with imprisonment if he preached without a license to more than 12 people."[9] Prospects for a Baptist preacher were poor, and John and Sarah decided to emigrate. First, however, they traveled to Ireland. Apparently John Crawford and his father were reconciled, and the visit was near the time of John's mother's death. While in Ireland, John and Sarah's second daughter was born; they named her Frances, after John's mother.

**John Crawford and Sarah Louise Hackett Crawford.
Courtesy of Barbara Cross McKinnon.**

Then they prepared to emigrate. To pay for their passage, John sold most of their wedding presents. Sarah, however, insisted on keeping a locket containing her hair and John's braided together and a topaz brooch that was his wedding present to her. It was probably in 1858 that the parents and their two young daughters sailed for Nova Scotia.

9. Notebook untitled [Miscellaneous 1950–53], Crawford to Taylor, February 16, 1950.

When they reached Halifax, John Crawford left his family among Baptist friends there while he set forth for Chicago. There he headed northwest on foot, looking for a community that had Baptists with both the desire and the means to support a preacher. He found it in the village of Cheltenham, about forty-two miles from Toronto. The Baptist settlers there began holding services by 1836, and in 1844 they organized a church.[10] When Crawford arrived, the congregation had been without a minister for one year, and they welcomed him heartily.[11]

First, however, he went back to Halifax, returning with his wife and daughters. The new situation was a challenge to Sarah Crawford. She had grown up without learning domestic skills, and apparently she had gained little knowledge in London, for she came to Cheltenham ignorant of basic household techniques.[12] Many years later, Isabel met Anna Hunter, who told her of the first time she showed Sarah Crawford how to wash: "We sorted the clothes and when the white things were ready I carried them to the boiler but before I could put them in your mother flew after me and taking the clothes from my hands said: 'Oh, Mrs. Hunter! Mrs. Hunter! Don't put them in that boiling water! They will burn and God only knows where we can get any more!'"[13]

Soon Emily and Frances were joined by a baby brother. He was named Hugh Frederick, after John's father, Hugh, and Frederick William Fogarty, in whose home Sarah had lived prior to her marriage.[14] Then Sarah gave birth to another daughter, Edith; soon sorrow came to the family, for Edith died at an early age. The Crawfords' last child, Isabel Alice Hartley Crawford, was born on May 26, 1865. Later in her life, Isabel whimsically told the story "of how as a baby a few days old she was placed in the arms of a cousin, who being a young man and much embarrassed demanded 'What are you going to do with this thing?' Miss Crawford said it was a question that was to weigh on the minds and hearts of my parents, for as the years went by, the puzzle grew.[15]

10. Nelles, *Cheltenham*, 2–7.

11. Luck and Gilmour, *Cheltenham Baptist Church*.

12. In that era, it was common for a family member to come into the household to help, and possibly Sarah received this sort of assistance in London.

13. Crawford, *Jolly Journal*, 19.

14. Hugh Crawford was listed on the 1861 census as being one year old—two years at his next birthday. Isabel said consistently that she was born in 1865, and on her seventh-sixth birthday, May 26, 1941, Isabel stated that Hugh had turned eighty two days earlier, making his birth date May 24, 1861. This seems highly unlikely in light of the 1861 census, but the ages for Hugh given on census forms for other years do not provide consistent information. He was presumably born in 1860 or 1859 (Census of Canada, 1861, Chinguacousy, Peel, Canada West, 72).

15. Notebook Illinois, clipping "Sketch of Miss Crawford's Life." There is no

John Crawford was an able and popular preacher. When Robert Alexander Fyfe heard of this "brilliant young Scotchman in the woods,"[16] he had an idea. Fyfe was a Baptist minister with a special interest in education. In 1860, the Canadian Literary Institute opened its doors in Woodstock, Ontario, and Fyfe left his Toronto pulpit to become its principal. Fyfe did all the teaching in the theological department, and each summer he traveled to raise funds for the institute. In 1867 he warned, "The principal *cannot* carry on his work any further in its present shape."[17] The trustees voted that Fyfe "secure the services of J. Crawford for the Institute if he can."[18] It took Fyfe three trips to Cheltenham to persuade John Crawford to join the faculty. According to Isabel, "Father felt called to preach the gospel above everything else on earth, but when Dr. Fyfe showed him that he would be preaching through every student for the ministry, he saw the point and 'followed where He led.'"[19]

The Crawfords moved to Woodstock in 1868, when Isabel was three. The parents were loving but careful of their children's upbringing, and out of necessity they were frugal. The children's clothes "were so good that they never wore out but were made over and over and over again, passing on down the line until they came to me for finishing touches."[20]

Isabel's first doll was wooden and, like Isabel's clothes, it was handed down to her. She wrote, "She was so ugly that . . . I just *couldn't* love her."[21] Isabel longed for something nicer. In October 1872, John Crawford's father died, and John made a trip to Ireland to settle the estate and to see that his stepmother was comfortably settled.[22] Isabel wrote, "Mother wanted me to have him bring me something sensible—something that I would always have, but I cried every time the subject came up. I wanted a *pretty* doll." John brought her a beautiful one, "but, alas, its beauty didn't last. First the flaxen hair came out in chunks, then the eyes stuck, and, finally, the peach

---

indication of who this "cousin" might be, for Crawford made no mention in her journals of Canadian relatives.

16. Crawford, *Jolly Journal*, 17.

17. Gibson, *Robert Alexander Fyfe*, 299.

18. Trustees minutes, annual meeting, July 9, 1867, 122, Board of Trustees Subseries 1: Minute Book 1858–89, Canadian Literary Institute Fonds.

19. Crawford, *Joyful Journey*, 19.

20. Journal 1920–21, 1.

21. Crawford, *Jolly Journal*, 42.

22. Hugh Crawford had remarried twice after the death of John's mother. His second wife did not live long, and then he married Jane McClernon, who survived him (Ward, *Ancestry of Emily [Crawford] Cline*, Hugh Crawford section).

complexion peeled off. Gum-chewing was strictly prohibited in our family . . . but I chewed that wax for weeks on the sly."[23]

Crawford house in Woodstock, Ontario.
Courtesy of Barbara Cross McKinnon.

Early on Isabel had a flair for drama. The first poem she recited in public was John Greenleaf Whittier's "Barbara Frietchie." Years later she remembered how "dramatically" she "roared" the lines "Shoot if you must this old gray head" and "'March on!' he said," as she marched off the platform.[24]

Isabel pictured herself as mischievous. She remembered that many times she "had to be spanked (after family worship) for some devilment committed during the day." She wrote, "[I]t was for telling lies that I got most of my spankings. I held no spite at father though, for I always knew I didn't get half as much as I deserved. I wasn't caught every time I 'digressed from the orderly practice of Baptist churches' and well brought up families."[25]

Isabel claimed to be "the terror of the town,"[26] and her stories about her childhood show that she was "full of pep," high-spirited, and independent-minded. Isabel's mother supervised her reading, and only once did Isabel read something that escaped her mother's scrutiny. Once a week, Sarah checked two suitable books out of the Mechanic's Institute library, one for

23. Crawford, *Jolly Journal*, 42.
24. Journal 1940–41, 124.
25. Crawford, *Joyful Journey*, 22.
26. Ibid., 54.

Isabel and one for Hugh. At school, Isabel noticed how interested boys were in a book called *Midshipman Easy*, but her mother ignored her hints. Finally Isabel took matters into her own hands: she sneaked her mother's choice back to the library and exchanged it for *Midshipman Easy*. At home she hid it under her straw-tick mattress. Stealthily she read it each night, relighting her lamp after she had answered—truthfully—to the question of whether her light was out. One night she was almost caught. When she heard her father return home, she hastily hid the book under her pillow and placed an open copy of *The Life of Elijah* in her hands. She feigned sleep as her father took the book, shut it, and blew out the lamp. The next day he chided her for going to sleep with the lamp burning, but her secret remained undiscovered. After she finished the book, back she took it to the library and exchanged it for the one her mother had chosen.[27]

Sarah Crawford did not simply oversee Isabel's reading: she was her daughter's first teacher. Well educated herself, she taught Isabel how to read and write and say the multiplication tables. At age ten, Isabel passed the necessary examinations and entered the Literary Institute. Study there was too advanced, however, and gradually she fell behind. As she described it, "The lessons were too long & reviews short."[28] Later, in the public school, she "set to work to 'catch up' with the children her own age, whose education had been well rounded out in contrast to the uneven development that had put Isabel Crawford in some things far behind and in others far ahead of them."[29] Of her education she wrote, "I learned enough history to know that my relatives were all well educated and prided themselves on their blue blood; enough geography to be in unknown quarters when there was music or a French lesson on the breeze; enough arithmetic to calculate by distance when I was forbidden to be on the street and caught sight of my mother turning the corner; enough grammar to puzzle strangers who couldn't reconcile such good English with such bad behaviour; enough music to alarm every living creature within sound, and enough physiology to know that I was in perfect health."[30]

Crawford had a reason for writing such self-deprecating remarks. Evangelical Christians anticipated an experience of conversion. Isabel was raised in a Christian home where she was taught to say her prayers, to participate in family worship, and to observe the Sabbath. But it was only with a conversion experience that the forms of religion became a part of the

---

27. Crawford, *Jolly Journal*, 30.
28. Journal 1926–27, 95.
29. Notebook Illinois, clipping "Sketch of Miss Crawford's Life."
30. Ibid.

believer's own personal faith. Yet the situation was complex. People might profess conversion, but how could others determine whether they were truly converted? If an obvious sinner was transformed, the evidence was strong. But with someone like Isabel who had been brought up in the faith and then experienced an early conversion, it was more difficult. For them, the test of changed conduct was more subtle, and the question was whether they became steadfast followers of the way. Isabel, in stressing her mischievous nature, prepared for the story of her conversion, her immediate zeal, and her lifelong attempt to follow God's call.

When Isabel was ten years old, the pastor of First Baptist Church in Woodstock held a series of revival services, and Isabel attended. When the preacher invited all who wanted to be Christians to stand, the young girl stood and "was surprised that every sinner didn't stand up."[31] Soon she was converted, and she asked to be baptized. But because she was so young, the decision was postponed to give the deacons the opportunity to observe her. Finally she was accepted, and Isabel Crawford was baptized on Sunday, March 21, 1875, about two months before her eleventh birthday.[32]

Following her conversion and baptism, Isabel had a new concern, that of "falling from grace." She wrote, "I simply couldn't sit up and be good, and say verses in a class any longer. I had to be up and doing."[33] And so, three months after her baptism, Isabel volunteered to teach Sunday school, partly out of new-found Christian zeal and partly from the fear that she would misbehave if she continued to attend her old class. Elbert Chute, a theological student, had rented a house in a poor section in the east end of Woodstock and had begun a Sunday school. It was to him that she offered her services. Chute was understandably skeptical about the capabilities of an eleven-year-old, and he told her that the school already had enough teachers. But Isabel persisted: "'How about seats?' I asked. 'Have you any empty ones? If so, I can fill them.'"[34] And so, with the prospect of two empty

---

31. Ibid., 10.

32. In her 1893–94 Journal, Crawford wrote that she "was baptized on Sabbath evening March 21st" (Journal 1893-94, 10), while in her *Jolly Journal*, published in 1932, she gives the date as April 21. March 21 was a Sunday in 1875, while April 21 was not. She regularly stated that she was born in 1865; that is the date of birth stated on her passport. She also said consistently that she was converted and baptized at age ten, before her birthday on May 26. But if she was born in 1865, she did not turn eleven until 1876. (Neither March 21 nor April 21 fell on a Sunday that year.) The ages given on census records are inconsistent for Isabel as they are for other members of the family, so they cannot be used to settle the question, which must remain a puzzle until new evidence is found.

33. Crawford, *Jolly Journal*, 35.

34. Ibid.

pews to fill, she went to work. To Chute's amazement, the next Sunday Isabel arrived with a small class of boys about her own age, "the toughest looking urchins ever to enter a Sunday school."[35] She continued to scour the neighborhood and add students to the class, many of them older than she, and both Isabel and the class thrived.

The first Christmas that Isabel could remember, she had made gifts for her family. She knit garters for her mother, bound little pieces of chamois to serve as spectacle wipers for her father, stitched yarn on perforated cardboard for bookmarks for her sisters, and hemmed a handkerchief for her brother. Now her interest in the east end mission brought Isabel a new challenge. The Sunday school Christmas tree was a widely-observed tradition. All those associated with the school received gifts. Isabel believed that this Sunday school should have a tree, and she went to work, making gifts "out of scraps of nothing & hand outs."[36] Her interest continued as the Sunday school grew, and when she was fourteen she made 120 gifts "for the poor."

Isabel devoted such attention to the Sunday school that she fell behind in her classes at the Institute. Furthermore she received a score of forty in "deportment." Professor James Edward Wells asked the parents of students with low scores "to look into the matter." John Crawford called Isabel into his study and admonished her, "'Isabella, you are giving too much time and attention to that East End Mission. If you don't do better during the coming quarter, and learn to behave yourself, you will have to give up your Sunday school class!'" Isabel, though converted, had lost none of her high-spirited nature: "I turned on Father with a look of horror in my eyes and said, 'Why Pa Crawford! Hasn't the Lord's work to be put first—ahead of everything else? Haven't I heard you and Dr. Fyfe say so, over and over and over again?' Poor father! He made no reply, but taking me to the door said: 'That will do, dear; but remember what I have said.'" Her narrative continued: "I don't know whether I did any better after that or not, but I *do* know that I taught my Sunday school class until we left town."[37]

Isabel's zeal reflected that of her father. John Crawford carried a heavy teaching load, especially when Fyfe's health declined. For a number of years, there had been suggestions that the theological department of the institute move to Toronto, but Fyfe had begged that the school would remain in Woodstock during his lifetime, for he was aware that such an arrangement would increase its already onerous financial burden.[38] Fyfe died in

---

35. Journal 1942–43, 20.
36. Journal 1937–38, 87.
37. Crawford, *Jolly Journal*, 37.
38. Ibid.

September of 1878. Soon after his death, the matter came up again, and now it became widely though unofficially known that the wealthy Baptist senator William McMaster was willing to give generous support to the move. The governance of the Institute was in the hands of its subscribers, and at a meeting in July of 1879, they approved the removal of the Theological Department to Toronto.[39]

On July 28, 1879, eleven days after the meeting, John Crawford submitted his resignation. He wrote: "According to the resolution passed at the meeting lately held in Guelph, it will be necessary for one of the present staff of professors in the theological department to retire, in order to make room for the forthcoming president. After mature & prayerful deliberation, it is my desire to vacate the position I have occupied for the last twelve years."[40] He expressed his intention to "proceed at once to seek other employment." Crawford did not, however, "seek" employment. Very quickly he made his own employment, for Crawford had a vision.

Soon after Crawford began teaching at the Canadian Literary Institute, Robert Fyfe had shown interest in the western parts of Canada that were opening up for settlement. He urged the Baptist Convention to send a missionary to the West, and in May of 1873 Alexander McDonald left Ontario to do pioneering work, opening churches in Winnipeg and elsewhere.

Though Crawford had initially been reluctant to exchange the pulpit for the classroom, he had come to see the importance of training men to become ministers. Now in 1879 he combined that interest with the concern Fyfe had shown for the West, and soon after his resignation, Crawford embarked on a journey of about three thousand miles to gather information. After he arrived in Manitoba, Alexander McDonald spent almost two weeks driving him to different parts of Manitoba and the surrounding Northwest Territories.[41] By the time Crawford returned to Woodstock, he had a plan.[42]

The settlers Crawford visited wanted pastors, but they could not fully support them. They needed pastors who could support themselves by farming; then, gradually, the church members could take on the responsibility. Furthermore, many prospective pastors were unable to pay much, if anything, for their education. They needed a school that had its own farm and

---

39. Soon after this, McMaster's name and gift were made known, and the Toronto Baptist College opened in October of 1881 (Gibson, *Robert Alexander Fyfe*, 324).

40. Crawford to Board of Trustees, July 28, 1879, Board of Trustees Series 1, Correspondence, Canadian Literary Institute Fonds.

41. When Manitoba became a province in 1870, it was about one-eighteenth of its present size. The Northwest Territories formed the eastern, northern, and western boundaries of the original small province.

42. Letter by John Crawford, *Canadian Baptist*, October 9, 1879, 1.

thus could become self-sufficient. The students themselves would erect the college buildings designed by Crawford. He assured his readers that his experience qualified him for both overseeing the farm and constructing the buildings.

Crawford believed he found the ideal location in Rapid City and its immediate surroundings: "It is a dry and healthy locality. The land is rolling and picturesque, with an excellent soil, a dark sandy loam upon a clay bottom.... This locality is well watered, and the water of excellent quality. There is also lime at hand, and abundance of fuel to burn it; also clay for brick, and stones for the foundation." Crawford and the current residents of Rapid City believed that it had another strong advantage: they expected the transcontinental line of the Canadian Pacific Railway to pass through Rapid City, which might become the first divisional point west of Winnipeg. The city would boom in population, and land values would increase.

In October, Crawford presented his plan at the Baptist Convention of Ontario and Quebec. Although the Convention could not officially take on work outside its boundaries, it "seemed very favourably impressed with the necessity of such a work."[43] Crawford enlisted the help of George B. Davis, who had been a student at Woodstock before going to Chicago to complete his theological studies. Both men visited churches throughout Ontario to raise money for the new Prairie College. They received small contributions but not the major donations for which Crawford had hoped, and funding for the college grew slowly. Following the settlement of Hugh Crawford's estate, John had purchased a house in Woodstock. Now he sold it, and with that $4000, an investment by Davis, and the gifts and pledges of those who had responded, it was time to begin. Early in the spring of 1880, Davis traveled to Rapid City with the first party of students. They secured land and went to work, starting to farm and also to build. On the first of October, the building was closed in.[44]

Isabel's brother, Hugh, was among those breaking land and constructing the building. Then shortly after the building was ready for occupancy, John Crawford brought Isabel's sister Emily and two other women, one a student and the other a cook, to take up residence. Emily had graduated from the Canadian Literary Institute with honors, and when classes began at Prairie College that winter, she and George Davis taught "without salary, to give the institution a start."[45] John did not stay long, however; he returned home to continue his quest for money to support the fledgling school.

---

43. *Canadian Baptist*, October 23, 1879, 5.
44. Davis, *Life Story*, 27.
45. Report by John Crawford, *Canadian Baptist*, January 20, 1881, 4.

While John Crawford was soliciting funds and Hugh and Emily moved west, Isabel remained in Woodstock with her mother, for Isabel had not quite finished her schooling. She had failed the entrance examination in mathematics and wanted another chance.

Finally early in the fall of 1881, sixteen-year-old Isabel passed the examination, and she and her mother were ready for the westward trek.[46] As they prepared to leave, a neighbor came over and asked to buy Isabel's canary for two dollars. Isabel offered to give her the bird, but when the neighbor left, the girl found two dollars on the table. Later she wrote, "I wondered *and* wondered what I would do with my wealth."[47]

At the farewell entertainment held at the Sunday school mission in honor of the family, Isabel was one of the entertainers. She sang a poignant song about a young orphan. She wrote, "Dr. Jones Farmer, Prof. Joseph Bates, Dr. George Sale, Rev. W. M. Corkey and others in the audience appeared interested in my plaintive voice, while the rest, including myself, were carried away with the words."[48] Then later in the evening, it was Isabel's turn to speak. Afterwards she recalled the climax of her talk: "'I have sold my canary bird for two dollars. I wanted to give Mrs. Cull the bird for nothing, but she left the money on the table. We pay two dollars and fifty cents a month for this place. We ought to have a building of our own some day. I am going to give one dollar of my canary-bird money to start a fund.' I got no further. I think everybody in the house, except those who were interested in my voice, was in tears."[49]

Soon Isabel and her parents headed west to make their new home at Prairie College. Many years later, Isabel reflected on the move: "Any man taking a delicate wife and family into the wild, woolly and frozen new West, after he is sixty years of age must be one of three things; either he is money crazy or plain crazy or is under the guidance of God Almighty for some special purpose."[50] To Isabel it was clear that her father was called by God, and so she and her mother were transplanted to the western frontier to participate in John Crawford's dream.

---

46. In *Joyful Journey*, Crawford stated that she passed the examination in October, while in her 1906-8 Journal she wrote that she left Woodstock for Rapid City on September 1 (Crawford, *Joyful Journey*, 24; Journal 1906-8, 37).

47. *Jolly Journal*, 38.

48. Ibid.

49. Ibid., 39-40.

50. McLaurin, *Pioneering in Western Canada*, 293.

2

On the Prairies

Isabel and her parents reached Winnipeg early in October, 1881. In May of that year the decision had been made to run the main rail line west, not through Rapid City, but through Brandon, and construction began quickly. Isabel and Sarah waited a few days in order to take the first passenger train going west to Brandon; John remained in Winnipeg. (Isabel suspected that "when he had paid for our tickets there was no money left for his own.")[1] According to Isabel's report, the train "ran out of fuel & the passengers had to get out & chuck wood to get up steam."[2]

Isabel, her mother, and three other passengers wanted to leave the train at Curries Crossing, about seven miles east of Brandon, but the conductor refused to stop. When one of the passengers gave him one dollar, however, he was induced to slow down. It was eleven at night; rain poured down, lightning flashed, and thunder rumbled. Isabel wrote, "One by one we were dumped along the tracks each of us rolling down the muddy grading almost into a creek. We called to one another like frightened prairie chickens, & decided to head for a dim religious light we saw in the distance. My! how we waded through the tall grass or weeds ½ or 1 mile. Several times mother almost gave out but we helped her along and finally we reached the tent where we were told to wait."[3] With an explosion of population in this area, tents were used for many purposes. This one was a hotel—and it was full.

1. Journal 1941–42, 51.
2. Ibid.
3. Ibid, 52.

Attempting to make room for the women, the manager took a stick from the wood box and vigorously poked at the burlap curtains that divided the tent into makeshift rooms. He called, "Get up! Women have come!" At first there was no response but finally, after a second round of poking and shouting, two men relinquished their places. Isabel wrote, "Then majestically the boss beckoned to mother & me & escorted us to a part of the burlap curtain where one of the refugees had evacuated. He lifted it & held it while we ducked under wet and muddy and all atremble. Mother shook out her shawl to full size, wrapped herself completely up in it—crawling over to the far side of the bunk & sat up with her back against whatever there was to lean up against. I laid down. We were both so thoroughly exhausted that we had to collapse someplace!"[4]

The rain still poured down the next morning as Isabel and Sarah set forth in an open wagon on the final twenty miles of their journey. When at last they reached Prairie College, Isabel found the large stone building a dreary sight, but even more startling was Emily's appearance: "Poor Em had gone out a year before us & met us at the door in a dirty old dress & a scrubbing pail & mop in her hands. Ma & I were perfectly shocked & started to cry for we had no idea that she had to do hard work. She went out to teach. It was the first time in my life I had seen her dirty & to think of one of us having to scrub fairly sickened me."[5]

Isabel was unprepared for what she saw partly because the previous February, Emily had written a more positive description that had been printed in the *Canadian Baptist*. The young teacher wished to stimulate interest in the new college. Although the "substantial stone building" was "quite common-place looking," it had to be seen in perspective: "By the time you arrive at Prairie College, you have learned to look upon a log house, with one room, a garret, and a fire, as the height of luxury; so that a stone edifice of three storeys strikes you as imposing. The idea of complaining because the dining room has mother earth for a carpet, because the table is made by driving stakes into the ground and nailing boards to them, because the walls are stone-gemmed sometimes with sparkling frost diamonds—to complain of these trifles never for a moment enters your mind."[6]

Emily Crawford had been teaching at the college since it opened, as had George Davis. But when John Crawford arrived in the fall of 1881, soon after Sarah and Isabel, he discovered that Davis had decided to resign to set up his own school in Rapid City. Financial matters lay at the heart of

---

4. Ibid., 52–53.
5. Journal Life Story, 3.
6. Letter by Emily Crawford, *Canadian Baptist*, March 17, 1881, 5.

the dispute.[7] Without Davis to share responsibilities, Crawford was overcome with work. The labor was not all academic, for the college had its own farm, and there was much agricultural work to do before the opening of the school term.

When winter came, the cold penetrated the eighteen-inch-thick stone walls of Prairie College, and the "sparkling frost diamonds" described by Emily could not be ignored. Eventually the walls were plastered. The Crawfords' apartment was on the second floor, along with three classrooms, while the top story was divided into twelve small rooms, each housing two or three students. The bottom story housed the dining-room and kitchen. Isabel wrote that the area "was always damp & disagreeable until we had it plastered & floored. Often we caught frogs & lizards [sic] wiggling about the corners, & one night we went to church forgetting to close the windows & on our return found the whole floor alive. The students got a boiler & sticks & gathered 53 frogs & 300 lizards [sic] off that floor!"[8]

The physical condition of the school was sometimes a distraction, but the heart of Prairie College was its academic program, which emulated that of the Woodstock institute. The students also took seriously their religious responsibilities. On weekends, many went to nearby settlements to preach, some walking "five, seven, or ten miles to fill their appointments," meeting with settlers who gathered in log houses.[9] During the summer, some of the students did pastoral work, and altogether five churches were organized by Prairie College students.[10] They had a strong role model in their zealous mentor. John Crawford once walked the forty-nine miles to dedicate a church. "This done he walked on preaching 4 more times in churches & school houses. When the last service was over & he was going to start for home, a man & a horse went with him father and the man taking turns riding the horse. At Minnedosa man & horse were sent back & father walked the 18 miles to the college, arriving in time for breakfast & taught his classes as usual Monday morning."[11]

Isabel, too, found her place in Rapid City, once again teaching Sunday school. It was "a class of young men that everyone else was afraid of. These young men would all pile into the back seats not to be taught but to throw wheat at everyone and make a general disturbance. They threw wheat at me

---

7. A good summary of the complex situation is given by David W. Remus in a biography of John Crawford printed in the *Canadian Baptist*, August 1, 1967.

8. Journal Life Story, 5.

9. *Canadian Baptist*, May 17, 1881, 5.

10. McLaurin, *Pioneering in Western Canada*, 291.

11. Journal 1941–42, September 18, 1941, 54.

the first Sunday but never after. This was in a union school and when we started one of our own the whole class followed me. Three were baptized and five converted."[12]

Teaching Sunday school was familiar to Isabel, but much about the environment was new. In Manitoba she had her first contact with Indians. She wrote that in the spring "the Indians used to leave their reservations & make excursions through the country, returning in the fall to harvest their crops. Their favorite camping ground was along the banks of the Saskatchewan at Rapid City so that all summer long rows of teepees could be seen as far as the eye could look."[13] When the Indians were camped, they would "come to the College by the dozens to get drinks of buttermilk & see the 'big teepee.' They always came in without knocking & wearing moccasins they made no noise so that any time we might expect to meet one of them, or more, in any part of the building. Many times I have turned to go into the kitchen & beheld a whole row of them along the wall pleasantly exhibiting their white teeth & awaiting their buttermilk. They were always well mannered & strictly honest."

While Isabel retained her diligence as a Sunday school teacher, she also retained her mischievous nature. She wrote that, due to the paucity of girls in the area, each girl "had many beaux. . . . One evening we were crossing the bridge on horseback when my escort halted & begged for a reply. If my heart & hand were not turned over to him he would leap into the river & be drowned. Being young I was a little afraid but replied 'I cannot give you both the heart wont come out but here is my strong hand to help you jump' My! goodness! How he fled far out of sight away from the river!"[14]

Alone or with a friend, Isabel enjoyed horseback riding. She wrote, "A wild reckless feeling enters the soul when seated in a saddle on the back of a wild Indian shaganappi pony, & you feel yourself flying over the boundless prairie. There is *nothing* like it!"[15] She also found another, more surprising attraction on the prairie: "The prairie fires are simply beautiful! . . . In the moonlight I have often wandered off alone matches in hand & lit fires all along the line (and I didn't have to run for the river & plunge in either)."[16]

Although Isabel found pleasures in prairie life, she worked hard. Everyone's work was needed, for the college was struggling. John Crawford had failed to recognize the difficulty of farming this part of the Canadian

12. Application, Crawford, Biographical Files.
13. Journal Life Story, 18.
14. Journal 1941–42, September 21, 1941, 56.
15. Journal Life Story, 8.
16. Ibid.

West. When he visited in 1879, the area was enjoying a wet cycle that continued for three more years. Then the much more common dry cycle returned.[17] Furthermore the newly-developing area had limited access to markets. Thus the farm was not providing the hoped-for support, and the price of supplies and of shipping donated stock and machinery was much higher than anticipated.

In February of 1883, the *Canadian Baptist* published a letter by "A Farmer." Its writer lamented how the Crawford family had "made slaves of themselves to do a work on behalf of the denomination."[18] Years later, Isabel used similar language when she wrote, "The work at P. C. was simply tremendous & when I look back now I pause & ask myself 'How did you do it'—The washings were awful & the simple making of the bread & butter for that family was one person's work. I baked every alternate day & washed the days intervening. No galley slave ever worked harder than I did rendering lard, corning *whole cows*, making soap, scrubbing, melting snow keeping my eye on a hundred & one things."[19]

By the time of the Baptist Missionary Convention of Manitoba and the Northwest in June of 1883, the situation was critical. Suddenly there was a new factor: Malcolm MacVicar had come to the meeting. He was a man with a mission, intent on persuading the Manitoba Baptists that all theological education should be centralized at Toronto Baptist College. After discussing the matter, the Convention decided to close Prairie College; John Crawford's dream had come to an end. All that was left for him to do was to close up Prairie College and search for a new situation.

The pioneering missionary Alexander McDonald had moved from Winnipeg across the border to Grafton in the Dakota Territory, and he invited John Crawford to visit him and to preach in the Baptist church in St. Thomas, in the northeast corner of the territory. There Crawford received a call to become the pastor. Thus, in the fall of 1883 he left to take up his new pastorate, leaving Sarah, Isabel, and some remaining students to wind up affairs in Rapid City.

One event brightened the season shortly before John's departure, although it did not pass without incident. At Prairie College on September 19, 1883, Isabel's sister Fanny married John Firstbrook of Toronto. The wedding was to take place in the family parlor, followed by a meal in the basement dining room. But the stove had been moved, the stovepipe did not draw, and the basement filled with smoke. Isabel wrote, "About 3 after 'High Noon'

---

17. Berton, *Last Spike*, 22.
18. *Canadian Baptist*, February 15, 1883, 4.
19. Journal Life Story, 30.

the ceremony took place & the smoked meal was partaken on in the lower region! Then came the farewells. I lay on the sofa crying hard because my sister was leaving us forever and I hadn't thought of it before! A friend bent over me kissed my forehead and said 'never mind Belle. It will be your turn next!' The next never came to me."[20]

The following months took on a darker tone, for closing the school was a challenge. Not just wheat prices had dropped. During its time of optimism, Rapid City had experienced a real estate boom, but that had ended dramatically, and land prices were low. The school and farm that once seemed to offer secure equity could not be sold. Crawford had poured all his assets into the venture, and now all was lost. Conscientiously he attempted to repay his debts, and in the process he lost possession of his personal library.

Isabel's hard work became even more difficult, and her robust constitution gave way. While there were still students at the college farm to do the threshing, she continued at her post despite her weakness. Yeast was not available for purchase, and so to make bread, Isabel made the starter "sponge" while she remained in bed. Then she dressed and was carried downstairs to knead the dough and was carried back up again. Finally her remaining strength gave way, and Doctor Cornell from Rapid City diagnosed her as suffering from "galloping consumption," or "acute phthisis." He put her on a diet of milk and gave her quinine, a commonly used medication at the time. She wrote, "For six long months I lay in bed wracked with fevers & pains of all kinds often times too weak to move a limb of my body. Once the household was called in to see me breathe my last but I was too mad to die & kicked the quilt over my mother's head instead."[21]

Reflecting later, Isabel wrote,

> [T]he Heavenly Father removed our family to Manitoba where He taught me some of the hardest & grandest lessons of my life. He swept all our earthly possessions from us & laid me upon a bed of suffering for six months. I couldn't see why I had been taken from the little school where I knew was doing good and brought out there to die. I couldn't pray—but at last I felt I must so I scrambled out of bed—dont know how—& knelt down & made the grandest prayer of my life. It was simply 'O Lord' accompanied with a flood of tears."[22]

---

20. Journal 1944–46, 80–81.
21. Journal Life Story, 31.
22. Journal 1893–94, 11.

Gradually she recovered, but the quinine that she credited with saving her life robbed her of much of her hearing. That impairment would remain with her for the rest of her life.

Finally, in the spring of 1884, Isabel and her mother were ready to join John Crawford in North Dakota. The best that John Crawford could do for their accommodation was to rent a little shoe shop consisting of two small rooms and a lean-to. The front room held a bed and a rocking chair, while the stove, three chairs, and a table were crowded into the back room. There was no space for Isabel to sleep; at night she would go to the room directly above Kermott's drug store, where she slept on a sofa.

In addition to ministering to the St. Thomas congregation, John Crawford preached at the little town of Glasston, six miles away. During Isabel and Sarah's first winter in St. Thomas, the Glasston congregation held a reception for the family in the schoolhouse in which the services were held. It was the first time that the Glasston people had seen Isabel, and she created a stir, well-dressed in a "cream cashmere dress with garnet plush front." She wrote, "The presiding officer failed to preside. The mob packed in like sardines, wiggled like fishworms and wouldn't behave."[23]

John Crawford was accustomed to using every opportunity for the edification of his audience. He had prepared an address on "Reconciling Difficult Passages of Scripture," and he attempted to give it. Isabel described his effort: "He quoted several verses that appeared to be in conflict and then proceeded to reconcile them. One said, 'And Judas went out and hanged himself,' while another read, 'He burst asunder in the middle.' The audience went wild, the rafters rang, the very lantern trembled. . . . He repeated his 'difficult Judas passages' once more. The applause was deafening! He retired, saying simply, 'I see that my subject is not suited to the occasion.'"[24] At the end of the evening, the proceeds of the entertainment were given to John. The eighty-seven dollars made a most welcome gift.[25]

After a time, the Crawfords were able to rent a house, still small, but with more space than their shoe-shop accommodations. In addition to the two rooms on its first floor, it had an attic. There they slept, John and Sarah in a double bed at the front of the house, and Isabel at first on a feather mattress on the floor at the back. Eventually their lives became more comfortable as they bought a bed for Isabel and a dresser for Sarah, but the attic had only rafters and roof boards. During the winter nights, Isabel slept with her blanket over head, and on many mornings she discovered that it had frozen

---

23. Ibid., 59.
24. Ibid., 60.
25. Ibid., 60–61.

stiff from her breath.[26] Then less than a year after they had moved into the house, the Crawfords received the wonderful news that their landlord planned to build an addition to their home. It ran the whole length of the house along one side, providing space for John Crawford to have a study at the front. Isabel and her bed moved into the small rear bedroom.

Their lives improved in other ways. Without his library, John Crawford found sermon preparation difficult. Each member of the family had a Bible, and Sarah had a copy of the 1635 *Emblems* by Francis Quarle, but that was all. In October of 1884, Emily Crawford married William Henry Cline; the wedding was held in the Toronto home of Emily's sister Fanny and her husband. As a Baptist minister, Cline was sympathetic to his father-in-law's plight, and he paid the seventy-five dollars due on the library.

Emily Crawford Cline, Frances Crawford Firstbrook, Hugh Crawford, and Isabel Crawford. Courtesy of Barbara Cross McKinnon.

26. Notebook untitled [Miscellaneous 1950–1953].

Isabel frequently mentioned her mother's delicate nature. She wrote that in North Dakota, "Father did the washing, I did the cooking and lots of laughing, while Mother worked harder than either trying to hold on to her faith in God."[27] Although Anna Hunter had attempted to teach Sarah how to do laundry when they lived in Cheltenham, laundry was John Crawford's task in St. Thomas. However, he did not wish to be seen by the neighbors doing something so unbefitting his role as hanging out the wash. That responsibility fell to Isabel, though she often teased him by asking, "'Father, why don't you finish the job and hang out the clothes? You always tell me to finish anything I start.' A knowing look would always come into his kindly face as he replied, 'I think you'd better attend to that, dear.'"[28]

Isabel's parents had provided their other children with good schooling, and it grieved them that they could not do the same for Isabel. They wished to send her back to Canada for further education, and in February of 1885 it looked as though they might be successful. The newspaper reported that "Miss Belle Crawford started Monday for Toronto, Canada, where she will attend school."[29] Isabel included nothing about this in her later biographical sketches, and she did not stay in Toronto to study. Only two bits of her writing give a glimpse of her visit. The Crawford children had heard from their mother about Jumbo, the elephant, who had been a great favorite in the London zoo. P. T. Barnum bought him and brought him to North America, and during Isabel's visit, Jumbo came to Toronto with the Barnum and Bailey Circus. Isabel, her sister Fanny, and Fanny's husband went to see Jumbo. Isabel observed that the animal looked down on them "with big kind eyes."[30] Within a week, Jumbo was struck by a train and killed in St. Thomas, Ontario.

On March 8, 1886, after Isabel had returned home, she referred to her time in Toronto in a letter to Mary Burdette at the Baptist Missionary Training School in Chicago:

> For some years back the Spirit of God has been working with me & has shown me distinctly that I am one of the called to "Go into all the world." ... The training the Lord has given me all the way through life points so clearly to the Mission work that I feel I must enter it or else live the rest of my life condemned before God.... During my visit to Toronto I spent much time among the poor & wretched and the success with which I met makes me think that I am more especially fitted to go about some big

---

27. Ibid., February 16, 1950.
28. Crawford, *Joyful Journey*, 29.
29. *St. Thomas Times*, February 26, 1885.
30. Journal 1934, August 15, 1934, 34.

city & search out the poor the blind the halt etc. . . . Oh do pray for me that the 'plain path' may be pointed out to me & I can distinctly here [sic] the voice saying: This is the way walk ye in it.[31]

The way was not made plain, and Isabel continued her accustomed life in St. Thomas. Her parents carefully though informally continued her education. She wrote, "For six happy years, night after night, in our simple home, full of books, mother instructed me in the best literature of the ages, having me commit the most famous passages of it. At 9. o'clock father came from the study and Bible topics were discussed till bed time. . . . I never realized till long after they were dead & gone that these wonderful '*home evenings*' were more for my special benefit than for their personal pleasure!"[32]

The family's finances were always strained, but a special blow came one year when John received word that his salary, like that of other missionaries, would have to be docked fifty dollars. The North Dakota General Missionary wrote, saying "We'll try & make it up to you by sending you a good barrel."[33] The news was well intentioned but not well received. The Crawfords knew that local churches often collected goods and packed items in barrels to send to missionaries for their own use or to distribute among the "natives." The Crawfords, however, found it humiliating to be the objects of such charity.

When the barrel arrived, Sarah fled upstairs to her bedroom. John wheeled it into the woodshed and opened it. Some of its contents were potentially useful. A warm, new Oxford gray shawl was marked "For Mrs. Crawford," but when Isabel tried to present it to her mother, Sarah responded weakly, "I have a very nice shawl of my own, dear."[34] For Isabel's father there was an overcoat with a silk velvet collar and chamois pockets. When Isabel encouraged him to try it on, he resisted: "In a voice that he might have used in depicting the awful condition of the Prodigal Son before he returned to his father's house, he replied, 'But my own coat is good enough yet, dear. It will last till I am able to buy a new one.'" Isabel hung the overcoat and the shawl out to air and then helped her father transport the barrel to the attic as Sarah exclaimed, "Do they think we are paupers to send us such rubbish!"[35]

Though the family was in strained financial circumstances, Isabel's high spirits could not be repressed. Months later she was to travel with her father to

31. Crawford to Burdette, March 8, 1886, Crawford, Correspondence, Mary Burdette Files.
32. Journal 1926–27, 95–96.
33. Journal 1893–94, October 18, 1893, 19.
34. Crawford, *Jolly Journal*, 89–90.
35. Journal 1893–94, October 19, 1893, 20.

a Baptist meeting. The night before their departure, she went to the attic and dug down in the barrel past the "nice good things" for the funniest items she could find. She outfitted herself with a wild combination of clothing. "But," she wrote, "the bonnet was the crowning glory! . . . On the left-hand side, shooting up like a fountain in the sunlight, sending forth gleams of navy blue, green and gold, was the whole magnificent tail of a black Spanish rooster! Holding this up and in place was a mother-of-pearl cornucopia with forget-me-nots on it and the words, printed in black, 'From Niagara Falls!'"[36]

Down the stairs she came. *Paradise Lost* fell from her startled mother's lap, and the even more startled cat ran from the room. John Crawford came in from his study to see what had caused the commotion. Nep, the family dog, barked sharply, and when Isabel reached up and wiggled the feathers, his eyes glistened. "He arose from his crouching position all atremble. His bobbed tail shot out straight behind, his nose went out in front, one foot left the carpet and if that blessed dog didn't 'set' just as if Father had shot a wild goose in a slough!"[37] Isabel made a flowery speech in which she bemoaned her parents' unwillingness to accept the "sacrificial offering" of the missionary barrel and urged them to "Repent!" She proclaimed that this was the costume she intended to wear at the upcoming convention, and the home was filled with laughter.[38]

Nep, the Crawford family dog. Courtesy of Barbara Cross McKinnon.

36. Crawford, *Jolly Journal*, 91–92.
37. Ibid., 93.
38. Ibid., 94.

Isabel's response to the missionary barrel illustrates the zest with which she embraced life in St. Thomas. The family's activities centered on the church, and once again Isabel took delight in teaching a large class of boys. She later described this as her "best work": "Thirteen of my class were converted and ten baptized."[39]

The church also held socials, oyster suppers, and Christmas entertainments. These provided pleasant social contact in the frontier town, and many of them also served to raise much-needed money for the congregation. In November of 1886, for example, the Sunday school society held a "sociable" at the new opera house that was nearing completion. The lively program included a cornet solo, recitations, and tableaux. According to the *St. Thomas Times*, "'Mrs. Jarley's Wax Works' was one of the interesting and entertaining features of the programme. Miss Belle Crawford, as Mrs. Jarley, did that old lady justice."[40] The Sunday school society collected over sixty dollars, and Isabel was discovering her talents.

Large snowfalls were among the hazards of prairie life, and the Crawfords awoke one morning to find their downstairs in darkness. They were snowed in. When John opened the back door, he met a wall of snow. He began to shovel—to no avail. But in the stable, Polly needed to be fed. Isabel bundled up warmly and crawled up a slanting board onto the snow. She rolled her way to the stable, and when she dug down and entered, she "found Polly more comfortable than we were in the house."[41] Isabel was able to get some hay from the haystack, and she provided Polly with snow instead of water. Returning to the house, she found her mother in tears. "'You will get your death of cold in some such escapade as this some day. You—are—so—like—your—father.'" Isabel continued, "Father turned with a twinkle in his eyes, saying, 'Tut, tut,' and walked off to his books."

John Crawford became concerned about the rising interest in the theory of evolution and its acceptance even by some ministers. In order to do his part to "ward off the enemy," he prepared a lecture presenting his own theories on the subject. He asked Isabel to accompany him on a lecture trip, to recite between sections of his lecture in order to supply "a *lighter vein* for the program."[42] The first lecture was in Grafton, south of St. Thomas, and the offering received there took them west to Park River the following day. But in Park River, stormy weather kept the audience small though, reported

39. Application, Crawford, Biographical Files.

40. *St. Thomas Times*, November 19, 1886. George Bradford Bartlett's script offered a series of monologues by Mrs. Jarley, each followed by tableaux featuring a waxworks character.

41. Crawford, *Jolly Journal*, 99–100.

42. Ibid., 83–84.

Isabel, "Father and I did our parts as earnestly as if the empty wooden seats had all been the heads of large families."[43]

Isabel Crawford on horseback. Courtesy of Barbara Cross McKinnon.

The next morning, at the train station, John discovered that, due to the small offering the previous evening, he did not have enough money to pay for tickets to their next appointments. Isabel observed, "Why, you *haven't* any money there.... And you don't mean to tell me that you started on this trip with no money in your pocket?" Handing him a ten dollar gold piece that she "had in safe-keeping," she said: "'There, go and get the tickets!' Taking it from me with his two hands and looking at me just a trifle reprovingly, he remarked, 'Now, my dear, just see how the Lord provides!'"[44]

Isabel also traveled on her own to visit friends. Once, when she went to see the Waldo family near Drayton, east of St. Thomas, she learned about the plight of the Hildebrands. It was harvest time, and thrashers were coming, but Mrs. Hildebrand was ill and Mr. Hildebrand could find no one to care for the children and cook for the workers. Isabel put on her oldest dress and an apron and went to the farm, where the farmer was happy to hire her

43. Ibid., 84.
44. Ibid., 85.

for three dollars a week. She learned from Mrs. Hildebrand where to find clean clothes for the children and what there was on hand to cook, and then she went to work. When Jennie Waldo arrived to see how the "hired girl" was getting on, Mrs. Hildebrand exclaimed, "O Jennie, I've got the smartest girl I ever saw. Why she has washed the children, swept & dusted & got the whole dinner ready."[45]

Isabel served the meal, and the men ate heartily. Jennie joined the group, and Isabel asked her whether she would like tea or coffee. Then Jenny "had to giggle & the cat was out of the bag."[46] Mr. Hildebrand stood up, and he swore, humiliated that a preacher's daughter had bathed his children, washed his dishes, and fed his thrashers. Later Isabel reflected, "I didn't collect my $3.00 a week but had satisfaction in helping a sick woman by deception!"[47]

In October of 1887, the women of St. Thomas organized a chapter of the Woman's Christian Temperance Union, and Isabel was elected recording secretary. St. Thomas was also home to a lodge of the Independent Order of Oddfellows. Isabel, as a woman, could not join, but her talents were well recognized, and at a program in the opera house in December of 1886, she presented an essay titled "Oddfellowship" that "added greatly to the enjoyment of all present and elicited well merited applause."[48]

The *St. Thomas Times* also listed the topics of some of her presentations at Baptist entertainments. In one program these included "Editorial," "Thanksgiving," "The second battle of Waterloo," "Ladies and the Polls," "Pigs Males and Men," "The History of our own times," "A Turkey Tragedy," and "Odds and Ends."[49] Isabel provided no details of these activities; in her 1926 journal, she merely mentioned that in North Dakota she "gave entertainments" and saved her money.[50] Later, in *Joyful Journey*, she explained the sources of the money that took her through the Baptist Missionary Training School in Chicago: she had earned it in North Dakota through "teaching painting, selling pictures, and giving entertainments."[51] Perhaps she did not write more about this because she was reluctant to associate herself with entertainers, for although her entertainments were of impeccable character, *entertainers* had a somewhat shady reputation among the pious.

45. Journal 1921, 14.
46. Ibid., 15.
47. Journal 1941–42, September 22, 1941, 58.
48. *St. Thomas Times*, December 17, 1886.
49. Ibid., November 18, 1887.
50. Journal 1926–27, 96.
51. Crawford, *Joyful Journey*, 42.

Isabel was more open about painting and selling paintings. Painting was among the genteel pastimes available to young women. In St. Thomas, Isabel became sufficiently serious and confident to place this ad in the *Times*:

> PAINTING CLASS.
>
> Persons wishing to take lessons in oil painting on silk, satin, crockery, wood, canvas, etc., can do so by joining Miss Belle Crawford's class, which opens Wednesday, February 18th. Terms 50 cents a lesson of three hours. Work done to order.[52]

These were happy times for Isabel, as she painted and prepared recitations; she taught her Sunday school class and was active in community groups; she assisted her father in his church work and labored to keep her mother from doing any housework; she visited with friends; and she had "beaux that overlapped like the prophets of old."[53]

In the fall of 1890, John Crawford left to make an extended trip to the East to attend church conventions in the United States and then to visit friends and family in Canada. He expected to be gone about two months.[54] Thus his letter, published in the December 12 edition of the *St. Thomas Times* came as a surprise. He addressed it to his St. Thomas church: "I would have written to you before this, but my mind has been considerably exercised for some weeks past whether it was not my duty to remain in Ontario. My friends here and my children, are anxious for me to settle in this Province, where I have labored some thirty years; and where a large proportion of the Baptist ministers are my old students. Here also my children reside; and it is proper, they say, that my old age should be spent among them. These and other arguments have been employed to persuade me to remain here."[55] He went on to explain that he "would return to St. Thomas, and take a more formal leave, but the expenditure of time and money seem to forbid" it. Thus again Isabel and her mother were designated to wind up affairs and prepare to move. Immediately Isabel went to work.

The Crawfords offered their household effects for sale. In addition to placing an ad in the *St. Thomas Times*, Isabel made 150 copies of a price list of everything salable, "even to the three brooms," and distributed them.[56] John Crawford became ill, and Sarah left to go to him, but Isabel was not finished. Next she "painted every single thing I could lay my hands on that I

---

52. *St. Thomas Times*, February 8, 1889.
53. Journal 1926–27, 96.
54. *St. Thomas Times*, October 3, 1890.
55. Ibid., December 12, 1890.
56. Journal Life Story, 51.

feared wouldn't sell (pie tins, jelly cake tins, meat tins, pot covers, patty pans stone ink bottles, saws, trowels, lots of old tools, dust pans, the coal scuttle & crockery churn.) I gave them all a coat of light house paint to clean them first & then put flowers & scenes on them."

Isabel placed another ad in the *Times*: "I shall have a sale of pictures rating from 25c. to $20. The sale will be at the house."[57] She wrote with pleasure, "The day of the sale the house was crowded & I made far more than I had expected."[58] Then she packed the family's books, and on January 15, 1891, Isabel left North Dakota to return to Ontario.

---

57. *St. Thomas Times*, December 19, 1890.
58. Journal Life Story, 51.

3

Training for Mission

"Papa met me at the Station in Toronto looking very sick & in a few days he & I started for Wingham where we spent eight very unhappy months & then his health broke completely & he & ma went back to Toronto while I came on to Chicago to School having fortunately earned & saved enough money to put me through."[1] This is Isabel's stark summary of the time after the Crawfords returned to Canada. Even when she wrote about hard work and lack of money in Manitoba and in North Dakota, Isabel had presented herself as someone who "couldn't help seeing & doing funny things."[2] But she found no humor in the next months in Ontario.

John Crawford was preaching in Wingham, a little more than 120 miles west and north of Toronto, but his tenure there was not long. Isabel wrote, "Within a year, before new ties were substantially formed, the blow fell. A deacon gave the right hand of fellowship to the new pastor, who walked slowly over . . . Poor father! I think he knew. I had never seen him sick a day in his life, or even 'indisposed,' but at last the cast-iron constitution collapsed and preaching days were over."[3] John and Sarah had no savings and now they had no income. Fortunately they had family members both able and happy to receive them. John Firstbrook, Fanny's husband, had entered the business started by his father, the Firstbrook Box Company, and John and Fanny lived comfortably. They invited John and Sarah to join them

---

1. Journal Life Story, 52.
2. Journal 1893–94, 12.
3. Crawford, *Joyful Journey*, 38. According to a list Crawford made in her 1906–8 Journal, his last sermon was on July 19, 1891 (ibid., 37).

and their four children, and soon the older couple left for Toronto. Isabel remained in Wingham for a while: once again it was her responsibility to close the family's home.

Isabel was twenty-six. An unmarried daughter often served as companion and care-giver for her parents, but she was no longer needed in that role. As she later expressed it, she had "a life that had to be placed somewhere."[4] But where? For years she had found joy as a Sunday school teacher, and her activity had always centered on her local Baptist church.

Five years earlier, in North Dakota, she had begun to consider a wider sphere of service. G. W. Huntley of Fargo, the traveling missionary for the territory, had told her about a Baptist training school in Chicago for women wishing to become missionaries, and he had urged Isabel to attend. She had written to Mary Burdette, Corresponding Secretary for the Women's Baptist Home Mission Society, hoping that a "plain path" would be pointed out to her.[5] None did at that time, and in summaries she made of her life story, she made no mention of the incident. Now things had changed. In her letter of application of 1891 Crawford wrote, "God didn't open the way then but now He has and I do so long to follow where He leads."[6]

The application called for a letter from the applicant's pastor, but because Isabel's pastor was her father, she suggested that it might come from Huntley instead. In his letter, he observed that "she is an active Christian, fairly well educated and has expressed to me the desire for Foreign Mission work. On that I advised her to attend the Training School. She has qualifications to make a good Home Missionary, also, is bright, energetic and ambitious to do good. If she remains single by all means receive her. She left North Dakota last fall for her present home in Ontario. It was generally understood here by those who knew her then that she was engaged to Rev. W. A. Waldo, who will finish his course at Morgan Park next may [sic]."[7]

As already noted, this is one of Isabel Crawford's silences. Although she claimed that in St. Thomas she had "beaux that overlapped like the prophets of old,"[8] she never mentioned Waldo. William Waldo had been a student pastor in St. Thomas when John Crawford first visited the area. Isabel and her mother arrived there in the spring of 1884, and Waldo apparently left North Dakota and resumed his studies at the end of that sum-

---

4. Journal 1921, 71.

5. Crawford to Burdette, March 8, 1886, Crawford, Correspondence, Mary Burdette Files.

6. Application, Crawford, Biographical Files.

7. Ibid.

8. Journal 1926–27, 96.

mer.⁹ If "those who knew her" were correct and there was an engagement, there is no indication of how it was broken, or when. William Waldo did not become a significant part of Isabel Crawford's life narrative.

John Crawford feared that the training school's instruction would be "too elementary."¹⁰ He had seen women as well as men successfully pursue studies at both the Canadian Literary Institute and Prairie College, and he felt that Isabel should take a "more thorough course" at a theological seminary. Isabel, however, doubted that her education was sufficiently advanced, and she preferred the training school.

She had just enough money for the two-year course—three hundred dollars—but she had nothing extra.¹¹ As the fourth child in the family, she was accustomed to hand-me-downs, and before leaving Ontario, she went through the available supply, making underclothes out of old linens and carefully cleaning and repairing dresses, "for there was no money to buy new ones."¹² Then she set forth for Chicago "with two trunks, a castiron constitution, a Scotch backbone, and a fully developed Irish funny-bone."¹³

The day after she arrived, Mary Burdette called upon her. She told Crawford, "I have your name here and have prayed for you every day since the Board voted to accept you as a student. You have come to prepare yourself for missionary service. I hope the Lord has called you and that you will bring great honor to His name."¹⁴

After Burdette left, Crawford pondered what she had said. Later she wrote, "It was the first time that I had ever heard anyone hint at the fact that God calls *women* into full time service as well as men. Father, as well as the other theological professors, was always on the lookout for 'suitable young men for the ministry,' with no reference whatever to women. They were supposed to become good wives, mothers, and housekeepers, able to wash and iron white cravats and chokers in such a way as not to choke the brethren."¹⁵ In her 1886 letter of inquiry, Isabel had expressed the belief that she was "one of those called to 'Go into all the world.'" Now, five years later,

---

9. Minutes of Proceedings, North Dakota Baptist Association, June 27–28, 1884, 60–61. W. 3A. Waldo is shown as pastor at St. Thomas (supply) and J. Crawford as pastor at Wheatland.

10. Journal 1891–93, 1.

11. Crawford, *Joyful Journey*, 42. In her application, she presented to Burdette a more complicated financial picture. However, not only in *Joyful Journey* but elsewhere she wrote about the three hundred dollars. See, for example, Journal 1926–27, 96.

12. Crawford, *Joyful Journey*, 42.

13. Ibid., 41.

14. Ibid., 42.

15. Ibid.

she received validation through Burdette's assumption that a *woman* might be called by God. In the future, her understanding of gender roles would be further challenged, and she might challenge other people's preconceptions, but for Crawford in the autumn of 1891, this was a new assurance.

The training school educated a diverse group of students, and the instruction, too, was varied. During their two-year course, the students undertook medical studies as well as instruction in Sunday School, Rules of Order, Physical & Vocal Culture, Music, Missionary, Kindergarten Methods, and Temperance. The "Industrial" studies included "Daily Practice Housework" as well as "Domestic Economy" and "Preparation of Work for Industrial Schools, etc."[16]

Crawford enjoyed the lectures in "Theological and Biblical" studies and discovered that she could listen to diverse opinions without "departing from the faith."[17] Though she did not agree with all the ideas presented by her professor Poindexter Smith Henson, she learned something important from him. One day Henson "came to give a lecture and, sailing up to the platform in his jaunty way over the newly waxed floor, he slipped and nearly landed on his back. On recovering, his first remark was, 'Ladies, this is no place for backsliding. You must always seek to walk uprightly, that those who follow after may not be led astray.'"[18] She had feared that her "Irish funny-bone" would prevent her from becoming a proper missionary, but she respected Henson and did not doubt his call to serve God. Crawford wrote, "Little by little my eyes were opened till I saw that the Lord could use me fun & all if I was only willing."[19]

Others noticed her tendency toward mirth, and one student tried to reform her. She came to Crawford's room and explained nervously that she, too, once had a humorous disposition like Crawford's, but through prayer she had overcome it: "[N]ow I can listen to a funny story and not even smile."[20] In reply, Crawford pointed out that "God made dogs and cats, horses and cows, and none of them can talk or laugh. Then he made people with the ability to do both. Don't you think that He meant us to use these gifts as well as singing and speaking?" Her would-be teacher departed, "showing all her front teeth."

---

16. *Baptist Missionary Training School, 1881–1893*, 6–7.
17. Journal 1921, 72.
18. Crawford, *Joyful Journey*, 45.
19. Journal 1893–94, 13.
20. Crawford, *Joyful Journey*, 43–44.

Isabel Crawford during her years at the Baptist Missionary Training School. Courtesy of the American Baptist Historical Society, Board of International Ministries, Missionary Biographical Files: Crawford, Isabelle.

While lectures formed an important part of the students' education, the real heart of the course was field work. In addition, students learned about "Daily Diaries, Abstracts and Time books, Prompt and Accurate Monthly Reports" to help them process their experiences as they did field work and to prepare them for the reporting that the women would do throughout their missionary careers.[21] Thus Isabel Crawford began keeping a journal.

On the first page of Crawford's first journal, she drew a map of "The Black Hole," an area roughly between the Chicago River and State Street,

21. *Baptist Missionary Training School, 1881–1893*, 6–7.

with Van Buren on the north and Twelfth Street on the south. Into this area the students went, two by two, every Thursday afternoon. This was not Woodstock or Rapid City or St. Thomas. Even Crawford's observations of "the poor and wretched" in Toronto scarcely prepared her for what she met in the Black Hole. She wrote in her journal, "The lesson God meant to teach us from the very beginning was—there is no more important work in the world than bearing the bread of life to the starving, but in the carrying of it we must be prepared for almost overwhelming obstacles."[22] Only gradually did she recognize that, not only were there obstacles, but bringing the "bread of life" was more complex than she initially recognized.

On her first day of field work, Crawford and her partner came upon three black women: "In my poor weak way I tried to tell these dark sisters that Jesus let trials & troubles come to them on purpose. He kept moving them about from house to house & from place to place to teach them that they were only visitors here below & mustn't act or try to act as if they had come to stay. I then read to them that lovely comforting passage in John XIV 'Let not your heart be troubled.'"[23] On her way back to the school, she reflected. "I must say I felt very much discouraged as I thought over what had been done." On another trip, Crawford encountered several very poor and drunken women. In her journal she considered the limited powers of the students and also how greatly the environment affected the innocent.[24]

Poverty was a problem, and so was the Roman Catholic environment; here Crawford reflected the attitudes common to many Protestants of her day. In one home, Crawford saw a "fearful" picture of Christ: "His bosom is bear [sic] & His flesh & skin are turned back revealing His heart which is blood red. It has six arrows sticking in it three on each side. It is vile."[25] Repulsed but wanting to learn more, she visited a Catholic church a short time later and "came out sick at heart"[26] Her conclusions were dire: "If protestants only knew the full meaning of the Catholic teaching they couldn't rest on their oars as they do. The devil is marching ahead with steady *determined* step & the first thing we know we will be in their power."[27]

Her concern about the Catholic Church did not keep her from exercising compassion toward Catholic individuals, whom she saw as imprisoned by their beliefs. She tried to bring them to the true faith, and her actions

22. Journal 1891–93, 2.
23. Ibid., 3.
24. Ibid., 21–22.
25. Ibid., 103.
26. Ibid., 110.
27. Ibid., 109–10.

toward the Lee family showed her willingness to minister to their temporal needs as well. Anton Lee and his wife had come from Germany. They were old, and they were destitute. She brought them food and warm clothing. As she developed warmer feelings for them as individuals, she became less able to categorize them simply as Catholics. She believed that they were longing "for the living Christ who had been kept hidden from them."[28]

The students' field work extended beyond calling from house to house. Crawford visited Waif's Mission, an organization that attempted to help girls as well as boys who were newspaper sellers, bootblacks, and the like. There she saw "two hundred ragged hungry children form in line & march up to the table & get their buns & eat them as ravenously as though they had seen nothing to eat since the last Sunday."[29] And when one of her friends was ill, Crawford taught a class at the Pacific Garden Industrial School.

During Isabel's first year in Chicago, she described to her father the theological problems discussed during her classes, and he wrote long letters in reply, as he tried to ensure that his daughter did not depart from the faith. She wrote later, "Father needn't have worried so," because he had already given her a firm grounding.[30]

Near the end of May, 1892, she asked him to write out the text of John 3:16 in all the languages he knew; she wanted to put it in her Bible. She reported, "He got all his books ready with my letter between them & lay down to rest a while before writing. When my mother went to him a few minutes after he didn't know her. He went 'Home' leaving to me the open gospel. If the Lord had spoken to me from Heaven He couldn't have made me feel more that He wanted me to take up my father's work & go forward with it."[31]

In a 1950 letter, Crawford wrote another description of his death: "One afternoon he took a walk of six miles, came home, went to bed and to sleep, and before morning, the poor man awoke a millionaire. In the only bank he ever made a deposit (his pant's pocket), mother found a jack-knife, a piece of string, and 38 cents in cash with which to carry on."[32] In her father's complete faithfulness to God, he had given all his material wealth. On the other hand, he had failed to provide for his own later life and for his wife's support.

---

28. Ibid., January 26, 1893, 85.
29. Ibid., May 28, 1893, 126.
30. Journal 1921, 72.
31. Journal 1893–94, 13–14.
32. Notebook untitled [Miscellaneous 1950–53], Crawford to Taylor, 16 February 1950. She also gave the amount as seven dollars; see Journal 1906–8, October 16, 1908, 453.

John Crawford's pure-hearted but short-sighted generosity gave Isabel both a model and a warning.

John Crawford's death affected his daughter deeply in an unexpected way. Three months after her father's death, Isabel and a companion visited John Cavenaugh. He was dying, and his drunken wife "refused to do for him as much as she would for a cat."[33] Twice before, the training school students had prayed with him, but on September 22, Isabel was overcome with the horror of the scene. In her journal she wrote, "A card that used to hang on Miss Burdettes desk passed before my eyes, and the big interrogation mark seemed to be waiting for an answer—'What would Jesus do?' Thoughts came thick & fast while my heart & will were melting. All in about a minute I saw my own father lying ill before me & I didn't need to ask myself what I would do for him. I certainly wouldn't read & pray. The battle with self was soon over & I asked if I might get a little water & cool his head." He responded eagerly, and she washed him as best she could. When she had finished, he pulled up his sleeve and showed her the tattoo of his initials, J. C., the same as those of her father and of her Lord. For Crawford, the barriers between her and those she had perceived as unlike her were breaking down.

Chicago in the early 1890s was a vibrant if rough city, and Crawford's education extended far beyond the classroom and field work. One day, she visited the Board of Trade, where grains and grain futures were bought and sold. From the visitors' gallery, she watched the merchants shout their orders and the telegraph boys rush about. In her journal she wrote, "I never want to hear another word against revival meeting excitement, from a person of the world, for I have been at genuine old time Methodist revivals & Salvation Army camp meetings but never have I witnessed anything that would begin to compare with the excitement at the Board of Trade May 21 1892."[34]

On the afternoon of Sunday, January 19, 1893, Crawford went to Chicago's North Side to see the famous revivalist Dwight Moody. During the early 1870s the former shoe salesman began to enjoy great success as a revivalist, and twenty years later his meetings remained popular. Because of her difficulty hearing, Crawford chose a front seat. The sight of him surprised her: "Instead of seeing a nice, gentlemanly, neat man with a winning face I beheld a person measuring about 100 inches round where the waist ought to be, medium height, coat open & flapping, full grayish frizzy beard & mustache, very thick red lips, & a penetrating dark eye."[35] Moody's style was as surprising as his appearance, for he "conducted the meeting in an off

---

33. Journal 1891–93, September 22, 1892, 55.
34. Journal 1891–93, May, 21, 1892, 34.
35. Ibid., 87.

hand way, giving out whatever came into his head & ordering every one to sing, here there & all over." After the singing, Moody gave a "wholesome, straight gospel talk." Afterwards Crawford reflected: "The meeting closed at last & I returned home feeling that I had seen one of the greatest men the world had ever known: Great because perfectly natural letting his heart lead him & not cramping his soul, by thinking about which foot ought to be put out first."[36]

In the early 1890s, Chicago offered a wide variety of attractions, the most eagerly anticipated of which was the World's Columbian Exposition, also known as the Chicago World's Fair. It was intended to celebrate the four hundredth anniversary of the arrival of Christopher Columbus. Many problems delayed the construction of the fair, but the dedication ceremonies were held October of 1892 among the incomplete buildings and landscaping.[37]

Chicago's streets were festooned with flags and banners when Crawford and a friend from North Dakota, C. A. Preston, set forth to see all they could of the colorful dedication day parade. They had been given tickets to the opening ceremonies, so they joined the throngs who crowded into the Manufacturers and Liberal Arts building, the largest covered building in the world. Crawford could not hear the recitation of the new Pledge of Allegiance, written by Francis J. Bellamy and circulated so that it could also be recited by schoolchildren across the nation. But she heard the five-thousand-voice choir sing "My country 'Tis of Thee"; the instrumentalists included a band just recently organized by John Philip Sousa. Reflecting on the event, Crawford observed, "The American people are more religious than they get credit for."[38]

When the exposition officially opened on May 1, 1893, Crawford watched another parade, this time with her roommate, Miss Berger. The procession was coming down State Street, only a short distance from the training school on Michigan Avenue. It was rainy and streets were muddy. By the time Crawford and Berger reached State Street, the head of the parade was near, and the women wanted to be on the other side of the street. As she crossed, Crawford found herself between the Liberty Bell and the open carriage carrying President Grover Cleveland. But her rubber pulled off in the mud. Unwilling to lose it, she took time to retrieve it despite the approach of the president's carriage. She "smiled & smiled & smiled in at

---

36. Ibid., 91.

37. The date had been selected so as not to conflict with celebrations in New York City on October 12.

38. Journal 1891–93, October 21, 1892, 80.

him but he never even raised his hat or said thank you."[39] She observed, "There may not be an aristocracy in America but the *spirit* is here whether the blood is or not."

As Crawford's two-year course came toward its end, she took time to visit more of the fair, until eventually she wrote, "Have done the World's fair till I'm sick & tired of it. I never want to see another 'sight.'"[40] The exposition offered much entertainment, but it had educational offerings, too. Outstanding among these was the Congress of Women or, more properly, the World's Congress of Representative Women, which opened on May 15. Crawford had wearied of "sights," but this was an event of substance, and she attended numerous sessions during the week-long gathering.

Much of Crawford's report focused on the dress of the participants. Bertha Honoré Palmer was president of the women's Board of Managers for the exposition and a leading figure in Chicago society. Crawford wrote, "Mrs. Potter Palmer was simply sweetness personified.... Her shoes were neat, her white kid gloves a good fit & her bonnet was sweet—all black with three little black tips & a buckle under them in front... her eyes are black, her teeth even & white & she has a sweet amiable expression lady like manner a wasp waist & lots of power."[41] Crawford's emphasis on appearance was perhaps due to her difficulty hearing, but it also reflected a traditional view of woman's role. The whole congress, she stated, "showed me how easily a woman could step out of her sphere & yet never know it."[42]

At one session, eight woman ministers were present. Crawford wrote that they "gave their experiences. I was thoroughly disgusted with the whole caboodle of them. One free Will Baptist said she had baptized fifteen on one occasion & I couldn't help but wish she had been drowned on the spot. *Rev. Anna Shaw* was the leading Spirit. She was a Methodist & was full of wit & was a Christian no doubt but—"[43]

Yet Crawford's remarks about those who stretched traditional boundaries were not all negative. She observed that woman suffrage leader "Susan B. Anthony was cute though rather masculine. She must be all of sixty & it did look strange to see her tip away back in her chair & cross her limbs. She was dressed in plain black silk with a white front covered with black lace. She is what we call clever & shrewd with lots of wit & is able to carry an audience anywhere she wants to—although to me her remarks were common

---

39. Ibid., April 29,1893 [sic], 119.
40. Ibid., 126.
41. Ibid., 127–28.
42. Ibid.
43. Ibid., 130–31.

place."[44] Another suffragist surprised her: "Lucy Stone was a dear old lady, not at all what I expected she would be. She was motherly & womanly. She was decidedly old fashioned in her plain black silk dress with pocket in the side gore & her big ugly bonnet." Crawford was particularly inspired by Julia Ward Howe. Although Howe was active in the woman suffrage movement, she was best known for writing the lyrics of "The Battle Hymn of the Republic." Howe recited the hymn, "first covering her eyes with her hand before telling what 'her eyes had seen.'"[45] In her journal Crawford wrote, "I could scarcely keep my seat. It was grand & she did give it with so much feeling."[46]

When the Congress of Women ended, Crawford could focus on her graduation. On June 9 she wrote:

> Tonight I receive my diploma & graduate from the Baptist Missionary Training School of Chicago. I thank the Lord for leading me to such a heavenly resting place. My soul & body are revived & I am now ready for life in earnest. . . . I go out into life afraid of nothing & ready for anything. I want the Lord to use me all He can & if I stand shivering round on one foot he may give me a cripples work. When the Lord said "Sic-cum" I want to go in the direction in which He points & when he says "scat" I want to run. It is the Lord God Almighty who brought me & I'm afraid to fool round & play with His work. It is Jesus Christ my Saviour who loved me & gave Himself for me & I am only too glad to show my appreciation of the great love by honest active service & self sacrifice.[47]

Thus with optimism and anticipation Isabel Crawford became one of the nineteen graduates of the Baptist Missionary Training School's class of 1893.

Two days later, Crawford was back in Toronto. She enjoyed visiting with her mother and with both of her sisters and their families. As she renewed family connections, she also waited—waited for the assignment that would tell her where she would begin her missionary career. During the summer she collected items for her missionary outfit, which comprised not only her clothing and other useful items, but also things that would help her to feel at home as she lived—so she anticipated—in an exotic culture. She would take a bit of North American gentility with her. All three of the

---

44. Ibid., 128. Anthony was, in fact, seventy-three at the time.
45. Notebook Illinois; with photo of Julia Ward Howe.
46. Journal 1891–93, 130.
47. Ibid., June 9, 1893, 138.

Crawford sisters had learned the fashionable skill of china painting, and into Isabel's trunk went painted china.[48]

The Baptist Missionary Training School as pictured on the diploma of Isabel Crawford. Courtesy of Barbara Cross McKinnon.

Crawford believed that she was ready to go anywhere God might send her, but when she received Mary Burdette's letter telling of her assignment, she had a rude awakening: "I told the Lord on my knees that I would leave the whole matter with Him & I really thought I meant it, but when the letter came saying 'You are appointed to labor among the Blanket Indians at Elk Creek Ok. T[erritor]y. I said 'I won't go one foot' and I tell you I was mad. I handed the letter to my mother who turned deadly pale, then flushed crimson & went upstairs."[49] In an earlier version of the episode, Crawford explained her anger and disappointment by stating, "I had planned to go to some *civilized* (?) place, where I could be *nice* & *good*." Above the line in different ink was added "India, China, Africa."[50]

Crawford's reflected the popular thought of her day, when writers in the developing field of cultural anthropology attempted to classify groups of

48. Journal 1893–94, 14.
49. Journal 1897–98, 41.
50. Journal 1893–94, 14.

people along a spectrum from primitive to civilized. For all their differences from North American and European culture, the people of India and China were placed among the "civilized," while American Indians were seen as "primitive."[51] Baptists had a long history of missions in these and other foreign locations. While not only pioneering missionaries but also later ones were often called upon to undergo great hardships, by the 1890s, some missionaries managed to create, in their homes and missionary enclaves, partial replicas of the "civilization" they had left behind. Thus Crawford seems to envision herself in a genteel home setting from which she would go forth to do God's work.

In a notebook dating from 1951, Crawford wrote that Burdette gave a reason for her appointment: "We have appointed you to work among the Indians because all the missionaries have to have interpreters & you being deaf wont interfere with your work." Crawford observed, "Why I never thought being deaf any handicap. I just took it for granted."[52] Crawford had successfully completed the required courses and the field work at the training school, and she saw herself as ready to go to one of the well-known foreign fields. She did not recognize that missionary candidates' ages and medical conditions could be factors in making assignments.[53] It was only when she was in her eighties that she acknowledged the reason given to her; it appears in none of the earlier reports regarding her assignment.

For a time she struggled with disappointment and rebellion. Then came a shift. In her earliest report of what happened she explained, "I started to pray about it & with every sentence came the words, 'My Jesus as Thou wilt' till at last my will was broken & I said, 'Lord Jesus I'll go to the Indians if *you* want me to go if I'm scalped twenty four hours after I arrive.'"[54] A year later, she tried again to describe the experience: "After thinking over it in a very business like way I decided that if I didn't go I was simply telling a lie to the Lord so I decided to go, feeling or no feeling."[55] Crawford's struggle to describe her decision suggests also a struggle to comprehend the change,

---

51. The presence of Africa on Crawford's list is problematic. Few of her contemporaries would have placed most of it in the "civilized" category with India and China. Crawford had heard missionaries from Africa tell of their experiences, but apparently she had not appreciated the dangers of some parts of the continent, for Africa was known as the "graveyard of missionaries."

52. Notebook 15 [1951], Barbara Cross McKinnon collection.

53. Gagan, *A Sensitive Independence*, 162, and Semple, *Missionary Women*, 27.

54. Journal 1893–94, 14.

55. Diary 1896–97, 72. In her 1897–98 journal she stated, "At last I clenched my fists & my teeth & said 'Lord Jesus I'll go to the Indians if You want me to go if I'm scalped twenty four hours after I land'" (41).

but her commitment to her decision was firm. She replaced the fine items in her trunk with things of a more practical nature.

When Crawford relayed her acceptance to Burdette, she included an anecdote about the famous British Baptist preacher Charles Spurgeon: "When Spurgeon became a Baptist his mother said 'Well Charles we did pray that you would become a Christian but we never prayed that you would become a Baptist,' and Sturgeon replied 'That is always the way with the Lord, Mother. He always gives us more than we ask.' I've got more than I asked for but I'll go."[56]

Isabel's reference to the possibility of being "scalped" illustrates the common perception of Indians as primitive and dangerous people—despite her own experience in Manitoba with Indians who were "always well mannered & strictly honest."[57] One family story, however, played into the popular picture of Indians as savage warriors. As Isabel recorded it, "My mother's youngest sister & her husband came from Ireland to the Yosemite on their Wedding trip and have never been heard of since. There was an Indian massacre about that time & it is supposed they perished with the rest."[58]

Early in September, 1893, Isabel Crawford received a letter from Burdette giving her first assignment: a speaking tour in southern Illinois. When she wrote asking Burdette what she should speak about, Burdette replied, "Tell how God has led you to the present time & no money in the treasury to send you out." Crawford refused. "Well, tell how God has led you." "All right I'll do that, but I won't hint or ask for money. It isn't my job."[59] She packed quickly and headed for Chicago. When she arrived there at ten-thirty in the evening, her brother met her and took her to the Training School for a brief consultation with Burdette.[60] Then Crawford left on an overnight train and began her career as a missionary.

After her first speaking tour, Crawford returned to Chicago. There she went to another event connected with the Columbian Exposition, namely the World's Parliament of Religions. Held from the eleventh through the twenty-seventh of September, the gathering brought together leaders of what the organizers considered the world's great religions. For Crawford, the Parliament was the high point of the exposition. She described the platform as "a riot of artistic colors from the flowing robes of the representatives

---

56. Journal 1897–98, 41–42.
57. Journal Life Story, 20.
58. Journal 1912–13, March 18, 1913, 148.
59. Journal 1893–94, 2.
60. Hugh Crawford had gone to Chicago to study nursing, though he did not complete the course (Doris Cline Ward, interview with the author, March 5, 2011).

of cults and so-called religions of the world. They looked well, spoke well, and left the impression of honest sincerity."[61]

On September 29, two days after the parliament ended, Crawford left Chicago to fulfill further speaking assignments before taking up her Oklahoma post. At Centralia, Illinois, the local minister conducted the Sunday morning service, but then he took a train out of town. This left Crawford fully in charge of the evening service—alone, "for the good deacons thought it was a sin for a woman to speak in church & so left me in full possession of the pulpit not even giving me an introduction.... Sailed through without any breaks & had no trouble holding the attention of the whole audience."[62]

After several more engagements, Crawford went to the Illinois Baptist Convention at Jerseyville. She and two other new missionaries would soon be leaving for their mission fields, and Crawford looked forward to having them received by the assembly and sent off with its blessing. Instead, to her dismay, she found that on the evening of October 17, while the men of the convention went on with their business, the women were scheduled to meet alone—in the *Methodist* church. At that meeting, Crawford recounted her experience, telling of her earlier life, her initial reluctance to accept her assignment, and her change of mind. Then she read from a small pamphlet that she had received just recently. It was an appeal from the Kiowa leader Lone Wolf, to whose camp she would soon be heading:

> When the Great Spirit created the world He divided the year into two great seasons, one warm the other cold. The warm season brings life & light, the grass springs up, the birds sing, there is growth & development & joy & gladness. The cold season brings death & desolation. The grass dies, the trees are bare, the fruits are gone the animals become weak & poor the very water turns hard, there is no growth no joy no gladness. You Christian people are like the Summer. You have life & warmth & light. You have flowers & fruit & growth & knowledge. The poor wild Indians are like the winter. We have no growth, no joy, no knowledge no gladness. Wont you share your summer with us? Wont you help us with the light & life that we may have joy & knowledge & eternal life hereafter.[63]

Lone Wolf's appeal had moved her deeply, and at last she was not simply reconciled to her assignment: she was eager to go.

---

61. Journal 1937–38, 11.
62. Journal 1893–94, September 29, 1893, 6.
63. Ibid., October 17, 1893, 14–15.

The women's meeting was successful, but Crawford still smarted from the slight to the new missionaries when she was called to the platform the next day at the general meeting. She first spoke of their missionary credentials, for they "have been called to the work as surely as any of you here today have been."[64] She next reassured the men that these women accepted their proper gender roles; the graduates were *"not preachers* or women wanting to usurp authority over our brethren in the ministry but we are humble followers of Jesus Christ willing in a sweet mild Christ-like way to carry the gospel into the homes & hearts of the women of our land & when we have won them to the blessed Master we bring them to you my brethren to baptize & to help strengthen you & uphold you in your greater work! Our one aim is to build up the Church of God in the least conspicuous way because we are striving to be like Him who made himself of no reputation for the sake of a ruined world."

Then Crawford spoke with unexpected boldness. The women had anticipated being sent forth with the blessings of everyone present, but instead, "You know you went on with your work as if nothing was happening while we were being sent forth by the women from a Methodist Church! It has cut us to the very hearts."[65] But the injury could yet be remedied: "I ask you if us girls may stand here & receive some parting words from Dr. Spencer. We ask that he may be allowed to come up here & give us some words of encouragement & that Dr Pierce our beloved professor follow him & then let us have Dr Tollman pray for us. . . . Will you grant us our request?"[66]

The women received their request. Then Crawford asked that the group sing "Blest be the tie that binds"; it was "very tremblingly sung for the audience by this time was completely broken up. I sang out like a lark for I felt somehow as if the Lord was in it all."[67]

On November 1, 1893, she met with Mary Burdette in St. Louis for some last minute discussion. After that, she headed for Oklahoma and her new mission field.

---

64. Ibid., October 18, 1893, 18.
65. Ibid., 19.
66. Ibid., 22.
67. Ibid., 23.

4

Elk Creek

AT THE BEGINNING OF November, 1893, the train bearing Isabel Crawford and Hattie Everts crossed from the state of Kansas into the Oklahoma Territory, and the two young women witnessed the West in transition. Only two months earlier, land known as the Cherokee Outlet had been opened for homesteading. Now Crawford saw "small new buildings about the size of smoke houses, on every quarter section & two or three on some I think. One row of sod is turned, round each claim & the stock stands round with 'no place like home.'"[1] Land-hungry Americans were staking their claims.

Crawford and Everts headed on to the southwestern part of the territory, to the Kiowa-Comanche-Apache Reservation. The Kiowas had gradually been pushed southward from their home in the northern Rocky Mountains. On the plains they became efficient bison hunters, obtaining food, clothing, and shelter from the buffalo they killed. But the once-vast herds diminished. Among easterners, there was a relentless hunger for western land, but the Indians stood in the way, and tension between settlers and Indians sometimes escalated into violence. As the native population decreased, many anticipated the disappearance of the Indians. While some might welcome their absence, others feared their ultimate extinction. As a solution for this "Indian problem," the government created new reservations. The Kiowa, Comanche, and Apache Indians were assigned land in the Wichita Mountain area. They were to obtain schools, churches, and protection from white hunters. In return, the government gained territory to open for settlement.

---

1. Journal 1893–94, November 3, 1893, 27.

The train took Crawford and Everts to Chickasha. There they ate and then went on by hack to Anadarko, to meet the Baptist missionary George Hicks, who was in the town because his wife, Ruth, had recently given birth. Tired from the long journey, Crawford retired early and slept through the next morning. In the afternoon, when she and Everts looked around the town, they saw that they had stepped into a new and strange environment. Because the bison were gone and the Kiowas were confined to their reservation, the people were now supposed to make the transition to farming—according to the government's plan. Many difficulties, however, stood in the way, and so the government was to provide them with annuities. This was the week they were to receive their rations, and they had left their homes and come to Anadarko.

Crawford was intrigued by what she saw: "The men have long hair hanging in two straight tails over the front of their shoulders & simply bound round & round from the roots down with otter skin. . . . Most of their faces are painted red down to the mouth & up through the division of the hair, while the lower part is colored bright yellow. Their blankets & moccasins are pretty & if they only had nice coverings for their legs would look charming."[2] Caught up in this exotic scene, she continued, "They do look so picturesque I do hesitate to try to civilize them, that is if civilization means a change of costume & dwelling places." But the whole purpose of the missionary enterprise was to "civilize" and Christianize the Indians, and not for long would she retain this romantic view.

The next day, while Crawford was looking out the hotel window, she "noticed a large corpulent Indian go by with a remarkably pleasant face"; he was wearing "civilized clothes" that fit him well. Half an hour later, Julia Given, interpreter for the Baptist missionary Marietta Reeside, came in and told the women to come outside to meet Chief Lone Wolf. "Of course we flew out for it was to his camp that we were to go. Imagine my surprise & delight upon being introduced to the same Indian whose face I had just admired. He met us very cordially & said to us through Miss Given, 'I am glad you come. Some of my people not want you. I will help you all I can. My people will not hurt you. Me glad—good—good.'"[3]

2. Ibid., 28–29.

3. Ibid., November 4, 1893, 29. An earlier Lone Wolf had been a Kiowa chief at the time of the Medicine Lodge Treaty. In 1872, the young warrior Mamadayte saved the life of his son, and two years later, when the son was killed, Mamadayte avenged his death. The elder Lone Wolf adopted Mamadayte, giving the young man his name, rights, and power. Since this book does not deal with the earlier leader, it follows Isabel Crawford's usage and refers to the younger man as Lone Wolf.

This was Lone Wolf, whose appeal for Christian missionaries had convinced Crawford of the urgency of her mission. In 1889, W. D. Lancaster was a carpenter living among the Kiowas to build houses and teach the men that skill, as part of the government's program to bring them into a Euro-American pattern of life. Lancaster was a Baptist lay preacher, and he and his wife opened a mission and a school for boys in Lone Wolf's camp. Lone Wolf's son was one of the students, and Lone Wolf came to recognize the value of mission work. Thus in the spring of 1891, he sent a message to Joseph Samuel Murrow, a missionary in Indian Territory now working under the auspices of the American Baptists. Murrow arranged a meeting with Lone Wolf and another Kiowa leader; they met with American Baptist missionaries and also with the corresponding secretary of the Women's Baptist Home Mission Society.[4] It was here that Lone Wolf made his appeal. The Baptists responded by opening missions at Rainy Mountain and at Elk Creek, where Crawford and Everts were assigned.

The next day, the two women were taken to visit the camps and meet some of the Kiowas. About thirty women and men attended the meeting led by Murrow in Chief Komalty's tent. Murrow introduced the two new missionaries, assuring the people that they "had not come to get their money or injure their property in any way but simply to tell them about Jesus & do them good."[5]

Finally, on November 21, Crawford and Everts started toward Elk Creek. Hicks drove them in a "prairie schooner" for the fifty-seven-mile trip.[6] At sunset on the third day they reached their destination. They had seen no houses during the day and, Crawford wrote, "the sight of two quite close together greatly cheered our hearts."[7] One was the home of the Lancasters, who had begun the mission work. It was in the other, the home of Komalty, that Crawford and Everts were to stay. Hicks and the two young women spent the night there. The next morning, Hicks started back to Anadarko, for he had decided to stay there until his wife and baby were strong enough to come to the mission. The two new missionaries were left at their post.

Komalty and Lone Wolf and their dwellings illustrated the transitions through which the Kiowas were passing. Though Komalty was "a wild blanket Indian," painted in the traditional way, his brightly-painted house was

   4. Corwin, *Kiowa Indians*, 113; Ellis, "The Jesus Road at the Kiowa-Comanche-Apache Reservation," 42.
   5. Journal 1893–94, November 5, 1893, 30.
   6. Burdette, *Heroine of Saddle Mountain*, 7. Late in her life, Crawford described it as a "lumber wagon" (Notebook 16 [1952–1953], Barbara Cross McKinnon collection).
   7. Journal 1893–94, November 23, 1893, 36.

well furnished in the Euro-American style, complete with "nice lace curtains & a very pretty heater."[8] Yet it was "dreadfully dirty." By contrast, Lone Wolf, when Crawford noticed him in Anadarko, wore "civilized clothes"; his home was a "nice clean teepee."[9] It was the goal of reformers and missionaries alike to assimilate Native Americans, to take the Indianness out of Indians. But even in such superficial matters as dress and dwelling, the process had uneven results. At deeper levels, the process was even more difficult and the results still more uneven.

On Sunday, Crawford and Everts attempted to hold a service, but no one showed interest as they sat outside singing hymns. Finally they entered one teepee and the woman inside let them hold a prayer meeting there, but only one other Kiowa came. It was a discouraging start. Also discouraging was the fact that so few Kiowas lived in the immediate area.

The next day, the two missionaries considered their situation in prayer and in conversation. They felt vulnerable since the Hicks family would not be at the mission for a considerable time. Was it risky for two women to remain there unprotected? In her journal, Crawford expressed doubts about the wisdom of staying, but she concluded, "Miss Everts believes He wants us to stay here so we shall stay although it is decidedly against my judgment."[10]

Then the two women set to work. Three days later, they held their first sewing meeting. Its purpose was in part religious, for the missionaries introduced the group to John 3:16, "God so loved the world . . ." Crawford wrote, "Lone Wolf interpreted with so much feeling that I could scarcely keep the tears back."[11] But their purpose was not just evangelistic. In the minds of missionaries as well as policy-makers, Christianity and civilization were intimately, perhaps inextricably, connected. One important mark of both was the Christian home, which must be clean, well run, and productive—like those of God-fearing Protestant families. Women missionaries played the special role of modeling it as well as giving instruction in the necessary skills.[12] At one meeting, Crawford took stove polish to Alma's tent and cleaned her stove. Crawford was realistic, however, about the results: "I'm willing to be a servant & do anything to win these people to Christ but it looks as if I were only winning them to myself & that very slowly."[13]

---

8. Ibid.
9. Ibid., November 26, 1893, 37.
10. Ibid., November 27, 1893, 37.
11. Ibid., November 30, 1893, 37.
12. See Dana L. Robert, "The 'Christian Home,'" 134–65.
13. Journal 1893–94, December 30, 1893, 41.

Some characteristics of "civilization" defied easy explanation. Crawford wrote, "Komaltah [sic] came in today with his hair all flying & I asked him why he didn't cut it off & pointing to the picture of Christ on the wall he said 'Jesus no cut his. White women no cut. Indians, no cut, like Jesus, but what's the matter with white men?' I was speechless. . . . I could have pointed to Jesus whiskers & said, 'Jesus no Indian: Indians got none' but I do feel that Jesus is an Indian to the Indian & a white man to the whitemen."[14]

Life was difficult, and in the privacy of her journal Crawford recorded her complaints. One day she counted 114 flea bites between her wrist and her elbow.[15] The two women had to chop wood for their fire, even during a blizzard. But hardest of all was their lack of success. In March Crawford wrote to the mission society, "Night & day almost have I labored for the salvation of their souls in rough physical work & quilt-patching & yet as I scan the winter's work there hasn't been one soul saved & only 1 quilt really finished. Satan often comes to me & says 'Crawford you're a failure. You better get back home' but I've had some dealings with that reverend gentleman before & do not pay any attention to his mean remarks."[16]

Everts and Crawford were aided by Crawford's quick wit and sense of humor. One day a white man arrived with a load of turkeys. He had heard that the missionaries were Baptists, and he claimed to be one, too. Crawford asked, "But are you a Christian? Some Baptists are not, you know."[17] The man laughed heartily and replied, "I hope I be. I hope I be." He then made his proposal: he usually sold turkeys for seventy-five cents each, but since they were Baptists, he would sell one for fifty cents. Crawford asked whether he had change, and after he had inspected his coins and said yes, she went to the house and returned with a dollar and a rope with which to tie the turkey. The vendor then pulled a quarter from his pocket and exclaimed, "Gee whizz! I thought this was a fifty-cent piece." The turkey was a big one, and with some reluctance, Crawford agreed to the purchase.

That night he camped nearby, and early the next morning Crawford returned, rope in hand. She inquired, "Are you still a Baptist?"[18] He answered, "I guess I be." She then observed that he must feel "mean" about yesterday's transaction. "I've brought the quarter back, and if you give me another turkey, we'll call the deal square. The Turkeys were to be fifty cents apiece to us, weren't they?" He roared with laughter as he gave her the sec-

---

14. Ibid., 54.
15. Ibid., December 30, 1893, 41; March 30, 1894, 56.
16. Ibid., March 22, 1894, 55.
17. Crawford, *Jolly Journal*, 137.
18. Ibid., 138.

ond turkey, and he laughed even harder when she assured him that she "was now thoroughly satisfied that he was a Christian Baptist."

In the middle of April, George and Ruth Hicks returned to Elk Creek with their baby. A church was under construction, and Crawford, Everts, and the Hicks family moved into the partially completed building, dividing the room with a curtain. Two days after their arrival, Crawford wrote in veiled terms in her journal, "It's queer old world after all and a Christian is never done learning. I've found out lately that there are Christians living right now who think nothing of going off piously to meditate on the Divine Word when it is a human dinner they ought to be cooking or some inhuman dishes they ought to be washing. Such is life."[19]

Isabel was learning other things, too. She saw how gamblers arrived with whiskey when the Indians received their supplies from the government and left bearing great loads of the Kiowas' possessions. She heard how Lone Wolf's blankets and hides were stolen. And she read.

While she was in Chicago, Crawford had read *Ramona* by Helen Hunt Jackson. Jackson had published *Ramona* in 1884, hoping that it would do for the Indian cause what *Uncle Tom's Cabin* had done for that of black slaves. When Crawford first read it, she "thought it all over-drawn."[20] Her experience at Elk Creek gave her a new perspective. She wrote: "I have read the book again after living with the Indians . . . It is a true representation of all . . . & as to the government's behaviour—I am horrified. They don't care two cents about the Indians. They want their land & minerals & they mean to get them if they have to kill every red man on the continent. That's their policy." Crawford saw the Indians as "poor & weak & blind," but increasingly she recognized the cause: "They are poor because the white men have coveted & taken their land. They are weak because the white men have killed & hunted & frightened off all their game & buffalo. They are blind because the white men have been selfish & have not taught them how to build & live in houses. They have had to live in smoky tepees till their eyes are nearly burned out. May god forgive us!"[21]

Many eastern reformers had become concerned about the situation of the Indians and thought they had a solution. In 1887, Congress had passed the Dawes Severalty Act, also known as the General Allotment Act because of its main provision. According to the act, each Indian would receive an allotment of 160 acres, and the government could negotiate for the purchase of the "surplus" lands and open them for white settlement. Five years later,

---

19. Journal 1893–94, April 20, 1894, 59.
20. Ibid., June 3, 1894, 69–70.
21. Ibid., May 26, 1894, 68.

a government commission negotiated the Jerome Agreement with Kiowa, Comanche, and Apache leaders. Following the meetings, the commissioners claimed that they had collected the necessary number of signatures required to open the reservation, although Lone Wolf and others charged that many of the signatures were fraudulent.[22]

The Dawes Act and the subsequent Jerome Commission negotiations fed the continuing white hunger for western land, but they were intended to do more than that. Isolating Indians on reservations had not resulted in the assimilation for which supporters of the reservation system had hoped. The new strategy was to break down tribalism and foster individualism by placing Indians on separate plots and increasing the pressure upon them to become farmers. If good, hard-working, Christian white settlers occupied lands, they could serve as examples and assist in the transition.

But not all settlers were good, and to some of the Kiowas, the danger was obvious. One young Kiowa said to Crawford, "We don't want it opened," and expressed his fear that "it would be the bad whites who would come in & they would steal & lie, act hateful to the Indians & pretty soon police would come in & take Indians to prison."[23] A few days later, he told her that "if any white man were to take his land from him he would split his head open or shoot it off." She confided to her journal, "I tried to preach him a little sermon but somehow or other I couldn't help sympathizing with the boy."[24]

On June 17, 1894, Everts and Crawford said farewell to the people of Elk Creek, and they did not know whether they would be returning. Crawford was discouraged. She wrote, "*We* opened the way for the Lord this winter and I learned the lesson that it is better to wait the Lord's time than to run on ahead at the risk of your health." She left "feeling sad at heart, weak in body & unable to understand God's dealings. There are precious souls here underneath the piles of rubish [sic] & God hasn't given us strength to do the digging."[25]

A train took them to Ardmore, Oklahoma. A few hours after they arrived, Crawford's "nerves snapped," and she was able to do nothing more than lie on a sofa.[26] She spent five days there, recovering her strength; she later attributed her collapse to "starvation."[27] She was not idle, however,

---

22. Pommersheim, *Broken Landscape*, 125–51.
23. Journal 1893–94, June 5, 1894, 73.
24. Ibid., June 15, 1894, 77.
25. Ibid., June 17, 1894, 78.
26. Ibid., June 20, 1894, 80.
27. Ibid., August 18, 1894, 100.

for into her journal she copied clippings about Indians. The items showed what she had been reading and thinking during the past months, and they supplied her with resources for the future. On June 20, she left Ardmore; two days later she arrived in Chicago.

From there she went to Toronto, where she visited her sister Fanny and her mother. Early in August, Crawford received word that some difficulties had been cleared up, and she could return to Elk Creek. She would live in the house of Kiowa Bill, who would spend fifty dollars to make it more comfortable. She could board with Mrs. Lancaster, and she would have an interpreter. Everything seemed in order. Meanwhile, she was to spend six weeks speaking on behalf of missions.

First she attended the South Central Association meeting in Norman, Oklahoma. Then Crawford began following the schedule of visits made by Martha Van Ness, general missionary for Nebraska. Crawford's talks, however, may not have been quite what Van Ness expected. When missionaries went on speaking tours, they usually told of their experiences in a way that would raise enthusiasm for missions—and contributions for the mission society. In 1893, Crawford had shown her independent spirit by refusing to ask her audiences for money. Now in 1894, she deviated from the formula in a more radical way.

Crawford had become deeply impressed by the wrongs suffered by the Kiowas, wrongs committed by the government and wrongs carried out by individuals who were not punished by the government. Now she spoke out against these injustices and worked to change the common perceptions of her white audiences. She told the story of the "Ruined Race" and tried to show where responsibility lay for the Indians' unfortunate condition. At one meeting, someone asked, "I believe you have been living among the Indians Miss Crawford, do the whites seem to have much trouble with them?" Crawford's wit was quick: "I said, 'I don't know whether they do or not but I do know that the Indians have lots of trouble with the whites!'"[28]

When Crawford returned to Elk Creek, she learned that the plans made by the Women's Baptist Home Mission Society had gone awry, and Crawford had to room as well as board with the Lancasters. She spent a day trying to make her "homely room beautiful to the soul for it will never look beautiful to the eye."[29] Everts had not returned, and Crawford was overcome with loneliness. Elk Creek seemed "a dreary desolate place after

---

28. Ibid., September 7. 1894, 104–5.
29. Journal 1894–96, 1894, 27.

all were it not for the few white tepees along the creek which contain real immortal souls."[30]

Komalty and his wife, Alma, were not at Elk Creek when Crawford returned, and she wondered why. She soon learned that their baby was gravely ill, and they had gone to Rainy Mountain so that he might die there. When a child died, it was customary to burn the house in which the death had occurred, but Komalty and Alma wanted to remain in their home at Elk Creek. After the baby died, Crawford painted a door panel for a grave marker. Looking at the burial place, Crawford thought, "Thank God, the Gospel has reached these Indians at last."[31] Yet not everything had changed. When Komalty and Alma returned from Rainy Mountain, Komalty had slashed his arms in a traditional rite of mourning, and Alma was crying inconsolably.

During her first year Elk Creek, Crawford had learned some Plains Indian sign language. Now one of the men felt particularly sorry about her lack of hearing, and he took it upon himself to teach her more signs. He came almost every day, and her proficiency increased. Early in December, she conducted a service without her translator, who was needed elsewhere. One of the Elk Creek men tried to interpret, but he found her signing better than his translating. Yet she still felt that she accomplished more with an interpreter, and she lamented his absence when he was pressed into service by the missionary.

The mission received boxes of clothing and other items from well-meaning church people. Many items were more valuable as patchwork than for their intended purpose, and Crawford cut them up and brought them to sewing meetings. She saw a larger usefulness in the simple activity of sewing. She wrote, "This whole Indian question is a perplexing one but there is a way of solving it & I believe the women have got hold of it. We go in with the Gospel rolled up in quilt patches & teach them something. The quilts warm their bodies, melting their hearts & making them ready to receive the word ... when we come to them with beautiful patchwork to teach them to make nice warm quilts, before they remember that we are white they are sewing as fast as they know how."[32] Gradually Crawford's close work with the women won them over, not only to herself, but to the work she was doing.

Because the land would soon be opened to settlers, the Lancasters and other white residents received orders to leave the reservation, and so Crawford again needed accommodation. Early in December, the Hicks family

---

30. Ibid., October 5, 1894, 24.
31. Burdette, *Heroine of Saddle Mountain*, 7.
32. Journal 1894–96, December 21, 1894, 48.

gave Crawford a room in their unfinished house, but she could tell that she had a cold and uncomfortable winter ahead: "The wind just whizzes round my head & I've had to tack a piece of chamois round the head of my bed on the floor to keep my head from blowing off in the night."[33] Crawford tacked felt paper on the walls, and George Hicks put some on the ceiling, "so that the wind doesn't whistle through quite so wildly."[34] She had no furniture, but she made a tick and harvested prairie grass to fill it; thus she had a bed.

As Crawford faced physical challenges, she was also challenged by the Kiowas' questions. One asked her, "If the Great Father loves his Indian children why did he let white men kill all our buffalo so that we are hungry like this? . . . I can't help hating white people when ever I see them because they killed them." Crawford recorded in her journal, "Again my heart got another blow but I tried to meet it by saying, 'All white men are not good. Maybe it wasn't right to kill all the buffalo but since it was so white men decided to pay the Indians for them.'"[35]

The policy-makers assumed that the solution to the disappearance of the buffalo was agriculture, but there were problems. The first was the land itself. Some might have been suitable for grazing, but the government was encouraging the Indians to grow crops despite the dryness of the climate; all too often the crops failed. The promised seeds and implements were often late or unsuitable if they came at all. And the Indians were to be taught by "government farmers," but they were too rarely present. So Crawford took on another role. In March of 1895 she wrote, "These Indians have had government farmers for 25 years & are so willing to learn. Yet nothing to amount to anything has been done. It's a shame, that's all, & if the Heavenly Father will give me strength I'll be government farmer as well as soul farmer for them. I do pray that the crops may be good so that they won't get discouraged."[36]

The Elk Creek men began plowing, and when the plow broke, Crawford fixed it and back to work they went, despite the heat. Next came seeding. Crawford first taught Lone Wolf how to hoe; then she taught him and his wife how to plant the different kinds of seeds they had received. She commented, "Think of a man of his age & willingness being unable to plant a bean & a government farmer paid to teaching him for 25 years."[37]

33. Journal 1894-96, December 6, 1894, 45.
34. Burdette, *Heroine of Saddle Mountain*, 9.
35. Journal 1894-96, January 13, 1895, 59-60.
36. Ibid., March 23, 1895, 94.
37. Ibid., April 17, 1895, 109.

As she taught, Crawford remained wedded to Euro-American gender expectations. Some of the farm work was carried out by men and women together, and this disturbed Crawford. While she was glad to see the Kiowas of Elk Creek progress toward becoming farmers, she looked forward to the "next generation" when one "may expect the woman to devote her time to the house."[38] Crawford's aspirations clashed with the pattern of Kiowas society, for traditionally it had been men who hunted and women who grew some crops. Crawford and others like her, in conflating "Christianity" with "civilization," were attempting to effect a radical change in native social patterns.

Lone Wolf was fortunate that he had received his seed. Another Kiowa, Charlie, came to Crawford and told her "with trembling lip" that the agent had refused to give him any, despite presenting a note from Crawford with her assurance that all the seed would be planted.[39] Crawford wrote to Frank Baldwin, a military officer who had arrived in Anadarko as Indian agent the previous year. She asked why some people received no seed and others received seeds that were unlikely to give good results in this area. She asked why there had been no government farmers and why farm machinery was not available when it was needed. Then in one brief paragraph, Crawford suggested the broader role that she was taking on. She wrote, "In three months I expect to go North to advocate the Indian cause & it is for this reason as well as for the sake of the Indians themselves that I write to you. I do not want to misrepresent government & yet I must tell why our Indians are called 'lazy.' I hope you will answer my questions fully, giving reasons for the apparent failure of government."[40]

In his reply, Baldwin expressed his opinion that the fault lay, not with the government itself, but with those entrusted with carrying out government policy. The work needed those who would "go into the field & work as they expect & want the Indians to work."[41] This must have pleased Crawford, for earlier she had written in her journal, "we have let them work long enough, now it is time to roll up our sleeves & show them *how*."[42]

Baldwin considered it important to teach the Indians not to accept charity but to support themselves by their own work. This, too, was Crawford's opinion. Some of the Elk Creek people complained that she was not as generous as the Rainy Mountain missionaries in distributing clothing that

---

38. Journal 1894–96, April 18, 1895, 110.
39. Ibid., April 9, 1895, 102.
40. Ibid., April 19, 1895, 112–13.
41. Ibid., May 23, 1895, 123.
42. Ibid., March 15, 1895, 89.

had been sent to the mission, but Crawford insisted on giving only to the ones who worked. As often as possible at meetings she had them sing "Work for the night is coming" because "they all understand the English 'word' 'Work' & we want them to associate it with religion."[43]

Elk Creek did not hold its Christmas tree until March of 1895 because Crawford had to make most of the gifts, using material that churches had sent to the mission. When the big day came, it was similar in many respects to those that Crawford had helped organize in Woodstock. All the Kiowas of Elk Creek, men, women, and children, received gifts. Then Crawford called to the front the seven men who had plowed. To each she gave a special treat: a raspberry tart.

About a month after the Christmas tree, Elk Creek observed another happy occasion. A colorful procession of men, women, and children walked to a small stream far out on the reservation. Three women were baptized: Lone Wolf's wife, Komalty's sister, and a woman from another part of the reservation. Hard work and crops, sewing and cleanliness were important, for they represented the values that missionaries believed to be the natural accompaniments of Christianity. But the baptisms were the first fruit of the mission's work. The missionaries sang "O happy day."

Three unexpected entries appear in Crawford's journal among the reports of her work. The first was on April 20, 1895: "Hugh arrived from home today & I was glad to see him although I had 6 weeks washing soaking."[44] Two days later she wrote, "Hugh & I started for Cheyenne arriving next day having got off the road. Drove over the land we are to file on, & liked the look of mine better than Hugh's."[45] Then on April 25 she recorded: "Took the oath of allegiance at about 11 today & feel mean enough to hang myself. Thank fortune I didn't have to do the writing."[46] Isabel Crawford's brother, Hugh, had come to Oklahoma as a settler, and Isabel, too, filed on land near that of her brother. This is one of the silences in Isabel Crawford's journals. Although she wrote the journals as resources for her reports to the mission society, she sometimes also recorded in them other, more personal thoughts and events. Yet in her subsequent journals she rarely mentioned her "farm." Crawford never lived on her land. Not only did she avoid presenting herself to the world as a land owner: she barely acknowledged that role even in the privacy of her journal.

43. Ibid., March 26, 1895, 98.
44. Ibid., April 20, 1895, 113.
45. Ibid., April 22, 1895, 114.
46. Ibid., April 25, 1895, 114.

Early in August, Crawford received a letter from the mission society instructing her that she had engagements in local churches from September 3 to November 10, and so she prepared for her leave. When she reached Anadarko, she called upon Baldwin. In her journal she reported, "He told me he was very much interested in my work. He could see great changes for the better in the Indians. He would depend greatly upon me when I returned & would fill any order I sent in for supplies. He saw my ideas about making the Indians help themselves were right & he would do all he could to help me—he enjoyed my letters very much."[47]

On the train from Chickasha to Chicago, Crawford observed that the farther east she went, the larger the women's sleeves were. "Women had to get off the train sideways."[48] She went on to Ionia, Michigan. Fashion made no difference on the reservation, but Crawford, always aware of style, "had to stay in the house all week till I got some sleeves made with a little dress added."[49] She did not wish to fit the stereotype of a dowdy missionary on furlough.

Crawford's schedule kept her busy, and by the time she reached Cincinnati she was tired. Harriet Rychen, state secretary for the Women's Baptist Home Mission Society, met her at the train. Rychen, "a tall, dignified-looking spinster with gray hair," told Crawford that she had scheduled no appointments for Crawford during the next two days.[50] What did she want to do that evening? There was a good concert in the city. Crawford replied, "Lady Fair, I am tired of *good* things and of being *thought* good. If there's a circus in town I'd like to go to that." They attended the Ringling Brothers circus and forged a fast friendship.

Once again Crawford's addresses were not routine reports of wonderful things accomplished at missions. She spoke of the plight of the Indians and how white Americans had been responsible and should work to right the wrongs. As she headed back to Oklahoma at the beginning of November, she reflected: "White people are responsible for the ruin & degradation into which our so called civilization has sunk them. . . . Are we Americans? NO we are all foreigners. There is only one race of real true Americans, the North American Indians, who today lie shivering & starving while we the usurpers of land & name stand well fed & clothed in purple & fine linen. . .

---

47. Ibid., August 19, 1895, 153.
48. Ibid., August 23, 1895, 153.
49. Ibid., August 30, 1895, 153.
50. Crawford, *Jolly Journal*, 10.

. Our mean dishonest treatment of these Indians has almost destroyed their lives & God up in heaven says we are responsible for their souls too."[51]

Back at Elk Creek, Crawford continued her work. Again she searched the missionary barrels for material for gifts for the Christmas tree, and again the tree was a great success. Yet although there were signs of progress, Crawford was becoming restless. Elk Creek's adult population was less than forty, and yet it was served by a missionary couple and Crawford, while other Kiowas had no one sharing the gospel with them.

Through her interpreter, Paul Zotom, Crawford learned of a settlement about thirty miles away, near Saddle Mountain. It had many more people than Elk Creek, and they had no missionary. Zotom, in turn, told the Saddle Mountain chief, Dumot, about Crawford and her work, and in March of 1896, Dumot came to Elk Creek to let her know that many of the Saddle Mountain Kiowas were ready to welcome her. He made a strong appeal: "It will be a good day when you come. We have nobody to tell us the Jesus way and we are all in the dark. We want you to come & if you do I will go all over & tell that you are there & all the men and women and children will come & give you their hands."[52] Crawford pondered making the move.

It would be a bold step, and so she traveled to Anadarko to ask Baldwin, the Indian agent, whether it would be "safe & prudent" for her to locate there. He replied, "It is perfectly safe if you can stand the roughing it, and a good location for a mission."[53] Two and a half years earlier, Crawford had doubted that it was prudent for Hattie Everts and herself to remain at Elk Creek without a male missionary present. Now she had grown much more daring. Although she had not yet consulted the board of the Women's Baptist Home Mission Society, Isabel Crawford agreed to go all alone to begin a mission at Saddle Mountain.

---

51. Journal 1894–96, November 4, 1895, 161.
52. Ibid., March 6, 1896, 188.
53. Ibid., inside the back cover.

5

Saddle Mountain

PAUL ZOTOM AND HIS wife, Mary, were moving back to Saddle Creek, and so on April 9, 1896, Isabel Crawford set forth with the couple to start her new mission. The wagon was piled high with belongings, and Isabel and Mary rode on top, seated on a bed tick beside a coop of hens. In mid-afternoon, they reached the home of Amonstake, who had married Mary's two sisters before he had learned of Christianity. That was common practice among the Kiowa—and it troubled missionaries, who generally refused baptism to those in *polygamous* marriages. Crawford recorded in her journal, "I'm beginning to change my views a little on this subject. I almost think that as long as the Indians live in camps it is better that some should be wife No 2. There are more women than men & a girl can't live a pure life in a camp."[1] The family received the travelers hospitably, and there they spent the night.

The next day, as they crossed Sugar Creek, a number of Kiowas met them. One was preparing to shoot a tired, thin cow. Then, reported Crawford, "In a few seconds he had wheeled his pony round, dismounted & was standing with gun in one hand & with the other reached up & shook mine vigorously. One by one the Indians came to shake my hand & say 'good,' while many of them said, 'You all alone come. Maybe so we scalp you.' After congratulations were over Buck Jim again mounted his steed & in a few seconds I heard a loud report & knew that a cow had fallen."[2] Crawford had not only been welcomed: she had achieved stature because she had shown no fear.

---

1. Diary 1896–97, April 9, 1896, 87.
2. Ibid., April 10, 1896, 90–91.

The wagon went on to Saddle Mountain, the community named for the saddle-shaped mountain lying a bit to the south and east. On Sunday, April 12, it was rainy, but people braved the weather to come to a nearby two-roomed house, and Crawford held her first meeting. People were curious about the odd apparatus she carried with her, a long, flexible tube with an earpiece at one end and a belled shape at the other. It was Crawford's "conversation tube," and they learned that if they spoke into the horn, she could hear them.

They assured Crawford of her welcome, and some of them indicated they were already acquainted with the Christian message. One of the men said, "I am glad you have come to us. You, one woman all alone with Indians and no scared. We like this. White people all afraid we will scalp them. They do not know our hearts. . . . We have no one to tell us about the Jesus over here & we all want you to stay & tell us & we will listen with our hearts & pretty soon some of us will be Christians."[3] Another explained, "We can't go to R[ainy] Mt. to church, it is too far, our horses poor. We almost forget what we know when we do not hear Jesus talk. You dont know how hard I try to walk a good road, but it is hard with nobody to help us & tell us the way. We will be your friends & help you all we can."

When Crawford held a meeting two weeks later, the sun shone brightly. Twenty-five people sat under the shelter of two wagon sheets, held up by six poles. Crawford asked: "Are there any Christians here?" No one responded. "Are there any who would like to give up the old roads and let the Holy Spirit teach the new?" At this, two men raised their hands, and the younger spoke: "Some Indians say when they are baptized that they bury all their bad roads and then they pick them up again and go off with them. I don't want to be that kind. I want to be a white-man Christian."[4] The speaker was Lucius Aitsan. His mother had been one of the four wives of the Kiowa leader Satanta before his death; she then married Lucius's father, Mokeen, who was a Mexican captured by the Kiowas when he was a boy. Aitsan had been educated at the Carlisle Indian Industrial School in Pennsylvania. Next he worked as assistant government farmer for one year and then was a member of the Seventh Cavalry. He became an interpreter for the Baptist preacher Joseph Samuel Murrow and for other missionaries. Aitsan wanted to know more about Christianity.

Crawford was there to teach Aitsan and the others, and soon the people gave her an Indian name: *Gee-ah-ho-ah-go-mah*, "She gave us the

---

3. Ibid., April 12, 1896, 91–92.
4. Crawford, *Kiowa*, 24.

Jesus way."[5] Though Crawford found that some were receptive to learning about the Jesus Road, as they called it, she also discovered quickly that others opposed it. As the Plains Indians had been forced to adapt to a new way of life, a religious movement sprang up, the Ghost Dance. Its prophets foretold the return of the bison, and Indians of several tribes grasped at this hope. After a while its popularity faded, but these were difficult times for the Kiowas, filled with disease and death as well as discontinuity with their past. In 1894 the Ghost Dance resurfaced. Its participants were hostile not only to Christianity but to the cultural practices encouraged by both missionaries and the government, such as wearing "civilized" clothing and building wooden houses.[6]

One evening when she had been at Saddle Mountain for less than a month, while she was holding a meeting, Crawford felt directed by God to tell those assembled "that I had not come to scold them & tell them their road was a bad one but had come to them to help them learn a better way."[7] She then learned the Ghost Dancers were holding a meeting nearby. When both meetings broke up, the Ghost Dancers came to talk with her, and they asked her to pray. The incident left Crawford resolved to learn more. Three days later she went with Paul and Mary Zotom to watch the "dreadful" sight. The people smoked to the Great Spirit, beat tom-toms, shook gourds, and wailed. One after another they came before the medicine man, who set them swaying gently at first, then faster and faster until they jumped up suddenly and collapsed. In the morning, when the people recovered their senses, they spoke of the wonderful things they had seen. They told Crawford that the Great Father "gave the Book to the White People and taught them to read it, but He gave to the Indians the dance road and told us to hold on to it tight till He came back to earth with our dead and our buffalo."[8]

Crawford had moved to Saddle Mountain on her own, without permission from the Women's Baptist Home Mission Society. In June, Aitsan sent a "strong talk" to Mary Burdette: "Dear Friend do not be afraid where Miss Crawford is. She stay with us. . . . I promise you . . . she will never be cold or hungry if I can help it because she stays away from her home to help us. I treat her best I know how."[9] On July 8, Burdette wrote to Crawford that "at the meeting of the Executive Board held yesterday the ladies voted to allow you to remain at Saddle Mountain as long as it is *safe* and *prudent*

5. Crawford, *Joyful Journey*, 65.
6. See Kracht, "Kiowa Ghost Dance."
7. Diary 1896–97, April 26, 1896, 106–7.
8. Crawford, *Kiowa*, 28.
9. Diary 1896–1906, June 11, 1896, 8–9.

and also to allow you $12.50 per month for an interpreter."[10] Crawford's decision had been ratified.

During her first weeks at Saddle Mountain, Crawford lived in a tent, and her dwelling was soon discovered by pigs who roamed the community. One night, during a thunderstorm, Crawford retreated to a nearby house and spent the rest of the night on the kitchen table. In the morning, she discovered that pigs had ransacked her tent and ruined all her food. Soon after that, when Crawford again withdrew to the house during a storm, pigs destroyed her new supply. After even more difficulty, Lucius Aitsan invited her to move into one of the two rooms of his house, a room with a cot and the cookstove. So on May 18, Crawford took up new, safer accommodation.

At her meetings, Crawford regularly asked whether there were some who would like to have Jesus as their friend. Once she was startled as a very old woman rose to respond, for the woman wore a child's dress from the missionary barrel over her Indian clothing. In the morning she had heard about "that Beautiful Home with water and fruit and no more 'hungry and crying,' and the Kind Chief who wanted to divide up with everybody." She continued, "I understand if we pick up this new road we must dress like white people so I have put on this dress to let everybody know that if I can have this Jesus as my Friend and go to live with Him after I get through with this life, I am willing to go round like this the few winters that are left, even if all people think that I am crazy."[11] Her action was extreme, but she demonstrated the conflation of Christianity and Euro-American culture that occurred in the minds of many.

Lucius and Mabel Aitsan had a much deeper understanding of Christianity. Late in June, at a camp-meeting at Elk Creek, both of them presented themselves for baptism. That spring Howard Clouse had come to the Rainy Mountain mission. On Sunday, June 28, he conducted the Elk Creek service as first Lucius and then Mabel walked into the water and were baptized. Crawford wrote, "Oh didn't I want to cry out for very joy when I saw [Lucius] going beneath the wave."[12] Lucius was already acting as interpreter; now he was an interpreter and a baptized Christian.

In August, Crawford went to Chicago and then to Ontario, where she saw her mother and her sister Emily. Then she followed the lecture schedule that the mission society had laid out for her. On September 10 she spoke on the Tuscarora reservation in northwestern New York State. She observed, "Poor people, how they do need strong loving hearts to pry them up & prop

---

10. Crawford, *Kiowa*, 47.
11. Ibid., 43.
12. Diary 1896–97, June 28, 1896, 121.

them for a few generations," never thinking that her own "strong loving" heart might be called upon.[13]

When she arrived at a church in Buffalo, she found that the program listed her as giving the sermon. She protested: "I told them I wasn't a preacher but a woman trying to do a woman's work in a womanly way."[14] In her talk, she stressed how the Indians had been ruined by the same people who now ignored them and took the gospel to foreign missions. Then the congregation rose to sing a hymn about "the faraway heathen who were receiving the good news," and she felt like ordering them to stop, for they had missed the point of her plea. Though she had once desired a mission assignment abroad, Crawford's loyalty was now firmly fixed on American Indians.

In her journal during this trip, Crawford mentioned for the first time the Indian Association. When Mary Bonney, a Philadelphia Baptist, became concerned about the government's plan to allow white settlement within Indian lands, she formed a group that came to be named the Women's National Indian Association. It developed many local chapters, and on October 12, Crawford spoke to the Poughkeepsie group. She received an invitation to call upon Bonney while Crawford was in Hamilton, New York. Bonney was eighty and feeble, but Crawford wrote that she "spoke very earnestly about the Indian question."[15]

Crawford arrived back at Saddle Mountain on November 30, 1896. As winter arrived, the kitchen in the Aitsans' house became cold, and Lucius and Mabel moved Isabel into their bedroom, a curtain for a partition. It was drafty, but resourceful Isabel used her umbrella and a blanket to provide a canopy to deflect the cold air. And so she continued to adapt to frontier conditions.

When the Aitsans' daughter celebrated her second birthday, Crawford gave her a dime for candy and two special coins to be used as the start of a fund to build a church at Saddle Mountain. They were a gold dollar that Crawford had received from her roommate at the training school, and a Canadian ten cent piece from Mary Burdette, who had no use for the foreign coin. Lucius recognized that when the new fund became known, "the Kiowas will all kick," and so they did, for the Ghost Dance members were strong in their opposition to having anything "white" constructed in the

---

13. Ibid., September 10, 1896, 134.
14. Ibid., September 13, 1896, 135.
15. Ibid., October 18, 1896, 142.

area.[16] But fabrics from the missionary barrel were turned into quilts, and through their sale and through gifts, gradually the little fund grew.

Early in May of 1897, Lucius left Saddle Mountain to get lumber and food. Rain poured down and Lucius was delayed—and Mabel and Isabel ran out of food, all except for salt and flour. There was a new litter of puppies, and one afternoon Isabel heard strange thumping sounds under the house, and the barking of a dog and the yelping of pups. Mabel was killing the puppies to feed her family. Soon Isabel overcame her initial horror and told Mabel, "if you will cut off two of the hind legs of one of the pups, skin them so there won't be a hair left, wash them and put them on a clean plate, I believe I am hungry enough to eat them."[17] And so Isabel's adjustment to the harsh conditions of the frontier continued.

In the spring of 1897, the Saddle Mountain Christians offered to host the early July camp meeting. In preparation they built a large arbor, their traditional shelter from the scorching summer sun. They set corner posts for the framework, then made a roof of saplings, and finally placed branches on top. When the time came, about five hundred Indians camped on the grounds, in addition to missionaries and teachers and two special visitors, the missionary J. S. Murrow, who had come to preach, and the Indian agent Frank Baldwin. At the close of the meetings, eighteen Christians were baptized in the clear, spring-fed water of Saddle Creek.

Late that summer, Crawford left Saddle Mountain to visit her mother, who was seriously ill. She returned by way of Chicago. The Women's Baptist Home Mission Society recognized that Crawford needed a helper, and the ideal woman was available. Crawford had known Mary McLean in North Dakota; when she saw her again in 1892, Crawford urged her to go to the training school. While McLean was there, she wrote of her desire to come to Saddle Mountain. "I cannot do the missionary part of the work," she said, "but I'm sure I can take some of the responsibilities off your shoulders."[18] The time had come; Crawford had paid for lumber and Aitsan had built another room onto his house. Thus in October McLean and Crawford traveled by train to Oklahoma.

There had been no mail at Saddle Mountain for some time when, on November 13, 1897, a whole sackful arrived. One letter brought Crawford the sad news that her mother had died on October 25.

> Coming sadly out of my tent this morning I was surrounded by a number of old Indian men wrapped in faded blankets.

16. Crawford, *Kiowa*, 55.
17. Ibid., 70.
18. Ibid., 74.

> They had laid aside their bright colors to show sympathy in their own way. Placing a brown arm about me and pressing my aching head upon his shoulder ... Dumot prayed while the others cried aloud. "O Great Spirit! Our leetle Jesus woman has lost her mother and her heart is all broken to pieces. Gather it together again and put it back strong. You have given her to us now and we will take the best care of her we know how. That is all. I have spoken."
>
> How I cried!
>
> The brown arm and nasty blanket were repulsive to me. The whole life was horrid. I hadn't a taste in common with it. I couldn't love the Indians and I wouldn't give up because I believed God had called me to give them the Gospel. The only blow that could crush the spirit within me had fallen! I was entirely bereft.
>
> Sob followed sob and the climax of misery was reached when I felt Dumot's warm tears falling down on my cheek and neck.
>
> A convulsion seized me. Then wonder of wonders! Into my heart there crept gently, silently, sweetly, a perfect calm.
>
> Tears ceased, a big sigh escaped and love was born. A love for the Indians not my own.[19]

Although Crawford had overcome her initial resistance to her assignment and had later take up the Indians' cause, she continued to feel a barrier between herself and them. Only now, when she recognized their empathy with her grief, did the barrier fall; for the first time, she was able to love the people among whom she worked.

Gradually not only the number of converts but the sense of Christian community grew, and by March of 1898, Crawford felt that she could "push a little."[20] At a sewing meeting that May, she presented a new idea. She told the group about the missionary society that had sent the gospel to the Kiowa, and she explained that they, the Christians at Saddle Mountain, could form a local society to spread the news to some other tribe. The people were surprised and enthusiastic, for they had not realized that they could help share the word. With the permission of the Women's Baptist Home Mission Society, their mission society would include men as well as women, "*especially if they paid their dues.*"[21] And so on May 10, 1898, "God's Light upon the Mountain" missionary society was organized. Little by little, through gifts and quilt-making, the small society gathered funds.

19. Ibid., 78–79.
20. Journal 1897–98, March 19, 1898, 33.
21. Crawford, *Kiowa*, 87.

The fund for building a church grew, too, though it was unclear whether the non-Christian Kiowas would permit its construction. When a woman from Dayton, Ohio, contributed three hundred dollars, to be used only for a small house for the missionaries, the issue had to be faced. On October 4, 1898, Crawford was summoned to a gathering under the arbor. She was told to sit in the middle of the circle, and after prayer, she explained what she wanted. Then she waited in silence for two hours as the men talked. Finally she received the verdict: "You may build your house on Lucius' land. After a while white men are going to come in here and cut up the land and take all that is over. They are dangerous. We must hurry up and look for land for Jesus and put His brand on it. . . . Then when the Jesus House is built you can move yours over to it with no trouble."[22] Though they anticipated opposition from the Ghost Dance people, they stated bravely, "We will let their talk hit us like the wind. We don't fight the wind or look at it; it hits and passes over us and pretty soon it is gone and we are not hurt."

The men agreed to look for land nearby so the missionaries would not be isolated, and for land with water on it. Then they said "Now you can tell the white friends we are ready for the church."[23] To their consternation, Crawford stated that they needed to build the church themselves, raising the necessary money. She believed strongly that the Indians should not be dependent, and she promised that the missionaries would show them the way. The people worked, and the fund continued to grow.

Crawford had an idea for how the Kiowas might earn money. She had observed the artistry of their drawings and paintings, and it occurred to her that if they learned the popular art of china painting, the products could be sold to benefit the building fund. She had first shared her dream when she had visited in the Ohio home of her friend Harriet Rychen, and when Crawford returned to the reservation after that tour, she was surprised to receive a letter promising a kiln. She hesitated briefly, for she had hoped to save the money and purchase it herself, "for to fail on anothers capital would be very much more unpleasant than to fail on your own."[24] However, she decided it was time to move ahead, and she accepted the offer. The equipment arrived in March of 1899. But there was no time to begin the experiment, for in April Crawford left for her vacation.

Crawford headed for San Francisco, where she was to attend a mission society convention. Before the meeting began, she visited the Golden Gate Park and saw bison. She wrote that her eyes filled with tears "when I thought

22. Ibid., 102–3.
23. Ibid., 104.
24. Journal 1897–98, October 24, 1898, 111.

of the far away Indians . . . I secured several hands full of the hair off their backs however greatly to their disgust, & this I sent back to the Indians to remind them of the past."[25]

One day at the mission society convention, Mary Burdette announced that at the women's hour the following morning, Crawford would present something in Plains Indian sign language. Crawford wrote,

> When I woke in the morning I lay in bed wondering what I would give. Not having a good memory I knew few things off by heart. I went over them. The multiplication tables (especially five times) & "Now I lay me down to sleep," The Lord's Prayer, The 23rd Psalm. All of which mother had *caused me to know* by constant repetitions. "Five times" would be a crazy thing to give. *Prayers* with signing out of the question. Only the 23rd Psalm was left & with the others in their beds quietly snoozing I thought out how I would give it to the Indians if I had no interpreter. I gave it at the devotionals and the Good Shepherd blessed it.[26]

By the time she arrived back at Saddle Mountain, on August 22, 1899, some things had changed. Mary McLean was gone; she had been transferred to the Rainy Mountain mission. Lucius Aitsan had worked for a while at Rainy Mountain as a government farmer, but now he had returned to serve as interpreter at half his government salary. And Frank Baldwin had left his post as Indian agent and moved to another assignment.

Less than two months later, McLean's replacement arrived to serve at Saddle Mountain: "She hopped off the train like a robin and we all knew that the new missionary, Miss K. E. Bare, would fill the bill to a T."[27] Kittie Bare, originally from Michigan, had graduated from the Baptist Missionary Training School and was ready to assist Crawford.

At Christmas in 1899, Crawford introduced a new concept to the Saddle Mountain Christians: self-support. They had been contributing money to one barrel for sending the Gospel to another tribe and to another for building their own church. Now Crawford set out third, for Aitsan's salary. He objected, saying "It makes me feel 'shamed."[28] Crawford replied, "Some white women take in washing to help pay our salaries, Lucius. . . . He wants us to take care of ourselves over here, as soon as ever we can, that the money that now comes may be used in sending other missionaries to other

25. Ibid., May 24, 1899, 144–45.
26. Notebook California, May, 24, 1898 [*sic*].
27. Crawford, *Kiowa*, 117.
28. Ibid., 119.

tribes." At the end of the meeting, $9.70 had been contributed toward the interpreter's salary.

In 1892, the government had negotiated the Jerome Agreement regarding opening the reservation for settlement, but it had not been ratified in the United States Senate. When it was presented for ratification in 1899, the news caused much consternation. Crawford wrote that "the Indians are running everywhere gathering up the bones of their dead and bringing them to the different missions. Living or dead it seems as if they must 'move on.'"[29]

In June of 1900, when the Jerome Agreement was finally ratified, Crawford realized that time had come to obtain land for the church. Hearing rumors that the Saddle Mountain mission might not receive land because it was not organized as a church, Crawford took action. She wrote to Indian Commissioner William Arthur Jones, asking whether he remembered the deaf missionary to whom Indian agent Frank Baldwin had introduced him. Then she explained her fears that "the government should say, 'Because you are a woman who endured the hardness of frontier life among the Indians like a man but did not organize a church like one, your Indians can't have any land for their mission and all you have done must come to naught.'"[30] She received the reply from the Acting Commissioner that the Saddle Mountain mission could have forty acres of land—or less if it preferred.[31]

James Randlett had replaced Baldwin as Indian Agent, and Crawford wrote to him when she learned that the mission was to receive much less than the 160 acres they anticipated. "Why," she asked, "should the Indians at Saddle Mt. have less than the other missions. Is it because I am a woman? . . . I am not a believer in women's rights but I am a believer in Indian rights provided they are really 'rights,' and are equal rights."[32]

Forty acres would have been one fourth of 160 acres allotted to the America Baptist Home Mission Society, but the Saddle Mountain mission was a project of the *Women's* Baptist Home Mission Society, and Crawford fought hard to have the women's organization receive its full portion. Eventually, with the help of Randlett and Jones, Saddle Mountain received 160 acres in two parcels of 80 acres each, plus 40 acres for a cemetery. Later Jones wrote, "It was a close call and had I not visited you and known personally the conditions surrounding the Mission the allotment would not have been approved. . . . If you had not taken the bull by the horns I could

---

29. Ibid., 117.
30. Journal 1898–1900, 131.
31. Ibid., 132.
32. Ibid., 134–35.

have done nothing."[33] Crawford had won the battle, though in doing so she probably antagonized the men of the denominational mission society that had to divide a 160 acre allotment among the other Baptist missions.

While Crawford was working to ensure that the Saddle Mountain mission received its land, she was also carrying out her usual duties. Kittie Bare had a gift for making useful items out of the strange contents of missionary barrel, and she worked vigorously at the laundry, but she did not like cooking or housekeeping. Mary McLean had relieved Crawford of more of her responsibilities than did Bare, but Bare gave Crawford much-needed support. Crawford believed in traditional gender roles, and she may not have noticed that she served in a role similar to that of a married male missionary while she had associates who took on many activities of a missionary's wife.

Crawford proceeded with the china-painting experiment. Though her immediate goal was to raise money for the building fund, she came to see a broader purpose: "It was our plan in the first place to teach these people to earn their living by farming but the Lord interfered because I was a woman, sent out by a woman's society and asked me to teach them a more womanly art.... Many of the older Indians cannot farm enough to earn a living. They simply can't plough day in & day out. Something less fatiguing must be introduced."[34] She judged the first results of the china experiment "neither good nor bad but good enough to convince me that we shall succeed!"[35] She had accepted the gift of the kiln in faith that the Lord was "trusting in me sufficiently to believe I would not let His investment be a failure.... If I fail I fail but if I succeed the Lord succeeds."[36] However, after mentioning china painting in her 1890 report, Crawford said nothing more. If it failed and if she accepted responsibility for the failure, she did so in silence.

Late in the summer, both Crawford and Bare took vacations; they were heartily welcomed back on September 16, 1900. Early in October, Crawford went to Arapaho to take the oath of allegiance and become a United States citizen. She described the experience: "I didn't hear a word of the oath but held up my hand with the rest. The judge had to repeat this question twice—'Do you believe the laws of this country to be better than those of Canada? I couldn't *honestly* say yes & so I said, 'I don't know enough about the laws of this country to judge.' I think the question an absurdity."[37]

---

33. Journal 1901–2, 0–1.
34. Journal 1898–1900, 116–17.
35. Ibid., 89.
36. Journal 1897–98, October 24, 1898, 112–13.
37. Journal 1900–1901, October 6, 1900, page facing page marked QRST.

In the spring of 1901, it was time to select land for the allotments. Crawford met with the allotting agent, and two eighty-acre parcels for the mission, half a mile apart, were chosen and registered.[38] For the moment, all was well. On August 6, 1901, the land was opened to white settlers, an event long feared by the Kiowas. Lone Wolf had gone so far as to initiate legal proceedings on the grounds that the Jerome Agreement violated some terms of the 1867 Medicine Lodge Treaty. His appeal was still making its way through the legal system, but that did not prevent the opening of the land.[39] A lottery determined who had the right to select land, and on the opening day, the winners "poured over the prairie like burning oil set afloat on an open sea."[40] After sixty days, those who had not been lucky in the lottery were permitted to snatch up any unclaimed land. In *Kiowa*, Crawford wrote vivid descriptions of the whole process; then she reflected: "Dumot expressed it exactly when with trembling hand he signed: 'We are afraid of everything that is coming except the Jesus House.'"[41]

The building fund for the church contained $425.22, and since Crawford insisted that the Saddle Mountain Christians raise the funds themselves without "begging," they did not anticipate starting construction for another year. But there were supposed to be "improvements" on the newly acquired land. It also needed the appearance of being settled, for miners were staking claims on unoccupied land. And so two buildings were moved onto the property, a smaller "den" and then, with much effort, a larger shed. Already miners had started staking claims on the mission's land but, Crawford wrote, "[w]ith a stick & a revolver (not Winchester) the mineral claims 'Located' on the mission land were 'Dislocated,' and the stone piles sent helter skelter down the mountain side."[42]

Gradually Crawford made a comfortable home in the relocated building. As she unpacked her books, she mused, "Poor books! . . . Once I

---

38. "Later developments proved it was not all registered in our capitol at Washington, as Miss Crowford [*sic*] wrote in her journal, nor was it even put on record at the County seat at Hobart. The eighty acres on which the church was later built, along with an adjoining forty acres for a cemetery were duly recorded. But the other eighty acres one half a mile distant, and on which a mission house was built seems to never have been recorded" (Corwin, *Kiowa Indians*, 130).

39. The Supreme Court did not render a decision on the Lone Wolf v. Hitchcock case until 5 January 1903. At that time it decided against Lone Wolf on the grounds that Congress had plenary power over Indian property because it had guardianship over their interests.

40. Crawford, *Kiowa*, 163.

41. Ibid., 168.

42. Journal 1901–2, 43. For a discussion of mineral claims made by non-Indians at this time, see William T. Hagan, "Adjusting to the Opening," 19.

thought I couldn't live without reading and at graduation promised myself that I would spend fifty dollars for books every year of my life. I did it once. Freight bills on missionary boxes and barrels and absolutely no time for self-culture prevented the repetition."[43]

On October 30, 1900, Hilon Parker, vice-president of the Rock Island Railroad, invited the Indian Agent, James Randlett, to join a train ride he had arranged for officials of the railroad. Parker inquired about the Saddle Mountain mission. Some time earlier he had been in the area and had wished to water his mules on the mission's property. Crawford had denied him permission because water was scarce. It was at that time that Parker first learned about the mission. Now the listeners became interested in Parker's praise and his comment that the mission deserved their help toward building a church. One of the men took out a twenty dollar bill and said, "Here is a starter; let us raise the two hundred dollars she needs." One man went to the other train car to extend the collection. When the money was assembled, the count stood at $240. At that point someone added a ten dollar bill to make it an even $250.[44] Randlett sent the money to Crawford, explaining its origin. The Kiowa Christians received the gift with gratitude, and Crawford wrote: "It was the turning point in the history of the church building fund. There was no more begging or groaning."[45]

While the Saddle Mountain Christians contributed to their own church building fund, they continued to collect money to send a missionary to another tribe. Mary Burdette of the women's mission society searched for a good location, and in November of 1901, Crawford was able to report Burdette's decision. For about five years, the Indian Association worked toward establishing a mission at Second Mesa, in Arizona. Learning of the Baptist women's interest in opening a mission, the association's president, Amelia Quinton, suggested to Burdette that the Baptist society accept the transfer of the association's property and rights there.[46] Burdette approved the idea, and when they learned of her decision, the Kiowas expressed their delight: "God's-Light-Upon-the-Mountain has borned a papoose!"[47] Mary McLean, Crawford's first helper at Saddle Mountain, was sent to open the new mission.

---

43. Crawford, *Kiowa*, 171.

44. Ibid., 183. The date is given in the Hilon A. Parker papers, along with the information that Lone Wolf was also present for part of the trip (October 14, 1900, Diary 1900, Hilon A. Parker Papers, Box 5).

45. Crawford, *Kiowa*, 184.

46. *Thirty-six Years among Indians*, 48.

47. Crawford, *Kiowa*, 178.

In April of 1902, when it was time for Crawford to take her vacation, she went first to Chicago and appeared before the woman's mission society board. After visiting her family in Ontario, she headed next toward Minneapolis, taking a steamship to Sault Ste. Marie. The ship hit a rock and the passengers were delayed, so Crawford arrived in Minneapolis on a Sunday morning. She had always kept the Sabbath faithfully, but this was a real test. Instead of taking a streetcar, she walked thirty-one blocks, carrying her satchel. When she found that arrangements had been made to have dinner a mile further on, she bathed and then set forth. Afterwards she wrote, "By the time I had walked back again I was more convinced that *Sunday travelling was wrong*! (especially on foot!)"[48]

In an address that she gave in St. Paul, Crawford showed a new concern. White settlers had entered the Kiowa territory since her last speaking tour, and she feared their influence on the Indians. She told her listeners the sad news that Dumot, the Kiowa chief who had invited her to Saddle Mountain, was dead. He was "[t]he Indian who pressed my aching head upon his shoulder when my mother died and prayed with the tears streaming down his paint cheeks!"[49] He had become drunk, and had sickened and died: "Gone down in the march of civilization!" Now Crawford's plea was for a pastor for the white settlers both for their own sakes and so that the Indians might not be destroyed.

After traveling to the east coast, Crawford again headed west, arriving at Saddle Mountain on the August 1, 1902. Soon she was faced directly with the question regarding the white settlers, for a request had come for the missionaries to hold services for them. Already overworked, Crawford felt conflicted. She wrote, "I tried like Jonah to get away from the 'go' of the Master but finally decided that I would have to obey."[50] When two men volunteered to build an arbor, she agreed to hold services every Sunday night. The Kiowas were momentarily speechless when she told them of the plan, but they agreed to help. They could bring the gospel to the whites as well as to the Hopis. Then early in the new year, they discovered another opportunity for service. A black family had settled on a claim nearby. When Lucius Aitsan returned from a visit, he reported, "The Kiowas is poor but nothing like that."[51] The Kiowa Christians adopted the family as their mission.

Another issue had arisen when Crawford returned to Saddle Mountain. What sort of church should be built, wood frame or stone? Crawford wrote

48. Journal 1902, 4.
49. Ibid., page opposite UVWYZ.
50. Ibid., August 21, 1902, 13.
51. Diary 1896–1906, January 25, 1903, 68.

in her journal, "They all talked about the building & seemed more inclined to have frame than stone because they didn't want to work for nothing [hauling stone] . . . but Miss Bare & I both feel that the Master never piled up all that stone for nothing. He expects us to use it."[52] Most of the Indians feared that their horses could not stand the strain; they preferred wood.[53] Crawford got financial estimates for both types of building, but her preference was clear: "we will pray & scheme & plan on & give up only when we have to."[54]

The women exerted what influence they could, but the Saddle Mountain Christians were frank about their opposition. One of them said, "If we build of stone everybody will look at Miss Crawford & say: See what she done. We voted for lumber & the society voted for lumber & she & Miss Bare pulled away from us and everybody will say she done it all. We don't like this."[55] Finally Crawford gave in. She wrote that "for the sake of preserving the unity of the spirit it had to be done."[56] According to her principles, the Indians ought to control their own affairs; in this instance, she had to surrender her will to follow the principle.

Hugh Crawford came to help oversee the construction, and he and C. C. Cooper from Michigan served as contractors. Excitement increased, and everyone helped haul the lumber. On November 9, 1902, the cornerstone was laid with all due ceremony. After it had been covered with small stones and mortar, Kittie Bare declared "this stone well and properly laid," and Lucius Aitsan closed the service with prayer.[57]

Construction continued through winter, and the church was ready for its formal opening on Easter Sunday, April 12, 1903, exactly seven years after Crawford had held the first gospel service at Saddle Mountain. The opening was a quiet event, with no visitors from afar. Crawford wrote, "We had planned for a simple building in order to send the Gospel to others. . . . The Great Spirit, the Creator, saw the mission in Hopiland, knew the living burning sacrifice it represented and breathed upon the poor little plans for our church. Instead of four walls He gave us six, instead of plain ceilings He gave us panels, instead of cheap windows He gave us stained glass and instead of an empty belfry He gave us a bell and a clock. It was truly the beauty of the Lord that filled that place."[58]

---

52. Journal 1902, August 3, 1902, 10.
53. Journal 1902, 32.
54. Ibid., August 3, 1902, 10.
55. Ibid., September 29, 1902, 45.
56. Ibid., October 3, 1902, 47.
57. Crawford, *Kiowa*, 198.
58. Ibid., 214.

As soon as construction of the church ended, the contractors began work on the mission house; the missionaries handled the arrangements on behalf of the Women's Baptist Home Mission Society. The two-room building that had been constructed by Aitsan and moved earlier from its original site became the dining room and kitchen of the new home. The moment they took possession of the house, Crawford and Bare began preparing it for an influx of visitors, for the Saddle Mountain Church was to be dedicated and the Saddle Mountain Christians would be organized into a church.

Late in August the guests arrived. They included Hilon Parker, the Chicago railroad executive who had shown interest in the mission. With him came his wife, Dr. Grace Rowley Parker, and other family members. Mary Burdette was there, as were other missionaries from the area and Indian Agent James Randlett. Bare and Crawford took great pleasure in showing all of them the church and hearing their delighted comments. Burdette remarked, "My dear Isabel, you have not been a model missionary. You have given us many a merry chase, but this church certainly is a model. It goes beyond my highest expectations."[59]

Gathering for the dedication of the Saddle Mountain Baptist Church, 1903. Courtesy of the American Baptist Historical Society, Notebook American West.

There was one small incident that Crawford did not mention in her journal until much later, but it was fixed in her memory. She wrote, "Years ago at the dedication of our little Indian Church in Okla. Dr Parker did me a favor that riveted her to my heart. She handed me a 'hot drink' in a little brown shiny bucket when I was about all in & nobody else noticed it. It reminded me of the 'cup of water' mentioned in the Bible, but I was glad

---

59. Ibid., 217.

this drink was hot."⁶⁰ The two had met before, but the closer friendship that began at this time remained a vital one for decades.

J. S. Murrow presided at the Sunday ceremony and asked Aitsan the necessary questions. "Is there any debt on the building?" Aitsan answered proudly, "No sir!"⁶¹ Burdette gave the prayer of dedication, and instead of God's-Light-upon-the-Mountain mission circle, there was now God's-Light-upon-the-Mountain Baptist Church. Deacons were solemnly elected. At the afternoon service, Captain Parker presented the congregation with a United States flag. Then six converts were baptized. Saddle Mountain members of the Rainy Mountain Church transferred their membership to the new congregation, and thus sixty-three people in addition to Isabel Crawford became charter members of the Saddle Mountain Church.

Crawford wrote "An Indian woman summoned up the feelings of the whole Kiowa settlement in these words: 'When I seen our Jesus House going up with my two eyes my heart began to grow and as the church got bigger my heart got bigger and bigger and bigger. Today it is all busted to pieces.'"⁶²

Saddle Mountain Baptist Church. Courtesy of the American Baptist Historical Society, Board of International Ministries, Missionary Biographical Files: Crawford, Isabelle.

60. Journal 1921–22, December 20, 1921, page marked RSTU.

61. Crawford, *Kiowa*, 218. In *The Heroine of Saddle Mountain*, Burdette reported his reply as a more sedate "There is no debt" (42).

62. Crawford, *Kiowa*, 221.

6

The "Jesus Eat"

The dedication of the church building and the organization of the Saddle Mountain Church in August of 1903 raised a new question. Now the church members wanted to receive the ordinance of the Lord's Supper, which they termed the "Jesus Eat." Since the new church had no pastor, how could they have it? The Rainy Mountain mission was twenty miles away; travel was difficult, and Howard Clouse, the missionary, was overworked.[1] Isabel Crawford had grown up in the home of a Baptist minister, and she was fully imbued with Baptist principles: the ordinance was a command of Jesus, and the right of holding it belonged to the church, not the pastor. So Crawford told the members that since they had no pastor, they could elect one of their own to administer it. On September 12, Crawford carefully explained the Lord's Supper. She told them that it belonged to the church and only to the church, and she explained that "Jesus wanted to give His children some simple things to do in remembrance of Him."[2] Unanimously the people chose the interpreter, Lucius Aitsan, to administer it.

One week later, on September 27, the joyous service was held. Henrietta Reeside and Lauretta Ballew were visiting; they had come from Rainy Mountain, where they had gone as pioneering missionaries more than a decade earlier. After the church covenant had been explained, Crawford's associate, Kittie Bare, read the story of the first Lord's Supper. The deacons

---

1. Elsewhere she said seventeen miles; see Journal 1906, August 3, 1906, 35.
2. Crawford, *Kiowa*, 223.

took their places with Aitsan in the middle, Reeside and Ballew on one side of him, Crawford and Bare on the other. Aitsan handed first the plate and later the cup to the two deacons, who distributed the elements to the people including the missionaries. For the first time, the Saddle Mountain Baptist Church had celebrated the Jesus Eat. In her annual report, Crawford wrote that the service "was conducted with so much tenderness of feeling that tears rolled down many cheeks and ten dollars was given to Jesus as a thank offering for leaving such a wonderful road."[3]

Lucius Aitsan and Isabel Crawford. Courtesy of the American Baptist Historical Society, Board of International Ministries, Missionary Biographical Files: Crawford, Isabelle.

Privately, however, Crawford was anxious, though more about her gender role than about church practice. In her journal she wrote,

> Why has the Lord asked me to do work without a *clear pattern*. There were no women preachers among the 12 or the 70. A

3. Journal 1903–5, 66.

woman's place is making home happy not parading in public. If she hasn't a home of her own she may try to make other homes happy. If public work is not a woman's sphere & a woman tries to do a man's work she surely must be wrong, & if we are to shun the appearance of evil I am surely not shunning it. O for a plain path! . . . If the Indians had not consented to Lucius taking the lead in this matter I don't believe I could have gone ahead with it. Then what? Would I have been right or wrong?[4]

At the end of September, Crawford left Saddle Mountain to spend two months visiting churches in Iowa, Kansas, and Nebraska. When she returned to Saddle Mountain, she read the mail that had accumulated during her absence. In the collection was a letter from Mary Burdette, Corresponding Secretary of the Women's Baptist Home Mission Society. Burdette exclaimed:

> What have you been doing? Several weeks ago I received a letter forwarded from headquarters expressing grave apprehension and disapproval of the report that you had administered the Lord's Supper in the Church at Saddle Mt. I intended to write to you then but have been so incessantly occupied that I fear I neglected to do so, as I have received another letter from another source, a high dignitary of the ABHM Society calling attention to it in a way that indicates trouble for you, for the Church & for the Society. Did you do it? I hope not. You certainly would not have made so radical a departure from Baptist usage as that while bearing the commission of the Society without the approval of the Board. If you did it was even without their knowledge. I hope you will set yourself right in this matter. You have so emphatically disclaimed any intention of taking the pastorate & we have done the same that it would seem very strange for you to assume functions pertaining to that office. I shall await with some anxiety but in hope your explanation.[5]

Crawford replied quickly, expressing nothing of the uncertainty she had earlier recorded in her journal. She explained that she had not administered the ordinance, but she also made it clear that she did not consider it against "Baptist usage" for a duly elected deacon to do so in a pastorless congregation. Then she wrote, "Can it be possible that I have misunderstood the teaching I have received. Surely the New Testament teaches that the Church

---

4. Journal 1902–3, September 27, 1903, 46.
5. Journal 1902–3, 63.

is responsible for the observance of the Lords Supper & not the pastor."[6] She waited anxiously for Burdette's reply, and on December 6 Crawford wrote in her journal, "Mail after mail has come in but Miss Burdette hasn't written & Communion Sunday is here. Lord what wilt *thou* have me to do? I must choose between what I believe to be right & what others may think wrong.... It is never safe to follow other people unless your conscience approves so I deliberately choose to follow the Lamb whitherso ever he leadeth. The second communion was celebrated in church today."[7]

Seeking support for her position, Crawford had written to three men whom she greatly respected, and their replies arrived a few days later. William Cline, Crawford's brother-in-law, concurred with the church's action and offered precedents for the practice.[8] Also affirming was Augustus Strong, whom she had met in Rochester, New York, in 1896. He was a leading Baptist theologian and the president of Rochester Theological Seminary. He replied, "I have no doubt that you are right in advising the Church to celebrate the Lords Supper even though they have no pastor. The responsibility of observing the Supper is laid by the New Testament upon the body of believers."[9]

The response of Joseph Samuel Murrow, esteemed Baptist missionary in eastern Oklahoma, was more guarded, but in his letter, too, she found validation. He wrote, "I do not think any one will deny that a Baptist Church has a right to celebrate the Lord's Supper. The administration of the bread & wine is very much better of course by a regular pastor, or by a regularly ordained Baptist preacher. It ought to be an extreme case where a Church attends to this ordinance without the presence of a regularly ordained Baptist preacher. But this is not *essential* to the validity of the ordinance, and a Church cannot be justly charged with heterodoxy that celebrates the supper in the absence of an ordained preacher."[10]

Murrow wrote of the importance of an ordained pastor, and Crawford decided that she must speak plainly to the Saddle Mountain Church. She told them her "heart was troubled," and she felt "the time had come when they should have a pastor, that the white men chiefs & Miss Burdette were troubled."[11] After she had finished, the first to speak was Odlepaugh, half-brother of Lucius Aitsan. He observed that the Elk Creek and Rainy Moun-

---

6. Ibid., 65.
7. Ibid., December 6, 1903, 65.
8. Ibid., December 12, 1903, 65–66.
9. Ibid., December 8, 1903, 65.
10. Ibid., December 12, 1903, 66.
11. Ibid., December 13, 1903, 67

tain missions had trouble. By contrast "It is so nice & quiet over here—no quarrel & no any trouble & this Church is going ahead & the Kiowas all know it." He explained, "We are afraid of the white men ministers but the white women are all right. . . . We don't want the white people to take this church away from us."[12]

Crawford continued to wait anxiously for Burdette's reply. When it finally arrived at the beginning of January 1904, Crawford learned that the delay was caused by Burdette's illness, and that Burdette "thinks we have done nothing amiss."[13] But while the women's board was satisfied with her explanation, the denominational board was not. Elijah Eynon Chivers, Field Secretary of the American Baptist Home Mission Society, feared the political implications of the matter, for the American Baptist denomination was the northern group. Southern Baptists were also present in the area, and there had been strife between the two groups; although they were now cooperating under a system of "dual alignment," tensions remained.[14] Chivers wrote to Burdette, "I am very sure that when the fact becomes known it will provoke criticism; and that if the course be pursued will lead to dissension. The matter will probably come up when the new Church applies for admission into the Association. There is perhaps no other part of our country in which questions of Church order lead to such warm discussions as in the South West, and it would not be at all strange if some people who are not over friendly toward the work of our Northern Societies should use this matter greatly to our disadvantage."[15]

Howard Clouse, of the Rainy Mountain mission, openly expressed his disapproval at what had been done and claimed that he was willing to come to Saddle Mountain periodically to officiate at the Lord's Supper. Despite his intentions, however, weather conditions or his schedule sometimes prevented him from keeping the appointment. Occasionally he cancelled his visit so close to the time of the service that it was impossible to inform worshipers who might be coming from a distance. In April, a few days before Easter, Crawford went to Rainy Mountain. Mary Burdette of the Women's Baptist Home Mission Society was there, and so were E. E. Chivers and Nelson Rairden, the denominational society's General Superintendent of Missions west of the Mississippi. Crawford wrote in her journal cryptically and ominously, "A conference of revelations took place. The Lord over-ruled

12. Ibid., 67–68.

13. Ibid., January 2, 1904, 73.

14. For a discussion of the dissension and the union, see Gaskin, *Baptist Milestones in Oklahoma*, 139–53.

15. Journal 1902–3, copy of letter from Chivers to Burdette, October 26, [1903], 73–74.

& secret things were made plain. We cannot walk too carefully before the heathen, nor before some who are not heathen. 'My Soul be on thy guard. Ten thousand foes arise.'"[16]

Two years later, Crawford described the painful event. At the informal council, Clouse charged that when he first came to Rainy Mountain, Crawford wrote to Rairden, asking him to keep Clouse away from Saddle Mountain. Crawford vehemently denied this, while Rairden agreed. He said, "I got such a letter from the Post Office signed Belle Crawford. I sent it to Dr Morgan and he advised me to tell Bro Clouse to keep away."[17]

After further accusations and denials, the group calmed down somewhat. Then Chivers raised the matter of sectional differences: "In this great South Western Country we have to be exceedingly careful what we do lest we stir up friction. If this thing that you have done were known it would rend the denomination from the North to the South! You should have an ordained minister to conduct the Supper for you."[18] The discussion was unresolved.

Burdette, Chivers, and Rairden came to Saddle Mountain for the Easter service. After the Lord's Supper, Rairden walked with Crawford back to the mission house. His manner was kindly, and he suggested, "Miss C. you need a good rest. I wish you would come to Omaha. Mrs Rairden and I would be so glad to have you rest with us."[19] But Crawford wrote later, "This riled me all up inside." She replied, "I'd like above all things to come to Omaha to help you go through every letter & paper in your office till we found that letter." The conversation ended in disagreement.

On Monday morning, when Rairden came to get his suitcase prior to leaving, he found Crawford crying. He spoke some conciliatory words, and Crawford, unable to let go of the matter, retorted, "That is right. Dr Rairden you ought to be sorry."[20] Crawford wrote, "Then I don't know what happened. We fought like cats. Dr Chivers came in & stood at the door with his arms folded, but a Greater than Chivers was there who knew that the whole vile plot had been set on foot of the devil for the express purpose of undermining & humiliating one whose chief offence had been *that she was a woman* under the Women's So[ciety]."

Soon after this discordant time, Crawford left for a vacation and speaking tour, returning to Saddle Mountain on July 15. Six weeks later, Kittie

16. Journal 1903–5, April 3, 1904, 76–77.
17. Journal 1906, 37.
18. Ibid., 160.
19. Ibid., 162.
20. Ibid., 162–63.

Bare left the mission to go back to Ohio; she was marrying C. C. Cooper, the builder who had come to Oklahoma to share with Hugh Crawford the work of building the Saddle Mountain church.

In October of 1904, the question of the Lord's Supper arose again. On a Saturday evening, Crawford received word that the expected guest minister, E. R. Hosman, was unable to come to officiate at Sunday's ordinance. She wrote, "We had the regular morning service—followed by the lord's Supper administered by Lucius. I won't postpone & let the Indians think its observance depends on a minister. It depends on *the Church* & so it must be taught!"[21] One of the members expressed apprehension, but Crawford explained, "When Brother Clouse hears that we have followed Jesus there will be no trouble. He understands." And she wrote to Clouse at Rainy Mountain, explaining the church's action.

Clouse did *not* understand. In his reply he expressed his "great sorrow," and the reasons he gave were ominous. He restated the denominational mission society's fear that "these *Southern Churches* would hear of that kind of work and it would hurt the work of the Society." He also warned that the action made the church "liable to be tried" by the Oklahoma Indian Baptist Association "on the ground of such practice for the Constitution is against all these things." He concluded, "In behalf of myself I must here state my principles will not permit me to render you further assistance in the ordinances if you still persist in that course."[22]

In 1895, the Baptist missions in the area had joined together to form the Association to which Clouse referred, and in June of 1904 the credentials of the Saddle Mountain Church were presented and approved, and the church was received into the association. The association's constitution stated that "when any church shall in our judgement become corrupt in faith and practice, the association will be at liberty to erase its name from the minutes."[23]

Crawford wrote again to Augustus Strong and once more received his firm support: "No Church has the *right* to omit the Lord's Supper simply because it has no pastor. It needs only to appoint one of its own members to administer the ordinance.... If other Churches or pastors disfellowship you because you hold the Lord's Supper without a pastor you can endure it & can

---

21. Ibid., October 23, 1904, 107–8.
22. Journal 1903–5, 123–25.
23. Minutes of the Workers' Conference and Oklahoma Baptist Indian Association, 1.

wait till they are better instructed. But you must 'do this in remembrance of me' even at the risk of losing their good will."[24]

Christmas brought fewer missionary barrels than usual, and Crawford ransacked the mission house to find things that could be "converted into a present."[25] A Miss Davis arrived to serve as Crawford's assistant, but in February Crawford wrote, "Owing to mistaken ideas about climate and conditions Miss Davis left after six weeks of 'strenuous life' carrying with her loving wishes from all."[26] Crawford longed for the coming of a pastor, Indian or white, "but the Indians are divided on the subject & if the matter is pushed it will cause a split in the Church."[27] It was a dreary season.

Near the end of April, Crawford left to attend meetings, speak, and have some much-needed rest. When she returned to Saddle Mountain in August, she sensed immediately that something was wrong. She "saw trouble in every face," but at first the Indians were so happy to see her that they did not want talk business and spoil the good feeling.[28] Gradually Crawford learned what had happened. Lauretta Ballew, who had attended the first communion service at which Aitsan had presided, subsequently told George and Julia Given Hunt that Crawford had made a big mistake in teaching them that they could hold the "Jesus Eat." Now George and Julia were frightened.[29]

While Crawford tried to reassure the Saddle Mountain Christians that they had done nothing wrong, she saw no options for herself. On September 15, 1905, she wrote a letter of resignation. In it she stated, "After careful and prayerful consideration from all points of view I have decided to lay down the work at Saddle Mt. to take effect about a year from the present time or as soon as the pastor and new missionary are initiated and the different pieces of work that are begun completed. My reason for resigning is simply this: I am boycotted and it is killing me. I can't hold out under the pressure and wish to resign before I am a wreck."[30]

The letter mentioned the coming of a pastor, and for some time this had seemed a solution, for if the congregation had an ordained minister, there would be no problem. There were, however, complications. The Kiowas were painfully aware of the injustices that their tribe had suffered at the

24. Journal 1903–5, 126.
25. Ibid., 127.
26. Diary 1896–1906, 102.
27. Journal 1903–5, 128.
28. Ibid., 18.
29. Ibid., August 18, 1905, 25–26.
30. Ibid., September 15, 1905, pasted between 42 and 43.

hands of white men and so, years earlier, they had asked for assurance that no white "Jesus man" would be brought in to rule over them. Crawford tried to assure them that even if the church had a white pastor, it would still be their own Indian church, but their uncertainty remained.

Ever since her return in August, Crawford had observed the Indians' concern, and she heard rumors. Finally in December, 1905, she wrote to Clouse and asked directly: "You spoke in one of your letters of the Association *voting its disapproval* of our method of observing the Lords Supper. Will you kindly tell me where, when & under what circumstances the vote was taken & by whom voted upon. I can find out nothing about it from the Indians."[31]

At last she learned. Crawford had been away at the time of the Indian Association meeting held in June at Watonga. There the Association passed the following resolution:

> In this report, we desire, as an Association, to express our sorrow that one of our Churches has deviated from the orderly practice of Baptist Churches in the administration of the Lord's Supper, in that the ordinance has been administered by other than ordained ministers. This is not in harmony with the Constitution of the Association, and may be an open door to other irregular practices. We ask all the Churches that this irregularity be not further practiced. We make this request because we think the practice is not right. We do not censure the Church because it was done through ignorance, but we desire all the Churches in this Association to be alike, not only in faith, but in practice.[32]

Now Crawford saw clearly why the Kiowas felt not only uncertainty but shame.

Crawford and many others hoped that Aitsan might recognize God's call and be trained to receive ordination and serve his people at Saddle Mountain. Although Aitsan felt called, still he hesitated. Crawford wrote to Mary Burdette asking the Women's Baptist Home Mission Society to decide about a pastor, but Burdette replied that it was a decision that must be made by the church itself.[33] Crawford wrote again to Strong, and he replied that "You are theoretically right but practically wrong. The Church has the *right* to administer the Lord's Supper whether it has a pastor or not & the right to depute one of its members to preside at the ordinance. But *interdependence*

---

31. Journal 1905-6, December 13, 1905, 20.
32. Diary 1896-1906, 110.
33. Journal 1905-6, January 17, 1906, 41.

is as much a New Testament and Baptist principle as independence & the Church should consult the views & feelings of other Churches *near* it."[34]

In all of the confusion, Crawford began to wonder whether her own ideas of gender roles might sometimes be inappropriate. She wrote, "I know it is God's way for *a man* to be the head of the Church but there are exceptions to every rule. . . . I wonder if it would be wrong for a woman to feed these poor sheep longer. It's a man's work I know but very often in life a woman is compelled from circumstances to feed not only sheep but horses cattle & pigs."[35] Yet she rejected unequivocally the suggestion of her friend Harriet Rychen's pastor, who wrote, "If an ordained administrator is insisted upon why not ask for ordination yourself? Your knowledge of doctrine is sufficient to warrant it. Your ability to succeed in the work could not be questioned. The only objections would be that you are a woman and then some might falter at your position on the ordinances. Neither of these however need be unsurmountable."[36] In her journal Crawford wrote, "It is bad enough to be called an old maid' but to be called A Reverend Old Maid would finish me in 24 hrs!"

April of 1906 brought an unexpected distraction. Crawford reported, "Two men arrived on foot who introduced themselves as Elders of the Church of Jesus Christ of Latter Day Saints. They looked tired & respectable so we invited them to stay over Sunday."[37] She did not ask them to speak in the morning service, but she invited them to speak later if they would make no reference to their "peculiar doctrine." "In introducing them I told the Indians they did not believe as we did but they would say a few words. It was a few words indeed. Only a few sentences each complimenting the work. Some people wouldn't have asked them to speak at all but I'm of the opinion that we should be courteous to all men in church as well as out of it. These men were sincere in their belief."

The Women's Baptist Home Mission Society asked Crawford to come to its meeting in May at Dayton, Ohio, and to bring four Indians from Saddle Mountain. She chose Lucius Aitsan and three others. As they traveled, everything was an adventure, and many things were frightening. At last the group arrived in Dayton. The bigness of the meeting impressed them, but afterwards the Indians were tired and wanted to go home. There was just one more stop, a visit to Wyoming, Ohio, where Harriet Rychen had arranged for their hospitality. There they experienced the highlight of their

34. Diary 1905, 67.
35. Journal 1905–6, December 21, 1905, 27–28.
36. Journal 1905–6, 53–54.
37. Ibid., April 9, 1906, 95–97.

entire trip when at the zoo they saw bison. Crawford and Rychen sat on a hillside watching: "Most of the buffalo were lying down, but when the Indians came up it was not long before they were all on their feet, crowding as near to the fence as they could get. I asked Kokom afterward how it happened. He replied: 'We knew them, and they knew us. We called their name, and they stood up and came. White men don't know how to talk buffalo. We have said our last say. Now we are ready to go on.'"[38]

The group arrived back in Saddle Mountain on June 2, 1906, and in the middle of the month, the Indian Association held its annual meeting. Mary Burdette arrived with Naomi Donnelley, chair of the Women's Baptist Home Mission Society Board of Directors. It was Crawford's hope that the Association would rescind the previous year's resolution denouncing the Saddle Mountain Church. Burdette and Donnelley held many conversations with missionaries and ministers, trying to bring that about. But some who supported Crawford were unable to attend, and the attempt to remove the stigma of the resolution failed.

Burdette and Donnelley learned from Saddle Mountain Church members that they favored having Aitsan as their pastor; next they talked with him and found that he felt a clear sense of call. Then another question arose: What preparation did Aitsan need? The women from the society suggested that Crawford instruct him, but she insisted that such hasty preparation would be inadequate and that, after the overstrain of the previous months, she could not take on the additional labor.

Soon Crawford realized that Aitsan's preparation was not the only issue; she sensed a growing resistance to the idea of his ministry. Finally, in July of 1906, she persuaded him to tell her the source of the difficulty:

> It is this way. A long time ago when we had the Lord's Supper the first time . . . they talked to Julia & George & they were very skeered. When our two babies died, a whole lot more died all over . . . they came to me & gave me a very strong talk. They said Jesus was punishing me because I gave them the Lord's Supper and I was doing wrong. I felt awful, awful bad, but I never said a word. I thought I done right & I just kept looking to Jesus.
>
> . . . After we had the Lord's Supper and the trouble came upon us, everybody pointed his finger at us and we were so 'shamed. We never thought to have any trouble there & they just like burned us with fire. I did not vote on that motion. I didn't know what it mean. We were all so shamed. We thought you knew the Bible the same as the Jesus men & we never thought not to follow you. It was just like fire in my heart when they said

38. Ibid., 115.

the Great Father was not pleased with us and had taken my two children away."[39]

Crawford reassured Aitsan that the fault was with the Association, not with the Saddle Mountain Church. She also put forth a plan: she and Aitsan might suggest to the church that they ask for a white pastor for one year. He could minister to the church and at the same time he could teach Lucius. Lucius agreed to the idea. Soon she also tried to reassure the church, making a simple comparison: "If Leslie Aitsan did something awfully wrong his father would whip him & not Richard. If I had led this Church wrong on the Lord's Supper, I would be punished & not the Church. Jesus heart is hurt all over to think that some of you think He punished you & took your babies from you *because you obeyed his commandment.*"[40] Then she presented the idea of calling a white pastor for one year and asked them to think about it.

On August 19, the Saddle Mountain church held a council. Lucius told the group that he wanted to learn from a white pastor what a minister's duties were. The group voted unanimously to request a white pastor for a year. (Aitsan's half-brother Odlepaugh, who objected to the proposal, went to Elk Creek and avoided the meeting.) Crawford recorded in her journal, "Two tears stole down my cheeks. I had worked for my own downfall for the good of the Church. It was the only solution to the question. I can't teach any longer—they have 'lost confidence in me as Dr Chivers might say,' on account to [sic] the Lord's supper question."[41] Afterwards she wrote to the Women's Baptist Home Missionary Society, giving the history as well as the recent details. She stated, "The road is definitely settled now & both sides have agreed to stand together & push hard." Then she closed: "As I have withheld the knowledge of my retirement from the work from the Indians so I wish you to withhold the same knowledge from the ABHM Society in your correspondence relative to the pastor. My desire is to slip away into the darkness with as little murmuring as possible and only a prayer for those who have so despitefully used me."[42]

During the next months, Crawford carried on active correspondence in several directions. From J. S. Murrow she received a warm letter of support. She exchanged letters with Augustus Strong, and his sympathy was more guarded. He agreed with her in principle but suggested that she be more conciliatory; she reiterated her position and countered with additional arguments.

39. Journal 1906, July 30, 1906, 26–28.
40. Ibid., August 12, 1906, 42.
41. Ibid., August 19, 1906, 60.
42. Ibid., August 28, 1906, 72.

Lucius Aitsan. Courtesy of the American Baptist Historical Society, Journal 1905–6, 109.

Her major postal campaign concerned the letter that in April of 1904 Nelson Rairden had accused Crawford of writing, a letter requesting that he keep Clouse away from Saddle Mountain. She continued to deny emphatically that she had done this, and she wrote not only to Rairden but to others to whom he might have sent the letter, asking them to produce a copy or at least to recollect of whether they had seen such a letter. While the men continued to maintain that she had written the letter, none could produce it.

Crawford wrote to the woman's board that she had decided to leave Saddle Mountain early in December, and on October 30 she received

Burdette's reply. Although the women wished she could remain, they understood her decision. Burdette hoped that a rest would restore Crawford so that she would soon be able to resume her work "with vigor of body, soul and spirit."[43] In closing she wrote, "God has wonderfully blessed your services and notwithstanding the opposition and lack of appreciation on the part of some, the people as a whole, who know of the work, know, also to whom under God, the success is largely attributed."

The eleventh of November 1906 "was a hard Sunday, the hardest perhaps that I have ever known," wrote Crawford.[44] That was the day she told the Saddle Mountain Church of her impending departure. She began: "My dear Sisters and Brothers of the Saddle Mountain Baptist Church I have something to tell you today that will make your hearts cry out with pain and mine cries also. The time has come when we must part and I must say 'Goodbye' to all of you and leave Saddle Mountain. It is like a mother parting from her children to give you up for God has taught me to love every one of you very dearly. It makes my heart sick to think about it but it cannot be helped."[45] She recounted the history of the situation, and then she explained her position: "The ministers in this Association believe the Bible teaches that none but Jesus men should give the Lord's Supper. I do not think so. I believe that the ordinance belongs to the Churches and they should make the road to have it whether they have ministers or not. If you could read the Bible I would stay with you and we would follow Jesus out of the Association for no Association has the right to boss any Church. But you cannot read and I do not want you to follow me so I will leave the Association. Do not be afraid. Jesus will take care of you and give me other work to do for Him where I can teach what the Holy Spirit wants me to without stirring up trouble."[46] Crawford concluded, "Dont think about the parting. Think about how glad you are that Jesus brought me over here with His wonderful message and how happy we will all be when He gathers us into His beautiful home where there will be no more sorrow nor parting nor death."[47]

To Mary Burdette, Crawford wrote, "The W.B.H.M. Society is not responsible for this. I resigned a year ago and if you do not care to defend my position longer it will be all right. I have the approval of the Master & that

---

43. Ibid., November 11, 1906, 124.
44. Ibid., 125.
45. Diary 1896–1906, 132.
46. Ibid., 135.
47. Ibid., 139.

is sufficient. You have stood by me heroically so far. I shall cherish no hard feelings if you let me go the rest of the way alone with the Master."[48]

The people of Saddle Mountain said their farewells on December 2 with many tears and sad words. Then, kneeling at the communion table, Crawford prayed: "O Lord I only believe; that is all—everything is in confusion in my heart, but though Thou slayest me yet will I trust in Thee. I believe. I know I believe. Forgive everybody and help me to forgive everybody even that horrid man Dr Rairden. Forgive me for calling him horrid. I'm horrid myself for saying it. Forgive him & help me to forgive him. Go with me & stay with the poor Indians & don't let the Church suffer. I'm unworthy but I believe."[49]

On December 3, 1906, Isabel Crawford left her beloved Saddle Mountain. Lucius Aitsan and his family took her in their hack to Mountain View, where she spent the night. The next day she left on the train. There were several delays along the way, but on December 7, she reached Chicago. After brief visits at the training school and with the Parkers, she took the train for Toronto, uncertain as to the course her life would take.

---

48. Journal 1906, December 1, 1906, 188.
49. Ibid., 195.

7

Transition: New Work

"My! the snow, the beautiful snow!" Isabel Crawford exclaimed over the unfamiliar sight when she reached the home of her sister Fanny and her family in Toronto on Saturday, December 8, 1906. That evening they were joined by her other sister, Emily, and her husband, who were also living in Toronto. It was an evening of reunion and celebration. On Sunday, Isabel did not go to church, "not because I was fatigued from the journey but for the wicked reason. I had no decent hat." For years she had struggled with the challenge of looking presentable each time she returned from her mission field. The next day she went shopping and with great delight bought her first ready-made clothing. She proclaimed that the practice "hereafter would be mine by adoption. I hate patterns & cutting & fitting & ripping & tearing."[1]

A few days later she received a letter from E. E. Chivers. He had found, not the letter Crawford had written, but one from Nelson Rairden to Harold Clouse. Rairden had reported to Clouse that Crawford wanted no "*interference*" at Saddle Mountain from the missionaries or The Home Mission Society.[2] Now that Crawford read this, she recognized that once, at one of the camp meetings, she had expressed her opinion that the "promiscuous giving" of clothing to the Indians should cease; Crawford wanted the Indians to work and take responsibility for themselves.[3] Clouse had nothing to do with this, and Crawford's words may have been misconstrued, inadvertently

---

1. Journal 1906–8, December 8, December 9, December 10, 1906, 3.
2. Ibid., December 13, 1906, 4.
3. Journal 1898–1900, pasted between pages 126 and 127.

causing hostility between her and not only Clouse but officials of the American Baptist Home Mission Society.

Crawford thanked Chivers for finding the "missing link" but noted in her journal, "There is nothing like giving people a scare when they deserve it."[4] Her letter continued, "I have retired from the work at Saddle Mt. and am now busy preparing my journals for publication. . . . I shall hasten the work hoping to complete it within a year." In her journal she continued, "I don't think I'll publish a word *of the trouble* in the journals but I mean to have some fun out of it all!"

Later in the month, Crawford again exhibited a combination of playfulness and resentment when she constructed "Indian shields," using parts of a hair switch from a missionary barrel and a miniature tomahawk. She sent one to Mary Burdette, secretary of the Women's Baptist Home Mission Society, and one to Burdette's counterpart in the American Baptist Home Mission Society, Henry Lyman Morehouse. To Morehouse she wrote, "I feel that it is yours by right of conquest and I am only sending it to you in acknowledgment of the superior strength of your forces. Hang it on the walls of 'the rooms' with your other trophies of the chase."[5]

Morehouse sent the "Christmas present" to Burdette "for interpretation."[6] When Crawford learned this, she observed, "My but it is fun! . . . Of course I've got to get a lecture from Miss Burdette for it yet, but I'll apologise as easy as a wink." Chivers, on the other hand, expressed no reaction to the implied threat of what Crawford's journals might disclose. He simply said he would "await with interest" their publication, and he commended her mission work. Crawford observed, "This D.D. is smarter than the other—he not only ignored but blarnied."[7]

Crawford planned to publish her journals, but early in 1907, when she read them, she was disappointed: "They are badly composed and only the novelty of the experiences makes them worth reading."[8] But if she were to do something with them someday, she was adamant: "I'll never hint at the difficulties & mean tricks that have been played by the good brethren." Without knowing Crawford's change of plans, Burdette wrote urging Crawford to accept the board's offer of a paid furlough of six months. Burdette also cautioned Crawford that she would need to submit the manuscript to the society's Publishing Committee for approval.

4. Journal 1906–8, December 18, 1906, 5–6.
5. Ibid., December 24, 1906, 9–10.
6. Ibid., 28.
7. Ibid, 29.
8. Ibid., February 1, 1907, 39.

Crawford felt unsettled, both about the question of publishing and about the path her life should follow. She had felt a divine call, and she did not feel that she could respond to it through settlement house work or the Salvation Army or temperance activity. She wondered whether a call was "indelible." If it was not, she might go to Oklahoma City and open an art studio and make her living with her paint brush.[9]

As she waited for a "firm conviction" to "settle down upon" her spirit, she settled down to painting china and to reading Shakespeare. She wanted intellectual stimulation, and she also hoped that the study would assist her in "catching a more cultivated style in writing for the King."[10] She "winced at the vulgar allusions & nasty parts," but she kept reading until she came to *Measure for Measure*. It "floored" her: "Mother never made me familiar with this play & I never knew why till I read it."[11]

By the end of June, Isabel Crawford was fed up. She wrote, "I've painted till I'm sick of it. I've read Shakespeare till I hate him. I've thought into the unfathomable till I don't know 'where I am at' and I'm completely tired of myself.... *Things* don't satisfy. Think of opening a studio & painting for ever, making impressions on canvas & china when there are real live souls waiting for impressions! Working for time is not to be compared with working for eternity! My dream studio in Oklahoma City has gone up in smoke. I must strive for souls while yet I may."[12]

Crawford wrote to the minister in Batavia, New York, concerning the Indians she had visited two years earlier. She wondered whether the way was open for her to work there. He wrote that she would be welcome, and at the end of September, she left for New York. Her sister Emily's husband had recently accepted a call to the pastorate in East Aurora, New York, and Isabel stopped there along her way. On Sunday, October 1, 1907, she was deeply saddened by the news of the death of Mary Burdette, Crawford's friend and staunch supporter at the woman's mission society. In her journal she could only write "Such a blow—personal and denominational!"[13]

Isabel visited Emily again at Thanksgiving. That evening she went to Emerson Hall, on the campus of Roycroft, an arts and craft community founded in by writer and publisher Elbert Hubbard. Two years before Isabel's visit, a cowboy poet named John Wallace Crawford ("Captain Jack") had come to see about publishing a book of his poems, and he and Hubbard

---

9. Ibid., 55.
10. Ibid., May 19, 1907, 102.
11. Ibid.
12. Ibid., June 28, 1907, 132.
13. Ibid., October 1, 1907, 181.

had become friends. Now Jack was back to present a program of his poems and stories. Isabel found him "jolly and witty . . . gentlemanly throughout & decidedly entertaining."[14] Besides sharing a Scots-Irish background and a last name, they had "the same frank manner, open heart, and 'funny streak,'" and Isabel quickly decided that she and Jack must be distantly related.[15]

Plate painted by Isabel Crawford. Plate in the Barbara Cross McKinnon collection, photograph by the author.

During the first year after she left Saddle Mountain, Crawford got glasses in hopes that her "head derangement comes from the eyes."[16] She visited a doctor whose verdict was "nerve waste, kidney trouble and grippe, with perfect heart & lungs."[17] But in December, 1907, still felt the need for help, and so she traveled to Clifton Springs, New York, for treatment at Clifton Springs Sanitarium. It had been founded by Dr. Henry Foster, who had come to the village in 1849 to develop a water cure facility. Foster was strongly religious, and he directed that the income from the enterprise should be used for the medical treatment of missionaries and ministers.

14. Ibid., November 29, 1907, 212–13.

15. Ibid., December 20, 1907, 239. For the life of Jack Crawford, see Miller, *Captain Jack Crawford*.

16. Journal 1906–8, February 14, 1907, 44.

17. Ibid., March 16, 1907, 57.

Although Foster died in 1901, his deed of trust ensured that the sanitarium continued according to his plan and principles.[18]

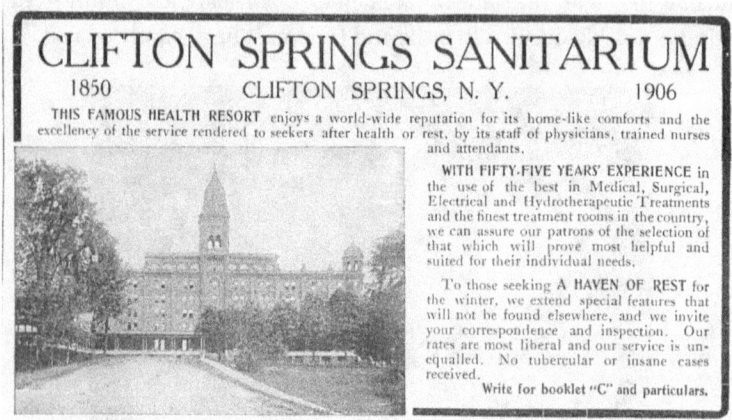

Clifton Springs Sanitarium newspaper advertisement, 1906.
Collection of the author.

When Crawford presented herself as a patient, she was told by her doctor that she had "overworked physically & mentally & the blood was not flowing naturally—too much was going to the head & not enough to the rest of the body." He determined the program she should undertake.[19] Although the sanitarium was located at Clifton Springs because of its sulphur springs, it offered various types of treatment.

Crawford's program included salt rubs and massages, medicated packs, a medicated foot-bath, Turkish bath, and a treatment called High Frequency. One morning she had a "Static": "I sat on a table with glass legs & my back up & they hit it all over with a metal ball that shot sparks & felt like needles. Then they made me turn my back backward put my feet on a copper plate that had a bar on it coming from an electric machine & they turned what they called a 'spray on me' which felt like a draught. Pretty soon I felt currents of electricity running up my feet & down my back."[20] Finally on January 8, 1908, she departed, recording in her journal, "None of these things have changed me & I go out into the world again as *stiff necked & perverse as of yore*."[21]

18. For information about Foster, see Samuel Hawley Adams, *Life of Henry Foster*.
19. Journal 1906–8, December 10, 1907, 213–14.
20. Ibid., December 20, 1907, 243–44.
21. Ibid., January 4, 1908, 280.

It was an apt self-appraisal. Before she left Clifton Springs, Crawford again sent Henry Morehouse of the denominational home mission society a "holiday reminder."[22] She sent one to Chicago, but since Mary Burdette's death, the headquarters of the Women's Baptist Home Mission Society was no longer presided over by someone so tolerant of Crawford's free spirit. When Ida Nuveen, president of the society, received a copy of Crawford's letter to Morehouse, she reprimanded Crawford. To Morehouse she wrote apologetically, "I cannot express to you the deep humiliation we feel, nor can I understand how it is possible for Miss Crawford to so lose her womanliness as to write such an impertinent letter."[23] Morehouse replied to Nuveen, "I think this will be a disclosure to you and to members of your Board, of the very great difficulty experienced by our missionaries in their relations with Miss Crawford in the work at Saddle Mountain; . . . I regret to say that she has shown a very vindictive spirit in many ways."[24] Concerned about what Crawford might say in public, he recommended that Nuveen cancel Crawford's next speaking tour. Crawford's behavior had widened the breach between herself and the men of the American Baptist Home Mission Society.

After Nuveen had corrected her "pretty severely,"[25] Crawford sat down "to explain and *apologize if necessary*."[26] In this very limited apology, she described to Morehouse her circumstances at the time of each indiscretion; the first time she was "fighting with all [her] strength against an attack of nervous prostration," and the second time she was in the sanitarium. "Need I tell you what brought me to this nerve wracked condition? I think not. You know & I know & God knows."

After leaving Clifton Springs, Crawford went to New York City to begin the next phase of her career. Though she might test the patience of the woman's mission society, her work for that group had captured the imagination of its members. She was an effective emissary, and Nuveen did not cancel Crawford's schedule. Thus Crawford began traveling from place to place to tell her story and speak on behalf of missions. She frequently wore her Kiowa dress, and she usually closed by signing the Twenty-third Psalm.

At first she made her headquarters in New York so that, at the same time, she could study lip reading. Her lack of hearing caused great problems, and in New York there was someone who might be able to help. Like Isabel

22. Ibid., 234.
23. Nuveen to Morehouse, January 16, 1908, Crawford, Biographical Files.
24. Morehouse to Ida Nuveen, January 18, 1908, Crawford, Biographical Files.
25. Journal 1906–8, 295.
26. Ibid., emphasis added.

Crawford, Edward Bartlett Nitchie heard normally during his childhood. Then, at age fourteen, he lost most of his hearing. When he was unable to get a job following his college graduation, he began to study lip reading with a teacher. Soon, however, he came to believe that the skill was largely self-taught. Thus in 1902, he published his first book of graduated lessons, and the following year he opened a school. This was where Crawford studied, fitting her lessons around her speaking engagements.

Isabel Crawford in Kiowa costume signing the Twenty-third Psalm. Courtesy of the American Baptist Historical Society, Board of International Ministries, Missionary Biographical Files: Crawford, Isabelle.

At the end of January, 1908, Jack Crawford, cowboy poet, was in the city, and he appeared on the platform with Isabel at Hanson Place Baptist Church on January 31. They might seem a surprising combination, but Jack's father had been an alcoholic, and Jack promised his mother on her deathbed that he would never drink. He had become a strong temperance advocate, and the evening was a big success.

Isabel Crawford and Jack Crawford at Camp Adams. Courtesy of the American Baptist Historical Society, Journal 1908–10, 127.

On February 20, Crawford went to meet the blind hymn writer Fanny Crosby, who was eighty-seven at the time. Crawford wrote, "She was shorter & broader than I, wore false hair & dark square or oblong gold rimmed glasses. As their conversation ended and Crawford prepared to leave, "[s]he clasped her hands in enthusiasm saying, Oh! Oh! & throwing her arms about my neck kissed me vigorously on the lower part of the right cheek. Then she drew herself back & said, 'Dearie don't ever let anybody else kiss you there.' I didn't promise. She had spoken into my deaf ears & I had looked into her blind eyes and there was no sound of falling *tears*. We heard & saw through Him who is invisible."[27]

In May of 1908, Isabel Crawford and her companion, a Mrs. Bailey, decided to attend a performance of Buffalo Bill's Wild West show in New York City. When the women arrived, William Cody himself was at the door, and Bailey introduced herself and Crawford. Cody asked Crawford in Plains Indian sign language what she wanted. She signed that she wished to talk with the Indians, and Cody agreed. Crawford had reservations about popular entertainment, but she was generally pleased by the performance. Only one aspect of the show disturbed her. There was a scene in which Buffalo Bill signed to the Indians, "I am your friend. I shake your hands." But in the next

27. Ibid., 322.

scene, as an Indian looked over a "scene of desolation," Buffalo Bill shot him: "The 'friend' who shook hands with him had betrayed him! The whole thing was true to life. A lie is not a lie when given to an Indian."

After the show, Crawford and Bailey were admitted to the dining room where the performers were eating, and through sign language Crawford soon engaged some of them in conversation. She reflected: "Poor people! . . . I don't suppose they hear the gospel when out on these trips & take back with them only the thought that the white people are interested in them because they can act in a show."[28] Thus before she left, she signed for them the Twenty-third Psalm, "& all stopped eating their dinners till I was through."

Crawford's schedule became so busy that she could not keep up the lip reading lessons, but now those with impaired hearing might receive help of another kind, a portable, battery-powered hearing aid. So on March 19, 1908, Crawford visited the Acousticon office. She discovered that she could hear using one of the models, and as soon as she had saved the required $50.00, she purchased one. The instrument had a cord between the earpiece and the microphone, and frequently Crawford was able to go to the front of a church or lecture hall ahead of time and place the microphone near where the speaker would be. She was delighted when the arrangement worked and she was again able to hear sermons and lectures.

At the end of July, Crawford returned to the Clifton Springs. This time her physician prescribed a High Frequency treatment. Crawford wrote, "It was terrible & I asked the operator to give it easier. She said she couldn't & one more charge made me jump, grab my things & run."[29] Her doctor provided a substitute. He did not require Crawford to use the sulphur springs that she disdained: "Such a lot of white, yellow & green people sit out under the Pavilion sniffing the sulphur water from the walled in spring. They sit there & smell *dead cat* for hours & think they are benefited! Others drink the stuff & others carry it off in bottles & pails. . . . A patient told me that when Henry Ward Beecher was here & tasted it he declared it reminded him of the last effort of an egg to be virtuous."[30] Crawford remained at Clifton Springs for two and a half weeks. Then she wrote, "Took my last treatment. It peeled the skin off my back and I fled."[31]

During the autumn of 1908 and the winter that followed, Crawford continued both working and taking advantage of any opportunities that presented themselves. In 1907, photographer Edward Curtis had published the first volume of his *North American Indian* series, and in May of 1909 in

28. Ibid., 380.
29. Ibid., July 31, 1908, 408.
30. Ibid., August 4, 1908, 409–10.
31. Ibid., August 17, 1908, 419.

New York, she visited an exhibit of his photographs titled The Pictured Story of a Vanishing Race: Enlarged Photographs of the North American Indian. Curtis was influenced by the view that Indians, declining in population and being forced to assimilate, would soon disappear from the land. Crawford commented that the photographs did not offer convincing support for this theory: the subjects were strong and muscular and did not look as though they were on the verge of extinction.[32]

Isabel Crawford in costume at a girls' camp at Northfield, Massachusetts, 1909. Courtesy of Barbara Cross McKinnon.

In September of 1909, Crawford had a new experience. When Albert Smiley was appointed to the United States Board of Indian Commissioners in 1879, he had been dismayed at the brevity of the board's annual meeting. Influenced by the Quaker practice of consensus, he sought a way in which people might share their concerns about Indian affairs. Albert and his twin brother, Alfred, owned a mountain-top resort hotel at Lake Mohonk, New York, and Albert invited a group to meet there in October, 1883. These

---

32. Journal 1908–10, March 3, 1909, 99.

meetings of Friends of the Indian continued annually and became a strong influence in the development of Indian policy.

Crawford was invited to the 1909 meeting. The assembled group was now called the Friends of the Indian and other Dependent Peoples; its concerns had broadened, but substantial time was still granted to Indian affairs. While the perspective of the group was Christian, Crawford had a complaint: "The speakers nearly all dwelt upon the political sides of the questions & proposed this plan and that that would accomplish certain ends. In a side room meeting the missionaries held a small but interesting session & I told them right out plain that without the power from on high the best plans would fail. Law & gospel are both needed in every work & it is useless to get results with the law only. It's the valley of dead bones over again."[33] Nevertheless she concluded her account, "the whole affair from beginning to end with the wonderful surroundings made one wonder if the Heavenly Portals were not somewhere near."[34]

After the conference, Crawford went to Wyoming, Ohio, to spend the winter with Harriet Rychen and to write her book. Carefully she went through each of the journals, making notes. She believed that the book would be "so full of the triumphs of the Gospel that people won't mind reading all the unearthly experiences that led up to the glorious ending."[35]

In the spring, Crawford went back on the road. In July she attended the Chautauqua at Boulder, Colorado. The Chautauqua Lake Sunday School Assembly of 1874 held in western New York had quickly expanded to offer a wide range of educational opportunities. Following the success of the original Chautauqua Institution, Chautauqua Associations were organized at many places to serve as centers of education, culture, and relaxation. The Colorado Chautauqua hosted an annual "School of Missions," and this year Crawford was one of the "Talent." She waited while all the others were introduced and said "such nice things." Finally she was called upon: "As usual, 'I put my foot in it' by saying: I have done missionary work in the slums, with the ragamuffins of the street, with the Blanket Indians on the reservation & now for three years I have worked among the Churches. Without any hesitation I say the last class is the toughest!"[36]

In August of 1910, Crawford, accompanied by her friend Harriet Rychen, paid her first visit to Saddle Mountain since she had left in December of 1906. Maggie Topping had come a year before Crawford's departure to assist her, and she was still there. So was Lucius Aitsan; his wife Mabel

33. Ibid., 143.
34. Ibid., 147.
35. Ibid., 154.
36. Ibid., 169.

had died and he was now married to Mabel's sister. Harry Treat had been assigned as missionary to Saddle Mountain, so the church had now been served by a white pastor for three years. The Kiowas greeted Crawford warmly, and quickly it became clear that they wanted Isabel Crawford back. Treat was with them only part of the time, and Topping could not provide the leadership given by Crawford. Aitsan was not ready for ordination, and the Indians were uncertain about what to do.

Next she headed to Clinton, Oklahoma, where she visited her brother and his family; she also got a horse and went out to see her farm. Then she resumed her speaking duties, following a busy itinerary: she recorded that in October of 1910, she had spoken fifty times and stayed in twenty-eight different beds.[37]

Beginning in January of 1911, Isabel Crawford was based in Boston and made her speaking tours from there. Then she began to work mainly in New Jersey. June was meeting time—for the Baptist Convention, and the General Convention of Baptists in North America, and the Baptist World Alliance. Crawford commented, "What a lot of 'business' the Lord's business takes. I'm glad I only have one 'constitution' to look after!"[38] On June 29, she arrived at the Chautauqua Institution in New York; her friend Harriet Rychen came the next day. The schedule of this, the original Chautauqua, offered an abundance of riches, and carefully Crawford and Rychen made selections from each day's program. Crawford herself spoke several times; then, after leaving Chautauqua, she gave presentations at several places in New York State. A September visit to the Cattaraugus Indian Reservation felt "like old times."[39] She was glad to be with Indians again, if only fleetingly. Then she was off to Indiana and Ohio.

In April of 1911, a small group of Indians had met in Columbus, Ohio, to plan for an organization. The resulting Society of American Indians opened its founding meeting on Columbus Day of that year. Only Indians could be full members, but non-Indians could become associate members. It was as an associate member that Isabel Crawford attended, and the amount of information she recorded in her journal attests to her interest. The full members were largely educated men and women who wore "citizen dress." They were mainly believers in assimilation, and they encouraged Indians to develop independence and help themselves, goals that Crawford supported firmly.[40]

37. Ibid., pasted between pages 196 and 197.
38. Journal 1910–12, June 13, 1911, 91.
39. Ibid., September 24, 1911, 145.
40. See Hertzberg, *Search for an American Indian Identity*, 59–78.

During the autumn, it became clear that Crawford's fame had spread well beyond the Baptist church that she called home. She spoke at meetings of the Congregational Women's Board of Missions, the Indian Association, the Women's Board of Domestic Missions of the Reformed Church in America, and Central Presbyterian Church. Then she returned to Wyoming, Ohio, and Harriet Rychen, for a period of sewing, writing, and preparing for "The World in Cincinnati," a large missionary exposition to be held from March 9 to April 6, 1912.

At the exposition was a low platform for Crawford and the four Kiowas who had been selected to come from Saddle Mountain; it contained a tepee and a large number of curios, sent by friends. The group spent specified times on the platform; at other times they visited more of the exposition and learned about a wider world than they had imagined. One woman asked Crawford to give the Twenty-third Psalm in sign language. Though Crawford had done this countless times in her speaking engagements, the Kiowas had never before seen it. When she finished, tears ran down all four faces.

In July of 1912, Crawford traveled again to Oklahoma. When she arrived at Saddle Mountain, Lucius Aitsan's son Amos lay dying. As his life drew toward its end, he had prayed that he would spared until Crawford arrived, and his prayer was granted. Three days after her arrival, the promising young man breathed his last. Crawford was also made welcome at the Rainy Mountain and Elk Creek missions. Things had changed, however, and Crawford wrote, "Again old missionaries should be blind as well as deaf & dumb. (If you can't be all three try to be one.)"[41] On she went to Clinton, to see her brother and his family before she headed for Arizona.

During her years at Saddle Mountain, Crawford had encouraged the converts to form the "God's Light Upon the Mountain" mission society, and its efforts led to the opening of the Sunlight Mission among the Hopi at Second Mesa. Now Crawford traveled to visit the mission, leaving the train at Holbrook, Arizona. When she reached the First Mesa compound, it seemed to Crawford as though it had been inundated by "a second flood, not of water but of sand," for the buildings were scattered among great boulders.[42] A few days later, when she arrived at the Sunlight Mission on Second Mesa, Crawford saw "another higgley-piggely settlement not founded on a rock but stuck on a sand pile. How the buildings keep from sliding downhill I do not know. There they were, the church the hospital & the house and 'all around was sinking sand.'"[43] Mary McLean, the founding missionary, had

---

41. Journal 1912–13, June 22, 1912, 4.
42. Ibid., July 20, 1912, 31.
43. Ibid., July 24, 1912, 41.

left at the beginning of that year, and Crawford regretted that she was no longer there. But Crawford was welcomed by the current missionaries, and following the Sunday service she had a collection of letters from the Hopi to send to Saddle Mountain.

Crawford returned to Holbrook and took the train to Williams. From there she went on to the Grand Canyon, where she "looked down over the battlements into the wonderful abyss & was quiet for once."[44] Crawford, however, was not content to examine the canyon from the rim. The next morning, she began her descent.

> The burrow [sic] clung to a narrow ledge of a path, hugging the rocks, not only with both feet but with all four. I'm a born rider but I confess as I looked "overboard" I wanted to turn back. The burrow had no room to turn but before I had time to jump off & run a photographer appeared like a Jack in the pulpit & told us "to look pleasant." Look pleasant with nothing between you and destruction but the off side of a Mexican mule! The "looking pleasant" stunt being over the party proceeded, preceeded [sic] by the guide. We could only see burrow's trail a few feet ahead of us for it kept circling round & round down & down till if one wasn't naturally "giddy" she would get there quick.[45]

From the Grand Canyon, Crawford went to California for a month's vacation. Here she visited with friends from Woodstock and from St. Thomas. When her holiday was over, she began an itinerary of speaking engagements. A vigorous suffrage campaign had brought the vote to California women in 1911, and in Los Angeles in November of 1912, Crawford witnessed women voting. Though a highly independent woman herself, she did not approve of this expansion of women's role; she wrote in her journal, "When I can vote women back into their homes I'll vote."[46]

44. Ibid., August 7, 1912, 57.
45. Ibid., 60–61.
46. Ibid., November 5, 1912, 104.

Isabel Crawford (marked with X) at the Grand Canyon, 1912. Courtesy of the American Baptist Historical Society, Album West.

In February, Crawford visited Yosemite. There, Inspiration Point lived up to its name: "A hush fell over the merry company & the words rushed into my mind. 'What is man that thou art mindful of him?'"[47] Yet the visit also brought to her memory a sad and mysterious part of her family's history. She recalled the story of her mother's youngest sister, who may have been massacred near there, and she wrote, "It is strange that I should want to visit the place but not so strange as my becoming a missionary to the Indians."[48]

Her next speaking itinerary took her to Nevada. From there she went on to Oregon and to Washington. In Pendleton, Oregon, she bought herself

---

47. Ibid., 154.
48. Ibid., March 18, 1913, 148.

two presents for her upcoming birthday "an Indian beaded bag & a string of real wampum."[49] Gradually she was building a collection of artefacts not only from the Kiowas, but from a variety of tribes.

A month later, on June 24, 1913, while Crawford was in Washington, Lucius Aitsan was successfully examined for ordination. Crawford learned the news from Katherine Westfall, Corresponding Secretary of the Woman's American Baptist Home Mission Society. With joy, Crawford pasted Westfall's letter and the minister's printed report into her journal. The event for which Crawford had hoped and prayed had finally come to pass.

After more work in the northwestern states, Crawford was ready for a rest. She sailed to Vancouver and spent two weeks at leisure. She longed "to be away from people & trains & churches & electric lights, artificial teeth, salads rats & hats. I was tired of fine choirs, beautiful jewelry stores & pictures by great artists."[50] And so she planned to travel to Alaska. Mrs. Charles Smith of Vancouver, the daughter of one of Crawford's Prairie College friends, agreed to go with her if Crawford would postpone her trip for a few days. That turned out to be fortunate, for the *State of California*, on which Crawford intended to sail, hit a rock and sank in Gambier Bay, Alaska, with considerable loss of life.

On August 23, Smith and Crawford left on the *Princess May* for Ketchikan. There they boarded a launch that took them to visit William Duncan and his mission. In 1857, Father Duncan, as he was commonly known, had come from England to the western coast of North America under the auspices of the Church Missionary Society. Due to disputes, Duncan's ties to the Church of England weakened; he and his colony were now at Metlakatla, Alaska. Here Duncan received Crawford and Smith warmly. The women spent three nights in the guest house, and each evening Duncan regaled them with accounts of his adventures. He enforced strict rules of conduct in the community, and Crawford admired both the results and the man who had brought about the transformation.

Following a visit to Sitka, Crawford and Smith headed south and docked at Seattle on September 9. After a few speaking engagements in Idaho, Crawford joined a party for a trip in Yellowstone. Then in September of 1913, Isabel Crawford returned to work, giving addresses in Idaho, Utah, Montana, Washington, and Oregon by the end of the year. In Seattle she heard the noted Baptist minister Carter Helm Jones preach on the text "How much owest thou to my Lord?" Crawford wrote, "It thoroughly upset

---

49. Ibid., May 23, 1913, 172.
50. Ibid., pasted in between 192 and 193.

me, for I couldn't help thinking that the Lord owed me *some rest* if He expected me to work for Him."[51]

She followed yet another rigorous schedule in Montana. Sometimes she was unusually tested. On January 25, in Butte, she spoke at the eleven o'clock church service, taught a Bible class, and spoke at Sunday school, before having lunch in a restaurant. At three she spoke "for the colored people," at seven to the young people, and at eight to the Swedish people. "Then we went to the Chinese mission & I spoke there & visited in two Chinese homes after I had just spoken *7 times & walked 63 blocks or 5 1/4 miles!*"[52] After this ordeal, Crawford asked to be released from her schedule for two months, and she settled down in Spokane to work on her book. On March 13, with a great satisfaction, she sent off the manuscript.

Then she took on her next assignment, General Missionary for the Inland Empire, or eastern Washington. As she worked, she also made time for "boiling down" her manuscript, for it had been returned to her for shortening.[53] By August, the mission society officers regretfully recognized there was not enough work in Washington to justify her time. Crawford would again take up assignments in the East, but first she had a vacation. Her sister Fanny Firstbrook and her family were visiting British Columbia, and Isabel joined them. In Vancouver, there was a cloud on the horizon; Crawford wrote, "The whole city was full of soldiers preparing for the awful war."[54] The family traveled to San Francisco, and soon Crawford left the party to head for Oklahoma. There she visited her brother and then went to Saddle Mountain. Most of the Indians were away during her first days there; this gave her the opportunity to repack the "few earthly belongings" she had left there; among them were Indian rugs, pottery, and baskets.[55] When the Kiowas returned, they greeted her with joy.

Crawford returned to Spokane. She then headed east, and in October she went for a second time to the Lake Mohonk meeting of the Friends of the Indian. There Crawford was particularly attracted to Amelia Quinton, who had assisted Mary Bonney of the National Indian Association and who later became its president. "She sat beside me & when I told her who I was she looked at me with wide open eyes. 'I have long wanted to meet you' she said 'but I had no idea you were so young!'"[56] Crawford especially appreciated

51. Journal 1913–14, December 28, 1913, 50.
52. Ibid., January 25, 1914, 76–77.
53. Journal 1914–15, July 31, 1914, 34.
54. Ibid., August 12, 1914, 37.
55. Ibid., September 1–5, 1914, 44.
56. Ibid., October 14–16, 1914, 57.

an address by Richard H. Pratt, founder of the Carlisle Indian School, who said that "the Indian problem was the white problem." Crawford wrote, "He is right. If the government would give schools, & churches gave missionaries and all political schemers eliminated the problem would solve itself."[57]

Finally, late in 1914, Isabel Crawford's work on *Kiowa: A History of a Blanket Indian Mission*, came to fruition. On October 14, when she had finished reading the proofs, she sighed with relief and proclaimed—inaccurately—"I'll never write another book. That is certain."[58] Although the book's copyright date was 1915, it came out in December, 1914. Crawford had prepared a long list of names and addresses to which copies should be sent, and on December 23, she received the first of many thank-you letters.

Crawford continued to give addresses on behalf of the women's mission society. On May 1, her monthly report proclaimed that she had traveled 2040 miles and given forty-one addresses. She wrote, "No wonder I feel all in!"[59] She fulfilled speaking obligations in New England, New York, and Pennsylvania until August of 1915, when again she spent a refreshing time at the Chautauqua Institution. Jane Addams was one of the speakers. Although Addams had Christian motivation when she and her friend Ellen Gates Starr founded Hull House in Chicago, Addams had no interest in evangelism. After hearing her speak at Chautauqua, Crawford wrote in her journal, "She—bah! Philanthropy without Christianity is dead!"[60]

In the summer of 1915, the international situation was much on the minds of Americans. Crawford observed, "There were Peace lectures galore. No one was to show fight; all were to be unprepared mollycoddles, sitting back loving one another and comforting one another . . . whispering one to another 'The battle is the Lord's' let Him fight it out! . . . Never in all my life did the Irish in me boil so furiously! Fight? I could have cleared off the platform without a shelalie. [sic]"[61] For Crawford, this discussion took a personal turn: oppressed by the itineraries she was given, she had tried to trust that the Lord "would provide a way of escape." Now "all this peace nonsense put fight into me & I decided to co-operate with the Lord instead of asking him to bear my burden longer." As soon as she had the opportunity, she would work to rectify the intolerable situation.

Back to work she went in September, making appearances in and around Chicago. There she received word that Fanny and John Firstbrook's

---

57. Ibid., 58.
58. Ibid., October 24, 1914, 65.
59. Ibid., May 1, 1915, 121.
60. Ibid., 148.
61. Journal 1915–16, 3–5.

son Jack was leaving for England to undergo training before he started active service as an airman. She "went weak all over" when she read the letter; then she "went down town to forget & didn't get back till after 10 o'clock. Saw the Battle Cry of Peace in which Cap Jack figured."[62]

Over the years, Crawford's pleas for more realistic and humane itineraries had failed. While she was based in Chicago, she tried again, in person, meeting with a committee of the Home Mission Society in November, 1915. Finally the women acknowledged the problem, and soon Katherine Westfall, the group's corresponding secretary, told Crawford that she had been appointed to work among the Indian tribes in western New York, to start at the beginning of September. The work involved four reservations. Crawford had previously visited three of them and "every time came away with the heart ache," for she recognized their great need.[63] She wrote joyfully, "Farewell to the 'fatigues of travel' overvisiting of the saints, midnight retirements, irregular down sittings & up risings, glad refrains such as 'From Greenlands icy Mountains and 'Speed away, Speed away' (with nothing to speed on but Shanks mare) Farewell to banquets where tables groaned, & luncheons where you did it yourself! Farewell to devilled ham sandwiches, sardines, cold potato salads, iced tea & strong coffee! . . . Farewell to all these funny things & welcome work that will need grace, horsepower & the guidance of the all seeing Eye!"[64]

---

62. Journal 1915, November 22, 1915, 48. The 1915 film urged military preparedness for war. It was the only film in which Jack Crawford appeared.

63. Journal 1915–16, November 17, 1915.

64. Ibid., December 1, 1915, 7–8.

8

New York Reservations

The fall of 1893, I said to the Master: Now I have done all I can to get myself ready for service. If you want me here I am.

He asked me to go to the Indians & I cried.

The fall of 1906. Again I said, Lord, what wilt thou have me to do? He said, "I want you to do platform work." I gasped but said: Thy will be done.

This fall of 1915 He said again to me, "I want you to go to the Indians" And this time my heart laughs! [sic]

All the way my Saviour leads me.

I have learned in whatsoever state I am there in to be content (except when overworked).[1]

IN NOVEMBER OF 1915, when Isabel Crawford received her assignment to work with Indians in western New York, she rejoiced that she would no longer be forced to rush from church to church "as to an hospital for an operation for appendicitis."[2] Now she would again be working directly with Indians, and she anticipated doing what had brought her success and satisfaction at Saddle Mountain. She was assigned work among the Indians on four reservations: the Tuscarora, a short distance north of Niagara Falls; the Tonawanda, east of Niagara Falls; the Cattaraugus, south and west of Buffalo; and the Allegany, a short distance north of the Pennsylvania border. Crawford recognized that there would be differences from Oklahoma; she observed that the Senecas and Tuscaroras had heard the gospel but they "had heard so much *more* about

1. Journal 1915-16, November 17, 1915, 6.
2. Ibid., 3.

other things & had seen civilization dominated by these other things that had it not been for the Holy Spirit in their own hearts, they would have supposed that the gospel was a mere fad with some of the white people & not a reality with any but the preachers."[3]

The Senecas and the Tuscaroras, two of the six Iroquois nations, had "seen civilization" much longer than the Kiowas. Upon gaining independence, the United States government "gave" land to Indian groups. Like much government policy toward the original inhabitants, this had unintended results. According to Anthony Wallace, the "reservation system theoretically established small asylums where Indians who had lost their hunting grounds could remain peacefully apart from surrounding white communities until they became civilized. It actually resulted, however, in the creation of slums in the wilderness, where no traditional Indian culture could long survive and where only the least useful aspects of white culture could easily penetrate."[4]

The Kiowas were in a difficult period of transition when Crawford went to Oklahoma, and some of their leaders recognized the potential of Christianity to help negotiate this transition. In contrast, missionaries had been among the Senecas and Tuscaroras from early years. When Crawford visited the Tonawanda reservation, she discovered that, besides a Baptist church, there were Methodist and Presbyterian buildings—three churches, but no missionary. She wrote, "Ministers of the faiths represented in the churches come out irregularly once a month more or less but it is the devil himself who attends to the pastoral work, & he does it well."[5]

Following that visit, Crawford also wrote, "A heathen long house is also on the reservation some place."[6] The establishment of reservations in 1797 had led to a period of anxiety and adjustment. Two years later, the Seneca leader Handsome Lake began to have visions, and the Code he taught as a result encouraged people to reform their ways and thus escape the destruction that threatened them. Though based on Iroquois religious traditions, his teaching reflected contact with nearby Christians, especially in its belief in heaven and hell. The longhouse, traditionally the dwelling of Iroquois family groups, became the ceremonial center for the followers of the Code of Handsome Lake.

Although these New York circumstances differed from those in Oklahoma, in January Crawford undertook a familiar task: she participated in "special meetings" on the Tonawanda reservation. She wrote, "From house

---

3. Ibid.
4. Wallace, *Death and Rebirth*, 184.
5. Journal 1915–16, December 5, 1915, 9.
6. Ibid., 8.

to house we went nearly every day for two weeks, singing & praying & exhorting.... I was thrilled through & through to the heart in witnessing such evidences of the working of the Spirits in lives which were all but snowed under."[7] In March, special meetings were held on the Cattaraugus reservation although, she observed, "It was a season of refreshing rather than of conversions!"[8] She considered it her mission "to give the Indians the gospel & the white Christians *hickory*!"[9] Through the special services she carried out the first of these duties.

Part of Crawford's assignment was to "help out in associational and other meetings, when it will not interfere with your plans for the Indian work," and that was when she applied the hickory.[10] Now when she spoke and wrote to white audiences, she expressed her surprise that so little was being done for the New York Indians when their need was so much greater than that of Indians in Oklahoma or "heathen" on foreign shores. She described the "degradation" that she observed, and she proclaimed, "It is the white people who are responsible."[11]

On June 11, 1916, at Red House, on the Allegany reservation, Fillmore Jackson, the native supply pastor, did not appear, so Crawford conducted the morning service. Then she was surprised to see the arrival of an old man, carrying everything needed for the Lord's Supper. He arranged things on the table in front of the pulpit and then signaled to Crawford that everything was ready.

> I fairly gasped & turning to the deacons said simply: "This is good. I am glad you are remembering Jesus as he requested. You deacons can conduct the service." Deacon Warrior shook his gray head & stepped away. Deacon Amos George sat down in the deacon's chair. There was no alternative. Rising from my seat in the congregation, after receiving the assurance & approval of the Holy Spirit, I said: "It is not customary for a woman to administer this ordinance. There is a command that we observe it and it is left with the church to arrange how it is to be done. I am not a member of this church, but if you vote to have me take charge of the ordinance I will do so." Deacon Warrior made the motion, Deacon George seconded it, & we broke bread together!!![12]

7. Ibid., January 8–21, 1916, 21.
8. Ibid., March 26–April 10, 1916, 69.
9. Ibid, March 7, 1916, 48.
10. Ibid., pasted into margin at page 7.
11. Ibid., January 29–31, 1916, 21.
12. Ibid., June 11, 1916, 81–82.

Thus Isabel Crawford did what she had been falsely accused of doing at Saddle Mountain. But here there were no reports and no repercussions. This was simply one part of Crawford's missionary service.

In August, 1916, she returned to Ontario for two weeks. Although Toronto was not far from western New York, the atmosphere was very different. The United States had not yet entered the world conflict, but in Canada "[e]verything flavours of war. Everybody seemed to be knitting socks & women in deep mourning were seen every time we went out. 'Your King & Country need You—*now*!' appeared every day in the papers & was seen on bill boards in conspicuous places."[13] Isabel found her sister Fanny and her husband filled with anxiety. Their son Jackie had received his flight training in England and begun service as an airman, and now he was missing. Isabel wrote, "we all feel that he is safe but a prisoner somewhere in Germany." She also visited her other sister; then she worked on her albums, documenting her activities in Oklahoma until she began her next New York itinerary.

On January 4, 1917, Isabel Crawford wrote in her journal, "Left for New York instead of for Toronto to say goodbye to my sister who sails for Switzerland to find 'Jackie' Jan. 13, with her husband. Such a time to go! But it can't be helped."[14] Although the United States still claimed neutrality, the nation felt the impact of the Germans' use of submarines. The Germans had temporarily ceased submarine activity, yet Americans watched nervously, and Atlantic crossings were fraught with hazard.

By the time Crawford wrote to the executive committee of the mission society in January of 1917, she had definite opinions about what was wrong on the four reservations. The area included about 3103 Indians and about 1000 nominal Christians. There were two ordained native preachers, but the church had given them no training. Thus the apparent failure of the native churches lay not with themselves, but with the home mission societies: "Civilization with little gospel and no law has plunged these Eastern Indians into depths of degeneration that I never saw equalled in the wild and wooly west."[15] Despite this, however, "[t]here are hundreds of both Christian and

---

13. Ibid., August 16, 1916, 102.

14. Ibid., January 4, 1917, 31. Although Isabel Crawford did not record the rest of the story, the family had learned that their son Jackie had been shot down behind enemy lines in July. He underwent surgery in a German military hospital; then in December he was moved to an internment camp in Switzerland. It was there that his parents were going to meet him. Two newspaper articles from the *Toronto Evening Telegram* (October 6, 1917 and October 15, 1917) have been transcribed by M. I. Pirie and are available on the Canadian Great War Project website at http://www.canadiangreatwarproject.com/transcripts/transcriptDisplay.asp?Type=N&transNo=725.

15. Journal 1916–17, 37.

Pagan Indians, on all the Reservations who live good, pure, honest lives in pretty homes surrounded by trees, flowers & mowed lawns."[16]

Crawford offered a partial solution: "It seems to me therefore a woman must be sent and a woman who has had experience with Indians and with 'roughing it.' She should be located in the City of Buffalo. . . . It should be her aim, under the guidance of the Holy Spirit, to plan for enlargement and the ultimate placing missionaries at each of these Indian Baptist Churches. If the Board of the Women's American Baptist Home Mission Society thinks favorably on this proposition, Isabel Crawford is willing once more to undertake a man's job in your appreciated employ."[17]

Crawford's next speaking schedule took her to Ohio. Before she returned to the Allegany reservation, she learned the sad news of the death, on February 28, 1917, of Captain Jack Crawford, in Brooklyn. Into her journal she pasted clippings about the passing of her "cousin."

Following evangelistic services at Red House, Crawford felt "dirty, cold, shabby, ugly, & worn out inside & out."[18] She "escaped" to Toronto for two weeks. Her sister and brother-in-law were still in Switzerland where their son Jackie was recuperating, so she was met by her nieces Ada and Mary Firstbrook. Isabel observed that the awareness of war hung heavily over the city, and she saw for herself the sorry sight of twenty-seven wounded soldiers just returning to Toronto from the front. Shortly after Isabel returned to the United States, that country, too, entered the war.

Crawford's next tour included engagements in Pennsylvania, New Jersey, and New York. While in New York City, she heard the popular evangelist Billy Sunday. When she first saw him, in 1914, she was not prepared to like the vigorous, colloquial preacher, but now she wrote, "the more I hear him the more I glory in his clear grit."[19]

Not all her activities were so pious. One afternoon, she went to Madison Square Garden to attend the Ringling Bros. and Barnum & Bailey circus. She particularly wanted to see a bear whiz around on roller skates and on a bicycle, and the bear did not disappoint her. When she returned to the YWCA where she was staying, she found three telephone messages instructing her to go to a hotel to meet home mission secretary Katherine Westfall. There Westfall exclaimed, "You've saved my life." Crawford explained, "It seemed that there was some bungling about the annual meeting at Elmira. I was on the programme & had never been invited. No one could find

16. Ibid., 40.
17. Ibid., January 29, 1917, 42–43.
18. Ibid., March 12, 1917, 48.
19. Ibid., April 15, 1917, 54.

me—telegrams & telephones had been busy & here I was at last. It meant an all day trip & an all night one back but I had got in some extra rest while in hiding & would go."[20]

In May, Crawford lamented the fact that she had not been able to spend more time on the New York reservations during the previous months, for she could fit in only brief visits. She wrote, "I do not feel called to go about telling the churches what Christ has done for the Indians. I feel called to tell Indians what Christ has done for them & will do for them in the future if they will let Him."[21] She judged the Indians' needs by her traditional standards; on the Tuscarora reservation she observed, "Poor Indians! They certainly need guidance & help. One afternoon I visited a number of homes & not one was 'normal.'"[22]

For a while, Crawford was able to work more on the reservations. In August, she went to Chautauqua as one of the speakers at its Home Mission Institute. In her journal she reported, "When my little turn came, I denounced the 'melting pot' that never let an Indian in it although he could contribute music & art that would surprise the whole world, if he got the chance." Those who "'study the Indian,' not for what *he is*, but for what they can make out of him, will never *know* the heart of the Red man! He will close it up tight till he knows whether you are interested in him or what he produces!"[23]

During the fall of 1917, Crawford attempted to combine a speaking itinerary with work on the reservations. She returned to Canada for Christmas, visiting Fanny and John Firstbrook. They had been able to leave Switzerland with their son Jackie and go to England. Then in October, they had returned to Canada, grateful that their ordeal was over even though the war still raged in Europe. Isabel also visited Emily and her family in Georgetown. After the rush of the previous months, she appreciated this interval of quiet. She returned to the reservations in January.

When she wrote her annual report at the end of March, she explained the difficulty of work on these reservations: "Please remember that there are no sidewalks or cement roads and all the Reservations but one are off the Rail Roads. Snow drifts appear everywhere in winter weather and in some places the roads can only be detected by post tops here and there higher

---

20. Ibid., April 16, 1917, 56.
21. Ibid., May 26, 1917, 59.
22. Ibid., June 17, 1917, 62.
23. Ibid., 73.

than the rest.... In spring, fall and summer we have quantities of rich and mellow mud."²⁴ In her journal she mused,

> That I am alive to tell the tale is due to the fact that I have exercised a "diversity of gifts." If our ministerial wanderers would ... do their own washing after preaching, clean their own shoes, mend their socks, turn their hat bands, press their suits, scrub their heads, learn to crochet & knit, read more poetry and less new theology, avoid fats, eat from shoe boxes, shiver half the time, roll in the snow, paddle in the mud, go and hear a Harry Lauder sing & take a turn on rollers sometimes I believe they would renew their youth like the eagles & retain their beaks & claws!²⁵

Her light mood was broken early in April by a letter from Mrs. L. K. Barnes, a representative of the women's mission board. Barnes reported that the Home Mission Council was asking the women's society to withdraw from the work on the western New York reservations because of overlap with the work of other denominations. Crawford was incensed. The problem was not overlap but a lack of thoroughness, constructing churches but leaving them unstaffed. They needed to strengthen, not withdraw from, the work.

In June, when Crawford returned following a speaking tour in New England, she learned that a team of visitors would be arriving—immediately. Besides Mrs. L. K. Barnes, the visitors included Lemuel C. Barnes, Field Secretary of the American Baptist Home Mission Society, and William Alexander Granger, also from that society. They were impressed by the extent of Crawford's work among the people. Though L. C. Barnes had to leave before the tour ended, Granger and Mrs. Barnes agreed with Crawford's request for a missionary at Red House, but the matter was far from settled.

On August 12, 1918, Crawford arrived at Chautauqua after a season of many engagements, "Tired & cross as 3 sticks. Was informed finally that the 'indications of providence' were that I was to speak on Sunday as arranged for, as there was no one else to be found. I declared that the indications of Providence were that if I didn't stop twitching at nights & get some rest & relaxation I'd go to pieces & have to quit the work.... I'll be a real heathen soon."²⁶

Some of the speakers had shifted their views. In particular, Shailer Mathews had been a strong peace advocate when Crawford attended

24. Journal 1917–18, 71.
25. Ibid., March 24, 1918, 78.
26. Ibid., 110.

Chautauqua three years earlier, before the United States had entered the war; now, in 1918, he advocated "'war to the finish.'" Crawford was also aware of the increasing theological distance between herself and many of the speakers. Mathews was a Baptist liberal who did not believe in the second coming of Christ in the traditional sense. Crawford wrote, "'Till I come' is hard to explain away."[27]

At the end of August, Crawford returned to Buffalo and to the reservations, expecting to make a speaking tour of Missouri and anticipating that a missionary would be sent to Red House. Both plans were overturned, and by the end of September, Crawford herself settled at Red House, on the Allegany reservation. With the help of a local woman, she cleaned out a "pen" that had been used for storage, and made it a "den" fit for human habitation. Crawford arranged to board next door with the Walquists, a Swedish family.[28] Carl was the section foreman for the Pennsylvania Railroad, and his wife, Hulda, was an excellent cook. In her quarterly report, Isabel rejoiced in eating "the best meals I have ever had since becoming a full fledged missionary twenty five years ago."[29]

After the United States had entered the war in April of 1917, Congress passed an act authorizing the sale of Liberty Bonds to raise money for the war effort. Isabel had purchased a one hundred dollar bond, and in September, 1918, she offered it to the Woman's American Baptist Home Missionary Society "in deep appreciation of the splendid treatment I have always received from every member of the official family."[30] She wanted to erect a *"living"* memorial to her parents. Later in the fall she was happy to learn that the women of the society responded enthusiastically to her suggestion of a prayer room in the training school. Crawford wrote, "Let the memorial then be to a sweet-faced mother in gray and to a father without gold who together suffered the loss of all things that they might win Christ!"[31]

On the eleventh of November, 1918, the nation thrilled to the news that the Great War had ended, and celebrations broke out across the land. Yet there were shadows. The cost of the war was high, and many would not return or would return maimed in body or spirit. And the lethal Spanish Influenza was taking its deadly toll. One of its victims, on October 31, 1918, was Lucius Aitsan, pastor at last of the Saddle Mountain Baptist Church.

---

27. Ibid., August 13, 1918, 110. This shift is discussed in Rieser, *Chautauqua Moment*, especially in pages 254 through 268.

28. Both in Crawford's journal and on census lists, the name is spelled sometimes Walquist and other times Wallquist.

29. Journal 1917–18, 134.

30. Ibid., September 17, 1918, 120.

31. Journal 1917–18, 155.

Isabel Crawford, "Today I sat down to write to the family, the church the deacons, the missionaries & poor old Mokeen. I have not shed a tear for years.... As I wrote one letter after another, tender, loving, sympathetic the flood gates of my soul burst and a torrent of tears has flowed ever since."[32] The interpreter, learner, and friend whom Isabel held in esteem and affection was gone.

The Presbyterians in the Red House area had no services of their own, and during the winter, some began to respond to the invitations of the Baptists. Crawford wrote, "There is only this one church in the town & all must be made welcome." Then at some point, in different ink she added "but some of the Baptists say the Presbyterians are to 'stay out.' My!"[33] A storm was brewing, and it was no simple denominational rivalry. Fillmore Jackson, a native Baptist pastor, was ordained but had no theological training. He was preaching that baptism was necessary for salvation: people could not be saved without it. Crawford was already aware of this, but now there were consequences. Some of the Red House Baptists failed to welcome Presbyterians because they did not view them as fully Christian. For Crawford, belief, not baptism, was crucial. She used as an example the words of Jesus on the cross to the converted thief beside him: he promised that the thief would be with him in paradise. To Crawford, this was no abstract theological point. Jackson was rushing people into baptism before they were truly converted, before they "believed," and then they were left to flounder.

All of this complicated what Crawford and the Red House Baptists considered a terrible threat, namely a proposal to give the Red House Baptist Church to the Presbyterians and receive instead the Presbyterian church building on the Tuscarora reservation. Crawford already knew of the proposal when, on March 5, 1919, there arrived at Red House "a man of middle age, pleasing and neat in appearance but with eyes nervously staring and hands trembling though not from cold."[34] He was H. T. Broughall, a Presbyterian missionary in the area. He had come, he said, "on very unpleasant business": he had come to take over the Red House Church for the Presbyterians. He appeared only with the greatest reluctance, and Crawford attempted to reassure him, explaining that the women's board had not been consulted, and that the proposition was not Baptist policy. In fact, the matter had not even been presented to the members of the Red House Church and the Cattaraugus Association of Baptist Churches, and their approval would be needed. In her journal she wrote, "The poor preacher's face brightened

32. Journal 1919, November 5, 1918, 54.
33. Ibid., February 2, 1919, 3.
34. Ibid., 31.

up here and he said joyfully: 'Miss Crawford I don't want to take this church over. I have eight as it is to look after and this would make nine. It is too much.'"[35] To the secretary of the women's society Crawford explained the history of the church. The women had raised money toward the building and the men did the construction work. Moreover they built the church without the help of a resident missionary. One church member still had the receipts. Applauding this history of self-reliance, Crawford exclaimed, "Talk about Saddle Mt.!"[36] She urged the mission society to support her attempt to "stand right with the Indians & help them save their church."

At the end of March, 1919, Crawford was summoned to a meeting in New York City. Speaking with representatives of both the women's and the denominational home mission boards, she asserted her usual independence of spirit, stating that she "wasn't working for Boards but for a Higher power! and it didn't make any difference to me what any Boards said. If a thing was right, I was with it, wrong I was against it & this whole Red House business was wrong & a tragedy before the Lord!"[37] When Crawford asked what to tell the people at Red House, a member of the women's board said, "Belle tell the Indians that there are no Baptists anywhere who want them to give up their church that it will not be taken from them without their consent." Crawford replied, "Then the matter is settled for they will never give it up and I will tell them not to worry for the whole thing is settled." "I didn't say that." "You said the same thing." "O no I didn't." "If the Indians refuse to turn the property over they are *to be let* go on as they are but our society is to withdraw its worker & put no more money in the field!! That is the decision."[38]

A week later, an automobile pulled up to the railroad section house at Red House, and this time Crawford received three callers. Along with H. T. Broughall and an elder from Buffalo was the elderly Henry Ward, of Buffalo, from the Presbyterian home mission board. Ward read to Crawford a letter from Lemuel Barnes, field secretary for the American Baptist Home Mission Society, stating that the Baptists were willing to give to the Presbyterians the Red House Church in exchange for the Presbyterian one at Tuscarora. Crawford declared the statement "unbaptistic in sentiment. No Board or representative of a Board can legislate any Baptist Church out of existence!"[39] The members of the Red House Church had not been consulted—nor, it turned out, had those at Tuscarora.

35. Ibid., 35.
36. Ibid., March 24, 1919, 43.
37. Ibid., April 2, 1919, 50.
38. Ibid., 50–51.
39. Ibid., April 8, 1919, 60–61.

Ward blamed the situation on the ecumenical sentiments of the day. He stated, "This whole affair is an after-effect of the war. There is a loud call for Church union and *you and I* cannot *stop it*."[40] For Crawford, that was no reason deviate from principles. But finally a practical note ended the conversation. She asked, "Dr. Ward do you mean to tell me that Brother Broughall can minister to 9 churches? He couldn't do it among whites much less among Indians! One service a Sunday once in three weeks won't fill the bill!" In her journal she commented, "This was the final crash. There was no more to be said."[41]

The next day, there was a "Called meeting of the Missionary Committee." Later, in a letter to women's board secretary Katherine Westfall, Crawford stated that she had just "let fly."[42] The resulting motion recommended that the effort to turn the Red House Church over to the Presbyterians be dropped and that Crawford continue to receive support as missionary there. The conclusive factor was that the Indians had built the church on their own; thus no denominational body had the authority to take it from them.

Work returned to normal at Red House. Crawford initiated a Bible school for the children on Sunday afternoons and turned the morning service into a similar class for adults. She also prepared for a visit by Mrs. L. K. Barnes of the woman's mission society, and Crawford had a mischievous idea. She was living in a small attic room that she had made habitable by dint of much hard work. Nearby was a storage room in which the Italian family downstairs had deposited junk over the years. In that room was a bed. She wrote, "Time after time I had listened to lectures emphasizing 'the importance of missionaries being able to adapt themselves to circumstances, no matter how uncongenial.' Here was an excellent opportunity to demonstrate the theory to one of the 'higher ups.'"[43] Crawford escorted Barnes to the house and upstairs to the attic. "The stark old junk room, arranged as if for her coming, overwhelmed her convention-conscious mind. No movie face ever gave forth so many changes of shocked expression as that of our distinguished guest." Quickly Crawford took Barnes next door to the Walquists' home and assured her that she was to stay there; only then did Barnes recover from the shock.

Following the church services, Crawford and Barnes set out on some visits. As they headed along a narrow path, a half-grown pig suddenly joined the procession. Crawford wrote, "all at once a violent squeal rent

40. Ibid., 64.
41. Ibid., 66.
42. Ibid., April 16, 1919, 69.
43. Crawford, *Joyful Journey*, 137.

the air and our guest stopped stock still and, breathing heavily, declared: 'That pig wiped his nose on my skirts, and I hit him over the back with my umbrella.'"[44] After protesting that pigs cannot wipe their noses, Crawford repeated the instruction that she had heard so often: "We must 'always try to adapt ourselves to circumstances, never giving up till we have accomplished that which we have undertaken.'" When the women reached their destination, the visit went smoothly until a horse and buggy approached. Abruptly Barnes rushed out of the house and ran down the hill, beseeching the driver to take her back to the Walquists' house. There was no room, but as Barnes and Crawford walked homeward, another buggy approached, and it had space for the city visitor. Back at the house, Barnes proclaimed "I know I couldn't do this kind of work. . . . I'd die."[45] Afterwards Crawford reflected: "It might have been better if I had not given my city guest such a strong dose but, strange to say, I felt no regret."[46]

At the end of July, Crawford left for a restful vacation in Manlius, east of Syracuse. Late in August she resumed her work at Red House, and she was received into membership in the small congregation. Then at the beginning of October, 1919, Crawford was once again on the road. She spoke during the morning service at Jordanville, south of Utica. Afterwards, she was introduced to an elegantly dressed woman, Corinne Roosevelt Robinson, who said to her, "Miss C, I did enjoy your address *tremendously*. My brother was a great friend of the Indians & *tremendously* interested in them. You are living a *tremendously* useful life. I did not agree with all you said about dancing, Church union, etc." Identifying herself as a "great admirer" of Robinson's brother Theodore Roosevelt, Crawford observed that "one of his best characteristics was that he believed not only that he had a right to his own opinions but that others had a right to theirs!" In her journal, Crawford quipped, "I had to make a *tremendous* effort to get this remark in!"[47]

During this period of speaking engagements, Crawford received a telegram reporting the death of her sister Fanny Firstbrook on November 7. Katherine Westfall wrote a letter of condolence. In reply, Crawford thanked Westfall for her sympathy. Yet she had the consolation of a firm faith in everlasting life: "He *is* going to give me back my loved ones just as soon as I wake in His likeness."[48] When she returned to her work at Red House, she found that, in trying to bring comfort to the people there, she forgot her

44. Ibid., 139.
45. Ibid., 140.
46. Ibid., 141.
47. Journal 1919, October 5, 1919, 133.
48. Ibid., December 2, 1919, 141.

own sorrow. She went to work fixing up the room in which she was to live, and she observed, "Work is the best antidote for sorrow."[49]

At the beginning of 1920, the women's mission society granted their workers a raise of fifteen dollars a month, but Crawford wrote to the board, requesting that she continue to receive her previous salary. In her twenty-six years of missionary service, she had managed to save $426.38. She had no debts, no wife to support, and no family to educate, and she felt that Christians should sacrifice for the sake of missions.[50] The board members expressed their appreciation but declined her request. Although Crawford kept scrupulous accounts of her salary and expenses over the years, and although her commitment to missions was high, her remarks do not fully reflect the basis of her financial security.

In October of 1915, Isabel's brother, Hugh Crawford, bought property in Clinton, Oklahoma, for eight hundred dollars. The following July, Hugh and his wife sold the property to Isabel for the same price. Isabel continued to own it until December of 1941, when she sold it back to Hugh, Maggie, and their two children for ten dollars.[51] Thus Isabel provided some support for her brother and his wife, probably based on profits she made on oil stocks that she purchased during her time in Oklahoma.[52] But her personal financial matters were something about which Crawford remained silent even in her journal. She felt it acceptable, however, to state that she had been able save from her salary an average of $16.40 a year over twenty-six years.

Early in 1920, Crawford received the happy news that the Missionary Training School had opened the prayer room dedicated to the memory of her parents. Writing about the memorial, she described her own certainty of her call: "Twenty-six years ago my dear father died without having one oft repeated prayer answered, that his only son might enter the ministry. A year later, as Aunt Lizzy Aiken offered the dedicatory prayer at my graduation, it seemed as if the heavens were opened and I heard two voices saying: 'This is my beloved daughter in whom I am well pleased,' for surely father understood then that his prayers were answered, only God had quietly called his daughter instead of his son!"[53] Now her parents had the "living memorial" for which Isabel had longed.

---

49. Ibid., December 9, 1919, 143.

50. Journal 1920–21, page EFGH and back side of EFGH.

51. Warranty deeds, Custer County, Oklahoma, July 21, 1916 and 19 December 1941, obtained for the author by researcher Rhonda Wood.

52. Doris Cline Ward, interview with the author, March 5, 2011.

53. Journal 1920–21, 1.

In June of 1920, the Convention of the Northern Baptists was held in Buffalo. That was near enough so that Crawford could attend. There had been an undercurrent of division within the denomination as some of its members—in particular some teachers in its theological seminaries—rejected the inerrancy of scripture and were open to German biblical criticism and to Darwinism. The anti-modernists rejected these trends and railed against their dangers. Curtis Lee Laws, editor if the Baptist *Watchman Examiner*, called for a General Conference on Fundamentals, to be held in Buffalo immediately before the convention. At the earlier meeting, Crawford heard the testimonies of men who had lost their faith while attending Baptist seminaries, and she was present when the Fundamentalists (a name that may have been coined at this time) took before the full convention their resolution that the schools, colleges, and seminaries be investigated. She observed, "Of course when the climax was reached & the split in the ranks avoided some one started 'Blest be the tie that binds,' but some of the singers were bound by compulsion & I fear did not sing from the heart."[54]

Crawford saw further evidence of change when she returned to Chautauqua that summer, and she did not find the offerings as interesting as usual. She wrote, "Perhaps I'm tired."[55] For the first time, Chautauqua's gates were open on Sunday. On a Sunday afternoon, she spoke at a children's meeting where "there wasn't a prayer offered."[56] But most of all she felt alienated by the liberalism of Shailer Mathews. She had already express disdain for his switch from peace advocacy to support for the war. Now she wrote, "Dr Mathews gave a talk in which he explained how when young men came to him with doubts about their father's religion because it was contrary to science, & their fathers didn't know it, he told them Genesis wasnt the history of creation but a myth etc. Bah! My father studied science as much as Dr M but he chose to stand by the creation in the old Book."[57] Crawford's heart was with the Fundamentalists.

Crawford left Chautauqua on August 25, and early in September she began to paint the church at Red House. Painting the window frames was especially tedious: on September 28 she wrote, "'Standing on the promises' is easy but standing on the *rounds* of a ladder is a different proposition because the flesh is weak I suppose."[58] At last, early in November, she finished. Both in celebration and of necessity she burned the dress in which she had

54. Ibid., 41–42.
55. Ibid., 48.
56. Ibid., 50.
57. Ibid.
58. Ibid., September 28, 1920, 62.

painted. In her quarterly letter, Crawford described the results of the effort: "It is all spic-and span, neat & clean and most patriotic in coloring: red inside white outside and blue in between! . . . We raised all we could among ourselves, worked hard, did no begging and came out with a balance of 44 cents."[59]

Isabel Crawford painting the church at Red House, New York, 1920.
Courtesy of Barbara Cross McKinnon.

Beginning on March 6, 1921, the Red House Church hosted a week of "special meetings." Fillmore Jackson took a leadership role, and things quickly went awry. As the meetings proceeded, Crawford found herself receiving instructions from Jackson, delivered by the sexton. Division grew within the small community, and it became clear to Crawford that Jackson and his supporter Elmer Jones had their own, independent plans and that the newly elected deacon, Harley Blinkey, was to take her place in leadership. Crawford was permitted to speak at the final meeting only when

59. Ibid., 88–89.

the program committee insisted on it.[60] After the services ended, Crawford requested a meeting of the Cattaraugus Association's missionary committee. The problem was perplexing, and a conference was called for April 14, 1921. There Jackson was questioned as to his views on baptismal regeneration. Crawford had long insisted that Jackson's views contravened Baptist principles, but his responses were too indefinite for the hearers to judge. In the end, wrote Crawford, "Jackson was requested not to come again without being invited by the missionary & he & Elmer said they were willing to shake my hand. They managed to head Elmer up my way but I counted five laboring with Jackson to none effect!"[61]

Before long, however, Crawford learned that the chairman of the missionary committee had "backed down," and the resolutions had not gone forward for signing.[62] Greatly discouraged, she wrote to Katherine Westfall of the home mission society, "It is a repetition of what happened at Saddle Mt." Seeing no hope for her ministry on the reservations of western New York, Crawford prepared to return to life on the road, visiting churches and making presentations to inspire her hearers with the importance of the missionary task.

---

60. Ibid., March 21, 1921, 126.
61. Ibid., April 14, 1921, 140.
62. Ibid., April 27, 1921, 161–62.

9

Coast to Coast

Isabel Crawford left Red House, New York, on May 2, 1921, to make a speaking tour in North Dakota. Things had changed in the past thirty years. Scandinavian and German settlers worked the farms near the prairie towns, and Norwegian, German, or Swedish was now heard in some of the formerly English-speaking territory. Some customs, too, were new: "I saw big men kiss each other right on their mouths with great vigour & women kiss each other as passionately. They certainly seemed an affectionate people and most earnest in their attention to the messages."[1]

Away from Red House, Crawford was able to reflect, and one week after her departure she sent her official letter of resignation to the women's board. She explained that from the beginning she had seen the need of an experienced white pastor on the reservation. She continued, "As the work is too delicate & complicated for a woman and as no recognition has been given repeated appeals for co-operation I feel it my duty to tender my resignation at once & report for new service."[2] A month later, she informed the Red House Church that she would not be returning.

When Crawford reached St. Thomas, North Dakota, the place looked very different from the village she had left more than thirty years earlier. Sapling trees had matured, and she hardly recognized even her own home. Other things had changed, too: the Baptist, Presbyterian, and Episcopal churches had all closed, and it was the Methodist church in which she spoke.

---

1. Journal 1921, 35.
2. Ibid., 26.

Crawford visited Red House in September. Ten days later, the community held a farewell for her on the Walquists' lawn. There was business to be attended to—the children and the ladies' aid wound up their financial affairs. There were cake and ice cream and the presentation of gifts, both to and from Crawford. On September 28, Crawford left the mission that had caused her so much frustration. Following a speaking tour in Vermont, she returned to Red House to finish "packing up *everything*."[3] Then she headed to New York City.

In June, Crawford had received an invitation from her friend Grace Rowley Parker. Her husband, the railroad executive who had been so supportive of the Saddle Mountain mission had died ten years earlier, and now Parker was living in Florida. Crawford wrote that Parker's invitation "set my heart atingling!"[4] Happily she accepted the invitation.

She traveled to Florida by train. Then an auto took her through the stately pillars that marked the entrance to Point Palma Sola, near Bradenton. Parker's house was located on a point of land, and to Crawford it seemed immense: until Parker reduced the number, it had contained twenty-three rooms. Crawford's bedroom confirmed her impression of luxury. She wrote, "I was so transported with joy that when Dr Parker put her arms round me & said: 'Now dearie this is your home & we want you to rest & rest & rest & have a good time,' I thought I had reached the land of corn & wine—prohibition or no prohibition! Poor little me! Think of getting a chance to 'rest & rest & rest'! I who have never known how it felt to be free from responsibility till this hour!"[5]

Christmas fell on Sunday in 1921, and Crawford shed her flannels and dressed in white "from head to foot" before she and her companions rode to Bradenton to attend church. Before he began the sermon, the pastor publicly welcomed Crawford and announced that she would be speaking on Tuesday afternoon at three o'clock. Crawford's vacation was not to be a time of complete rest. Soon Crawford's calendar was dotted with speaking engagements, yet she undertook them at a pace of her own choosing, and these serious endeavors did not curb her playful spirit. She wrote, "It's fun to be out of school. We used to have recess there twice a day. Why can't we have them when we are out of school? . . . It seems to me I've never had any play time till now. Responsibilities came when I was only sweet sixteen & new ones came in quick succession as soon as the old ones disappeared."[6]

3. Ibid., October 21, 1921, 57.
4. Journal 1921–22, page before A.
5. Ibid., December 20, 1921, page RSTU.
6. Ibid., February 9, 1922, 10.

Yet as she enjoyed the hospitality and the rest, Crawford also pondered the question of what she was to do next. She wrote to Clara Norcutt, corresponding secretary of the women's missionary society, stating clearly her decision that "without Christian co-operation between the societies it would be suicide for me to undertake Indian work again. Perhaps you may think because I laugh & try to throw off trouble that I don't feel the crushing set backs the poor Indians have had to stand but don't deceive yourself for there isn't a nerve in my body that doesn't quiver as a result of the double tragedy."[7] She was willing to continue in deputation work, and once again the home mission society assigned her to that task.

When Crawford received word that her first assignment would be in Kansas, she decided pay a visit to Saddle Mountain on the way, and so on April 3, she headed for Oklahoma. She arrived at Clinton late in the evening two days later. During her visit, Isabel went out from Clinton with her brother to see their farm property once more. Then she headed to Saddle Mountain. At the cemetery, she saw the graves of Lucius Aitsan and others whom she had known. The pastor invited Crawford to speak at the Sunday service, and she did so, with Sherman Chaddlesone as interpreter. Then "Hunting Horse started a 'sing' going over & over & over the same words or verse Indian way, gaining more & more voices & more & more volumn [sic] of sound till the little church fairly resounded with Indian Melody."[8]

After a visit to Rainy Mountain, Crawford embarked on her speaking tour in Kansas. She continued her work in Wisconsin and Illinois. Finally, on the Fourth of July, she caught a train that would take her to Red House. There she spent several days packing her suitcase for her winter itinerary and a smaller bag for Chautauqua. Again she was joined at Chautauqua by her friend Harriet Rychen.

In the autumn of 1918, Crawford had decided to undertake Chautauqua's home-study reading course "for recreation."[9] Crawford had completed the required list during the previous January, in Florida. Now she was eligible to receive her diploma at Chautauqua's annual Recognition Day. Thus on August 17, 1922, Crawford joined with the fifty-nine other members of that year's class to pass through the Golden Gate on the Chautauqua grounds. Two days later she wrote in her journal, "I've passed through one 'Golden

---

7. Ibid., February 26, 1922, 13.

8. Ibid., April 9, 1922, 37. The earliest missionary women had encouraged one of the first converts to make a song, putting Kiowa words to music that was also within the Kiowa tradition. Thus Kiowa Christians could connect the Jesus Road with their own culture. For a discussion, see Lassiter, *Power of Kiowa Song*.

9. Journal 1917–18, October 25, 1918, 127.

Gate' and feel about ready to hobble up to the other. Life at Chautauqua is strenuous."[10]

Chautauqua Home Reading Course graduation photograph of Isabel Crawford, 1922. Courtesy of Barbara Cross McKinnon.

Once again Crawford returned to Red House, but her relationship with the church bothered her. Still filled with loyalty and affection for the church at Saddle Mountain, she had decided to return her membership to that congregation, and during the summer she wrote to Red House asking for a letter of dismission. The church clerk refused, however, stating that Crawford must appear before the congregation "and make your Self good."[11] Following her visit to Red House, Crawford wrote to the Saddle Mountain pastor: "The Indian Church at Red House is not in a condition to do business, the whole work having run down since I left. Two or three attend the services but never enough to get a proper vote on anything. So I am going to ask that

10. Journal 1922–23, August 19, 1922, two pages before AB.
11. Ibid., page facing AB.

you receive me on the Churches knowledge of my Christian experience."[12] Thus Crawford returned—at least in membership—to her beloved Saddle Mountain.

After a season spent on the east coast and in the Midwest, Crawford was assigned to speaking engagements in California. She left Cincinnati on December 12, 1922. As her train crossed the southwestern states, Crawford read and crocheted. On December 16, she reached Los Angeles and traveled on to San Diego, arriving in the evening. There she stayed with George and Ida Kermott, good friends from Crawford's years in North Dakota.

On Christmas evening, 1922, Crawford went with friends to see the new, spectacular silent film *Robin Hood*, with Douglas Fairbanks. Crawford did not avoid motion pictures any more than she did circuses. She judged each according to her own standard of propriety, and *Robin Hood* fared well: she pronounced it "good and decent!"[13] She found other amusement, too, between her speaking engagements. San Diego had hosted the 1915–16 Panama-California Exposition, and during the second year of the exposition, a zoo had been established. Crawford visited the park, noting how the site had changed since she was there in 1912. She observed, "It is wonderful but I don't like the monkey cages though. They are the limit & if I thought they were my forefathers I'd almost be ashamed of my Creator for it certainly wasn't necessary for Him to give the race such a vulgar start."[14]

As she traveled, Crawford frequently made contact with people she had known in the past, and on March 20, 1923, she took the train to the town of Ceres. There she visited with Elbert Chute and his wife, Sarah. It was to Elbert Chute that eleven-year-old Isabel Crawford had volunteered as a Sunday school teacher almost forty-eight years earlier. After he had completed his theological education, he took medical training; then the Chutes departed for India. There they served long and well, and now they were living in California. The visit brought back warm memories.

While she was in Los Angeles in June, Crawford attended a children's service at Angelus Temple. The prominent and successful Canadian-born evangelist Aimee Semple McPherson had opened the tabernacle the previous January. McPherson appeared "gowned in white with a long black cape, large white collar, white shoes & stockings & bouquet (large also) of sweet peas at her waist."[15] Although Crawford herself had engaged in evangelism and although she agreed with many of McPherson's religious beliefs, she

12. Ibid.
13. Ibid., December 25, 1922, 19.
14. Ibid., February 1, 1923, 29.
15. Ibid., June 16, 1923, 65.

had reservations. In her journal she wrote, "The Angelus is beautiful & artistic, and everything about the place & service spoke of 'effect.' . . . God is using Mrs Mc undoubtedly *but*, I could not help but feel that the *spectacular* was put forward & that every thing nearly about the service was aimed at the immotions [sic]."[16]

After a brief vacation in Canada, the pace of Crawford's life picked up once more as she carried out assignments in Oregon. She attended a camp at the Burton Baptist Assembly Grounds on Vashon Island as a lecturer.[17] The serious nature of her work did not, however, suppress her playful spirit. Crawford entered heartily into the camp's activities; a report in the camp newspaper of a faculty-student baseball game began, "The mighty have fallen,"—for the faculty had lost. But it continued, "'Miss Crawford's' playing was the shining light of the game. Her thrilling catches were loudly applauded by the audience."[18]

After this, Crawford began an even more strenuous schedule that was made worse by various complications. By the middle of September, she had spoken twenty times in sixteen days and felt that it was "time something happened."[19] Yet when Crawford asked for Clara Norcutt's help in making her schedule less demanding, the mission society's secretary replied that nothing could be done from the New York headquarters. "[S]o," Crawford wrote with prescience, "I've got to speed till I drop, I guess."[20] Things grew worse. Her itinerary called for her to speak once on November 14. But after she had spoken twice, she learned that she was also to be the "honored speaker" at an evening banquet.[21] Then at Oregon City, when Crawford thought she was through following an early afternoon meeting, she learned that she was scheduled to speak at the evening prayer meeting, too. Afterwards she had laundry and packing to do, and she did not get to bed until the wee hours of the morning. She spoke with Ora Campbell Wright, secretary of the Oregon Convention, who had provided the schedule, but he paid no attention to her complaint, and problems continued.

Crawford was not only at her wit's end: she was at the end of her physical endurance. On November 30, 1923, when she went in to the hotel dining

---

16. Ibid., 65–66.
17. Kathleen Henderson, Executive Director, Camp Burton, e-mail to the author, January 22, 2010.
18. Journal 1923–24, page opposite GHIJ.
19. Ibid., September 13, 1923, 4.
20. Ibid., November 7, 1923, 34.
21. Ibid., November 14, 1923, 42.

room, "something happened."²² She collapsed, although in a few minutes she was able to eat. A doctor diagnosed her case as "Nervous exhaustion from over work," and she was forced to cancel the remainder of her Oregon tour. Wright's less than tactful response was that "it was an opportune time as it was hard to make itineraries in December!!" As Crawford rested, she read, and by the time she resumed her activities, she had read thirty books.²³

In the middle of January, 1924, Crawford started to fill speaking engagements once more, and during the next months she worked in Oregon, Washington, Montana, and Idaho. Following a less onerous itinerary, she was able to find amusement as she traveled. In Montana, when her hostess recognized Crawford's humorous nature, she said, "You are not like Miss Sindrell. They told me so when they asked me to take you. She stayed with me once & said: 'What are you making on the stove it smells like lemon pie. I hope it isn't for I don't like it & never eat it'! It was lemon pie but they said Miss C. won't be like that."²⁴ The next morning, when her hostess asked what she would like for breakfast, Crawford replied, "lemon pie."

In June, she visited the Chippewa Cree Indians of the Rocky Boy Reservation in Montana. After an interpreter introduced Crawford, she spoke with her own distinctive openness: "I told them I knew they were gathering for their sun dance, & I had no bad words to say against their religion. Indians had many religions. Some worshipped the sun, some worshipped the Ghost dance way, the Image way the mescal way etc. I knew Indians who tried all the Indian religions he knew of but his heart was never satisfied till he found the Jesus way, & that was the road I was going to tell them about the only one that had power in it."²⁵ She concluded by saying, "Go into your sun dance meeting but take with you this thought: Jesus made you & made your honest, kind hearts. He wants to set them right; . . . You will bring your hearts out of your sun dance council as hungry as ever. Take them to Jesus lift them up to Him. He made them & knows how to satisfy them."²⁶ As she left, she "breathed a prayer that the Sun light of the sun [sic] of righteousness

---

22. Ibid., November 30, 1923, 60.

23. The fiction included *Pride and Prejudice* and *Vanity Fair*, and also Sinclair Lewis's *Babbitt*, published little more than a year earlier. Among the non-fiction items were a number of titles about Indians, including three by Charles Eastman, the prominent Sioux reformer whom Crawford had met in 1911.

24. Journal 1923–24, June 8, 1924, 73–74.

25. Ibid., June 10, 1924, 76.

26. Ibid., 77.

might overshadow the Sun dance & bring peace to the Rocky Boy Band of Native Americans."[27]

At the end of a busy summer she went to San Diego, to stay once more with the Kermotts, from North Dakota. They had recently been injured in an automobile accident and had suggested that the three of them might "all rest together."[28] Crawford exclaimed, "Rest? I hadn't seen my trunk for over a year & worked at it & getting 'all things in order' for another year till 5 PM. Sep 2 when we all came to San Diego. Saw 'The Ten Commandments' which was horrid." While the first part of Cecil B. DeMille's 1923 spectacle was devoted to the story of Moses, much of the film depicted the lives of two brothers and showed the consequences of following and of failing to follow the commandments. The film highlighted the downfall of the immoral brother, and Crawford disapproved of portraying immorality, even if in the end it was duly punished.

From California, Crawford's speaking itinerary took her first to Arizona and then to Colorado, where she received an "uninterrupted itinerary" from November 16 to December 19. Finally on December 24, Crawford headed east. She stopped at Cincinnati and stayed a short time with Harriet Rychen. Then she was off for Salamanca New York, spending the night on the train "with hair up & shoes on, in order to get off the train at 4.15 am" on December 31.[29] The faithful Carl Walquist met her and took her to his home; he went back to bed while Crawford and his wife visited merrily. Soon she was off for a day on an important errand.

Grace Rowley Parker was planning a trip abroad, and she had encouraged Crawford to join her. While she was in Denver, Crawford had attempted to fill out the passport application, but she did not know where her naturalization papers were. Now her brother, Hugh, had succeeded in getting duplicates. The federal office most convenient to Salamanca was in Buffalo, so off she went, filling out the papers as the train passed through the countryside. A phone call to a friend brought a witness to identify her, and by three o'clock she had filed the application. Her passport arrived January 3, 1925. It described her as five feet, three and one half inches tall, forehead high, eyes hazel, nose retrousse, mouth medium, chin round, hair medium brown, complexion medium, face oval, and distinguishing mark deaf.[30]

One Wednesday evening, Crawford went to Red House for the church service. She gave the group an old-time gospel message. Then, in closing,

---

27. Ibid., 78.
28. Journal 1924–25, August 4, 1924, 1.
29. Ibid., December 31, 1924, 45.
30. Journal Abroad I.

she assured them that she knew they "did not mean it" when they refused to give Crawford her church letter until she "came back & made good."[31] She explained that she had been accepted as a church member at Saddle Mountain on her experience, and she asked to be removed from the Red House church roll. Elmer Jones, "as penitent as Peter," spoke kind words, and a vote by the congregation quickly acknowledged that the action had been a mistake.

Crawford visited with friends and then filled more speaking engagements during the next month. In New York City, on February 9, she made final arrangements for her trip and then arrived—half an hour late—for a farewell reception in her honor. On February 13, 1925, she set sail on the *S. S. Braga* for a new adventure.

---

31. Journal 1924–25, January 14, 1925, 48.

10

Interlude Abroad

ISABEL CRAWFORD BOARDED THE *S. S. Braga* on the afternoon of February 13, 1925. Immediately she was pleased with her stateroom's white enamel walls, shiny fixtures, and white and rose striped curtains; "every thing from carpet to ceiling was spic & span & invitingly clean."[1] It was also decorated with "7 boxes of candy a dolled up basket of fruit, flowers, 2 books & 52 letters." Though Crawford was tired from her recent activity, she looked over the letters and the other deliveries. Then she simply looked out at the sea and hummed "There is rest for the weary." During the next days she did nothing but read and write, sleep and eat. By the time they reached the Azores, she had forty-nine post cards and eleven letters ready to mail.

In Lisbon, Crawford joined a small touring group. It was Shrove Tuesday, and it was Crawford's first experience in a predominantly Roman Catholic country. The whole city appeared festive on this last day before Lent. The group visited the Estrella Church, and Crawford "felt awed" at the sight of its paintings and high arches.[2] Yet she was struck by the stark contrasts. She wrote, "A poor woman near me had only stumps of hands but over them she held her beads counting them & praying with a face expressive of the deepest sorrow. I think it was the saddest sight I ever looked upon." Crawford's sorrow was not simply for the woman's condition but for the futility of her belief.

---

1. Notebook Abroad I, February 13, 1925.
2. Ibid., February 14, 1925.

When the *Braga* stopped at Oran, Algeria, Crawford stayed on board and sewed. While she was at Saddle Mountain, she had received a beautiful bisque doll, a doll she "should have had" when she was a child.[3] In Oklahoma, she had no time for frivolity, so Crawford put her away. Before the trip, she had taken out the doll, named her Palestine (Pal, for short), and made a box in which Pal could travel. Now Crawford made clothes for Pal, and she became so absorbed in the task that on February 28, she sewed all day without realizing that it was Sunday.

On March 4, 1925, the ship reached Alexandria. The next morning after breakfast, Crawford left the *Braga* with a guide, passed through customs, and caught the train for Cairo. There she went to her hotel and hired a guide for the following days. The next morning she and her elaborately-dressed guide set forth by tram to see the pyramids of Giza. Crawford observed the striking contrast between the untold wealth on one side of the river and the poverty on the other, and she was intrigued by the "moving circus" that she passed: "camels, donkeys, goats, oxen, men in skirts & veiled women, children in rags & fixed up ones, two wheeled carts autos etc."[4] She rode a camel around the Great Pyramid of Cheops, and when they descended a hill, the Sphinx came suddenly into sight: "The ugliest thing I ever saw; far uglier than his pictures. He looked as if both Jess Willard and Jack Dempsey has had bouts with him and had beaten him to a frazzle. His expression was a little like Mona Lisa, a sort of haughty sickish smirk." After lunch she and her guide visited a bazaar. Crawford had seen the streets of Cairo replicated at the Columbian Exposition in Chicago, "but," she observed, "the real thing is somewhat different!"

The next days were filled with more sightseeing. At the Egyptian museum, she observed, "Ramses II mummy looks like an Indian. They were horrid looking all dried up and wrapped in veily stuff. If they had known how terrible they would look they surely would have preferred cremation."[5] Then it was time to join Grace Rowley Parker and the Temple Tour party with which they were to travel. Parker had been in Europe for several months. At the train station, Crawford bought a first class ticket for Jerusalem and boarded the train. Spying a suitcase with the initials "GRP," she knew she was in the right place. Along came Parker and the rest of the tour party at the last minute. During the night, they ferried across the Suez Canal, and the next morning, their guide pointed out the sights as they continued their journey.

3. Crawford, *Jolly Journal*, 43.
4. Notebook Abroad I, March 6, 1925.
5. Ibid., March 11, 1925.

The Temple Tours party arrived in Jerusalem on March 13, and after lunch, they toured. Crawford wrote, "Beggars, dirty children, sore & scabby individuals, Arabs in long robes, patriarchs in queer headdresses, pilgrims, tourists, donkeys loaded with junk, camels with 'heads up' made up the queerest procession eyes ever beheld. Never again shall I think of or hear the words, 'Our feet are standing within thy walls, O Jerusalem' without thinking of dirt & smells!"[6]

The next days were filled with new experiences. At the Dead Sea, Crawford reported, "I washed or dipped several handkerchiefs, washed my doll & tasted the waters."[7] While Crawford found Jerusalem's Church of the Holy Sepulcher "shabby" on the outside, inside "the imagination lost itself in astonishment."[8] The church, she observed, "is *supposed* to be built over the rock that held the sepulchre of Christ." She was not inspired by her visit to the tomb but "felt sorry that the old priest did not get out in the world to render service to the *living* Christ."

On March 17, the Temple Tours group headed for Bethlehem. Crawford was "somewhat disappointed" in the Church of the Nativity, which she found "all dolled up with glitter and tinsel."[9] About its "Grotto of the Manger," she wrote, "I went down & looked & came up feeling queer—not a bit enthused or religious even." After a final night in Jerusalem, the tour group set forth, stopping at Jacob's Well. Once more Crawford was disappointed by what had been done to a biblical site: "The water was good but the place so built over and fixed up with altar & pictures that no one could recognize it as the well by the side of the road where the women came to draw water."[10] They went to Nazareth and then passed through Cana. At the Sea of Galilee, Crawford delighted in their two-hour boat ride. She observed that "no one could be on 'Blue Galilee' & not feel His peaceful presence!"[11]

On March 21, the Temple Tours party left the British Mandate territory of Palestine and entered the French Mandate territory of Syria (which included modern-day Lebanon). Their first stop was Damascus, where they visited biblical sites. But Damascus did not only hold memories of the distant past. At an Armenian refugee camp, the tour party was forcibly reminded of a much more recent event: the Armenian massacres that had begun not quite ten years earlier. Crawford observed that the poor people

---

6. Notebook Palestine II, March 13, 1925.
7. Ibid., March 14, 1925.
8. Ibid., March 15, 1925.
9. Notebook Palestine and Syria III, March 17, 1925.
10. Ibid., March 18, 1925.
11. Ibid., March 20, 1925.

looked "thrifty and ambitious."[12] During the next days they journeyed to Baalbek and to Beirut, and then they returned to Palestine, to Haifa, to start the next leg of the trip.

Isabel Crawford with her doll Pal. Courtesy of Barbara Cross McKinnon.

On March 26, 1925, the group left Haifa. This time they crossed the Suez Canal by day, and they arrived at their Cairo hotel later that night. In the morning, they took the train to the dock in Alexandria. There they boarded a sailboat that took them to the White Star Line's *Adriatic*. It left the port late in the afternoon. Crawford recorded that it cost "$176.00 from Alexandria to Naples a 3 night & 2 days trip. Of course we had plenty of style but it was very de-pressing—to the pocket-book."[13] She spent the time working on her journal.

12. Ibid., March 21, 1925.
13. Notebook Italy IV, March 27, 1925.

On the morning of March 30, the group stepped ashore at Naples. Crawford joined a group for a trip along the Amalfi Drive. She was captivated by the gardens that appeared in most unexpected places, and she was pleased to see men, women, and children working and singing and laughing together: "'Sunny Italy' is the very name that suits it—for not only is the climate sunny but the people."[14] Roadside shrines were new to Crawford, and she wrote, "although I am not a Catholic, I couldn't help thinking it was a good idea to have reminders of Him here & there along the journey, 'lest we forget'!"

In Rome the group engaged in a flurry of sightseeing. While others in the group seemed entranced by Michelangelo's fresco "The Last Judgment" on the altar wall of the Sistine Chapel, Crawford "didn't care for it . . . the abode of the saved looked like the magic carpet scene in the 'Thief of Bagdag' [sic] Tastes differ of course."[15] She was also dismayed by the nearby picture of John the Baptist pouring water on the head of Jesus "from a clam shell." She exclaimed, "*Catholics know* Jesus was never baptized that way!"

On Palm Sunday, April 5, the group attended the "very showy" service in St. Peter's, and on Easter they attended two services.[16] First they saw "a lot of Catholic ceremonies" at the basilica of St. John Lateran, and then they went to an American Methodist church. There Crawford was delighted to see a marble bust of Methodist Bishop John Vincent, co-founder of the Chautauqua Assembly.

When Crawford left Rome, she may also have left the tour, for after this, Crawford only wrote of traveling with Grace Parker and a Mrs. M. B. Little, of Knoxville, Tennessee. After Rome came Florence, where she viewed the original of Michelangelo's mighty sculpture David. She wrote, "If David could see himself standing bolt upright with not so much as a shirt on, I feel sure he would have put his sling in action again with more vigor than he used on old Goliath, & 'do' Michelangelo."[17] Next they went to Venice, not "to see pictures but to see *the place*."[18] In Milan, the women were deeply disappointed to find that the section of the monastery housing Leonardo Da Vinci's mural The Last Supper was closed for a holiday.

They next traveled into Switzerland. Crawford found words inadequate: "The beauty of the varying landscapes can't be described but we saw snow covered mountains with clouds below & above the peaks, blue & green

14. Ibid., March 30, 1925.
15. Ibid., April 4, 1925.
16. Ibid., April 5, 1925.
17. Ibid., April 17, 1925.
18. Ibid., April 20, 1925.

& gray waters, castles & churches high upon mountain peaks & gardens & trees & men & women digging together with big children caring for little ones. Goodbye Happy-go Lucky Italy."[19] Crawford also admired the cleanliness of Switzerland; in Interlaken, she spilled some water on the floor. She "wiped it up with a towel which refused to show any spots or blemishes afterward."[20]

On April 29, they took the train to Montreux, where a street car brought them to the picturesque castle of Chillon, made famous by Lord Byron's poem "The Prisoner of Chillon." Like many tourists before them, Crawford and Parker hunted the pillar in the dungeon where Byron had carved his name. From there they went on to Geneva. Rain limited their sightseeing, but they visited the Reformation Wall, completed only eight years earlier. Statues of four Geneva Reformers stood in the center of the wall, but Crawford, a Baptist, took special pleasure in seeing a sculpture of Roger Williams included among the smaller statues at the side.

After Switzerland came France. For Crawford, the primary attraction in Paris was its art. At Notre Dame Cathedral she was struck by the rose windows and bas reliefs but disliked the gargoyles: she wished the builder had designed something more "churchy" looking.[21] One of the highlights, not only of Paris but of Crawford's trip so far was the visit she and Little made to the Louvre. She had never dreamed of seeing the originals of such familiar works. Crawford's distaste for nude art, however, remained strong. She wrote whimsically of Venus de Milo, "A woman without hands could never be beautiful to me. I suppose Mrs Venus couldn't dress herself & must be excused for appearing in semi nakedness."[22] The Three Graces by Jean-Baptiste Regnault, however, had no such excuse. Crawford ran from the painting: "These wretches *had* hands! Why didn't they dress first!"

One day Crawford and Little took a tour of Paris. When the guide pointed out a monument to the two men who discovered quinine, Crawford shook her fist at them, "for had they never made it I would have better hearing today."[23] On the following day, she joined Herbert and Elizabeth Evans, of Berkeley, California, on another tour. On the way to Rheims, they saw much evidence of the recent war, and Crawford found the cathedral "stricken looking," scarred by broken statuary and smoke.[24] From there they

---

19. Ibid., April 23, 1925.
20. Notebook Switzerland and Belgium VI, April 29, 1925.
21. Notebook France VII, May 3, 1925.
22. Ibid. May 6, 1925.
23. Notebook France VIII, May 11, 1925.
24. Ibid., May 12, 1925.

went north to Berry-au-Bac, where they walked carefully to avoid barbed wire as they followed their guide along a narrow path. Here the Germans had dug wide trenches and hidden devastating fortifications.

After their wonder-filled trip to Paris, Crawford and her companions moved on to Brussels. On Sunday, they attended a service at the cathedral. Although by this time Crawford had attended mass several times, she continued to find the Roman Catholic service "queer."[25] Yet she did not doubt the religious nature of those in attendance: "The people surely seemed devout & believing."

The following morning, the women traveled out from Brussels to see somber sights. At Malines, the results of the war were starkly evident: abandoned houses without windows or roofs, and fallen ruins where houses had been. Crawford wrote with surprise, "Churches seem to have been special targets. One would naturally think any one fighting would avoid harming the churches!"[26] From Malines the group motored to Louvain, which had suffered mass destruction at the hands of the German army in 1914. That afternoon they visited the site of fighting a century earlier: the Waterloo battlefield of 1815. In her journal Crawford noted, "From here we motored back to Brussels convinced that 'War is hell.'"

In Antwerp, Crawford lamented the perpetual rush. She reflected, "How one wishes for time to look into & study such works of art & genius! Life seems just the same. We are kept jumping at full speed day in & day out with no time to admire God's glorious sky & trees & flowers & fruit or trace His hand in all the leadings of our lives! . . . I want to understand this door—and I want to trace God's hand in my little life."[27] On they went to Amsterdam, where they enjoyed tulips in a riot of colors. That left them only one hour to visit the famous Rijksmuseum, but Crawford considered it "a perfect day, spent among God's flowers and man's glorious imitations."[28]

On the morning of May 23, they enjoyed their final sightseeing in Amsterdam. Then they went to the office of Imperial Airways. Crawford was always ready for new experiences, and she was about to have one: she and her friends were flying to England. They each paid $19.00 for their passage to London. The passengers were weighed; Crawford recorded hers at 114 pounds. She wrote, "Each passenger was given a supply of cotton batting

---

25. Notebook Switzerland and Belgium VI, 17 May 1925.
26. Ibid., May 18, 1925.
27. Ibid., May 20, 1925.
28. Notebook Holland, May 21, 1925.

to put in the ears to prevent the thud of the machine from interfering with their slumbers. Again I was fortunate in not having to use my portion."[29]

In her journal, Crawford described the experience: "And so we flew to London from Amsterdam without a jolt or unpleasantness of any kind. It was just like sitting in a dentists chair expecting the dentist to strike a nerve any moment."[30] They flew at eighty miles an hour, observing the fields, canals, houses, boats, and castles beneath them. Four hours after they left Amsterdam, they arrived at Croydon, south of London: "The wings dipped a little and we 'sat tight' as the machine went off the level. Then the little wheel at the back struck the ground and slowly the other two in front came to earth & after a little run the monster stopped, the door opened & we set foot in "Old England."

During the next days, Crawford both visited traditional sights and found things of special interest. She took particular pleasure in looking for familiar names in Poet's Corner of Westminster Abbey. And at the British Museum, her chosen destination was the Rosetta Stone; she thought "how interested the Indians would be in the 'talking stone.'"[31] She also had more personal quests. One was to visit Metropolitan Tabernacle, opened in 1861 to hold the vast congregations attracted by the popular Baptist preacher Charles Spurgeon. She cherished a letter she had received from her mother. Sarah Crawford described hearing him preach a dramatic sermon on "I am the good shepherd."[32] Now, long after Spurgeon's death, Isabel was able to attend a Sunday morning service at the tabernacle.

London also had closer family connections. One afternoon, Crawford took a bus toward Kings Cross station and then found her way to Percy Circus, with its gracious row houses built around a central terrace. There in number sixteen Isabel's mother had lived with William Frederick Fogarty, his wife, Emily, and his sister Emily prior to Sarah's marriage. Isabel rang the bell and was admitted. The building that had been a single dwelling was now divided into apartments. Crawford took some photos to mark the visit.

On May 26, she had the treat of spending her sixtieth birthday with relatives—her mother's sister Inez and Inez's two unmarried daughters. According to Isabel, her mother, Sarah Hackett, was one of the oldest in her family, and Inez the youngest. So great was the difference in ages that Inez did not remember having seen Sarah, but Isabel enjoyed making the connection, and her newly-met relatives received her cordially. Grace Parker

---

29. Ibid., May 23, 1925.
30. Notebook England I, May 23, 1925.
31. Notebook England II, May 29, 1925.
32. Ibid., May 31, 1925.

left for Edinburgh on June 2, but Crawford stayed longer, visiting Stoke Poges, Windsor, Oxford, and then Stratford-upon-Avon.

In a private boarding house in Stratford, she was pleased to find "a very clean & neat room splendid board & most congenial company."[33] She observed, "The A. Express Co gives me the names of the most expensive hotels always." The following afternoon she walked through the countryside to Anne Hathaway's cottage in the hamlet of Shottery. She was surprised at the sight of her destination: "Why they call it a cottage I don't know for it is a two storied long building—quite large." Thinking there must be another way to return to Stratford, she asked some children for directions. "The way led across Shottery Brook' which had a cement dam over it & over which water trickled. I dont get dizzy crossing such places so started to walk over. When in the middle I stepped on a slippery substance & over I went—down 'plunk' over the dam. I scrambled up of course & got across but before 'going on my way rejoicing' I took off my skirt & washed out the muddy plasters which decorated its folds. I was wet to the skin in spots but after walking 'through the fields' flapping the skirt before me everything got dry."[34]

Next Crawford traveled to Ireland. In Dublin she was met by a cousin, Walter Surrat, and dined with his family. After seeing some of Dublin's sights the next morning, she left for Cork. Through the train window, Crawford observed bogs with piles of peat drying in the sun, and a man with a blackthorn walking stick, things that she had heard her father describe years before.

After spending the night in Cork, Crawford took the train for Blarney and then walked to the castle. She climbed up the narrow circular stone stairway and walked along the parapet until she came to the famed Blarney Stone. Far below, the ground was visible between the floor upon which she had walked and the outer wall that held the Blarney Stone. Kissing the stone was an awkward if not dangerous activity: the visitor was to lie on his back and be lowered by an attendant while holding to two iron bars on the outer wall. The male pronoun was appropriate for, Crawford wrote, "Any woman who would attempt such a performance would have to be a born fool or worse."[35] She devised a method of her own: "I was fool enough to go down on my knees letting the attendant hold my feet while I slid down far enough to touch the stone. I tried to kiss it but my head refused to turn far enough round to do the kissing. I tried two or three times to reach it with my lips but couldn't get up to it for I was let down the wrong way round. However

---

33. Notebook England III, June 7, 1925.
34. Ibid.
35. Notebook Ireland, June 10, 1925.

I kissed my hand three times & carried the kisses over to it that way so I suppose I 'kissed the Blarney stone!'"

Next she went to Belfast and on to Magherafelt, in County Londonderry, near where her father had lived as a boy. There she was met by George McKillen, pastor of the Carson Memorial Baptist Church in Tobermore. The next morning McKillen drove her to Castledawson along the route on which John Crawford traveled to see Alexander Carson, a visit that resulted in John's conversion. They called upon an elderly woman who remembered Isabel's grandmother and then saw the old linen mill that once belonged to the Crawfords. When they drove to the house where her grandfather had lived, Crawford "sat in front of it in the car & read the will in which the place was very accurately described."[36] They also saw where Alexander Carson was buried. The following day, Crawford spoke both morning and evening in McKillen's church, which had been erected in Carson's memory. Both in England and in Ireland, Isabel Crawford had made connections with her past.

Her visit to Ireland complete, Crawford took a ferry to Scotland. In Edinburgh she toured the usual sights, including Saint Giles Cathedral. According to tradition, it was there that Jenny Geddes, in protest, hurled her stool at the clergyman who was attempting to use a new prayer book written by William Laud. Crawford commented, "Jenny Geddes must have been a crack shot if she hurled her stool *round a pillar* at the preacher in the pulpit if she sat where the tablet says she did!"[37]

The months of sightseeing were taking their toll. Regarding her visit to Saint Giles, she wrote, "I'm a bit tired of seeing Cathedrals & the wonders of man. I never get tired of God's wonders though—mountains, rivers, trees, flowers skies etc. They are ever new, & never tiresome."[38] Fortunately her journey was nearly done. The next day she took the train for London, and on the morning of June 22, she traveled to Southampton. After one night there, Crawford boarded the *S. S. Leviathan* and headed back home at last.

---

36. Ibid., June 13, 1925.
37. Ibid., June 18, 1925.
38. Ibid.

11

Looking toward the Future

WHEN THE UNITED STATES Line's steamship *Leviathan* docked in New York City on June 29, 1925, Crawford disembarked, passed through customs, and hurried to the missionary society office. In the evening she boarded a train for Salamanca, where she spent three days unpacking and repacking. When her brother-in-law, William Henry Cline, retired from the pastorate in 1920, he and Isabel's sister Emily bought a fruit farm in Grimsby Beach, Ontario, on the Niagara Peninsula, where the two had met long ago. Isabel went there now and wrote that she "had a *fruitful* season." She explained, "Never ate so much fruit per hr since I was a child in the old home where fruits of all kinds abounded."[1]

They had much to talk about, too, and not just concerning Isabel's recent trip. In a courthouse in Tennessee, the trial of John Thomas Scopes began on the very day that Isabel arrived in Grimsby Beach. Scopes, a high school biology teacher, was accused of teaching evolution, which contravened the laws of the state. Crawford wrote simply, "'The Scopes Trial' was *It* during my visit," but comments she made elsewhere in her journal about the theory of evolution indicate that she was pleased when, near the end of her visit, Scopes was found guilty.

Though she held conservative views regarding evolution, Crawford took a step that was still somewhat bold in 1925, especially for a woman of sixty: she bobbed her hair. Until recently, it had been assumed that respectable women would have long hair, but some women were now having

---

1. Journal 1924–25, July 10–27, 1925, 67.

their hair cut short. Crawford, with her characteristic independent spirit, embraced the new style.

Then Crawford went to Chautauqua, though she did not take in as much of the program as usual. She did go to hear Charles Gilkey, pastor of Hyde Park Baptist Church in Chicago, who "gave good material." She continued "I confess I was on the alert for heracy. [sic] How different we listen now to what we used to."[2] She also heard Edgar John Goodspeed, a Baptist and a professor of New Testament at the University of Chicago Divinity School. Two years earlier, Goodspeed had published *The New Testament: an American Translation*. Many fundamentalists objected to his efforts, and Crawford reflected their attitude. She wrote, "Dr. Goodspeed *tried* to defend his 'American Translation of the NT.'"[3]

At the end of August, Crawford returned to Salamanca, and she spoke to the congregation at Red House. She told briefly of her trip to Palestine and then—without realizing that the Presbyterian pastor was present— urged the Indians to cooperate with the Presbyterians. To her surprise, he came forward and commended her talk. Not everything was peaceful, however, for Crawford learned that Fillmore Jackson was still active and causing division. Then, on the evening of September 8, 1925, Crawford headed for Connecticut. She was going back to work.

During the autumn, Crawford labored in the northeastern states. She spent Christmas with friends in New Jersey and next moved on to Pittsburgh. Her schedule then took her to Ohio, and when she was in Cleveland, she went to see the silent movie motion picture loosely based on Zane Grey's novel *The Vanishing American*.[4] It depicted the oppression of Indians in a way that Crawford considered "so good & true & heartrending that I wish every many woman & child in America could see it."[5] In fact, she did her part to increase its audience: in Canton, Ohio, she took two women to see it, and she went once more, with the pastor's wife in Defiance. But she did not slacken the pace of her work, for on February 14 she spoke five times, in four churches.

For two weeks in late February and early March, Crawford rested at the home of Harriet Rychen. Then she was off again, to Indiana, Iowa, and Nebraska. During a bit of vacation in July, Crawford went to Rochester, Minnesota, for a check-up at the Mayo Clinic. She "got a clean bill of

2. Ibid., August 1, 1925, 69.

3. Ibid., emphasis added.

4. Crawford wrote, "The book is so good, the movie fine. wouldn't know the movie was any relation to the book—everything different" (Journal 1926–27, February 16, 1926, 14).

5. Journal 1926–1927, February 3, 1926, 12.

health,"⁶ and soon she headed west to Washington and Idaho. Then, by the middle of August, she was back in Illinois. In November, Crawford went to Traverse City, Michigan, to see her co-worker, Kittie Bare. Bare had left Saddle Mountain to marry C. C. Cooper, contractor for the Saddle Mountain Church, but, as Crawford expressed it, "Life is a problem to some and none at all to others. She thought she loved him. He thought he loved her. They married had a son—parted & now she washes for a living & he YMCAs in Cleveland. How the story will end God knows."⁷

Deputation work with its constant traveling had never brought Isabel Crawford the same satisfaction she felt during her years in Oklahoma, and her time with the New York Indian reservations was filled with frustrations. In December, 1926, she wrote to Katherine Westfall of the woman's mission society regarding a possible change, with a fixed base. Her preference was to go to Berkeley, California, to help with the new Baptist training school there. She wrote, "I don't like *easy* work. I want a hard job, with an abiding place."⁸ She went to Dayton, Ohio, anticipating an Ohio itinerary and was dismayed when it was cancelled. She settled down in the YWCA to remain until after the Christmas holidays, and she continued to write letters about her future, reluctantly conceding that "if the Board feels that I can accomplish greater things by continuing in the deputation work so be it. Like Faust I can see that the advancement of *a cause* is greater than any individual plan."⁹

As she mulled over her future, Crawford wrote a report more reflective than usual. She noted changes over the past thirty-three years, especially in the importance now granted to women's work, and she presented her views on how women had made this progress: "Not through fighting & scrapping & demanding our rights have we women come to the front in missionary endeavour but through patient ladylike submission . . . always remembering that we were called to serve, and serve we must *in our own way*."¹⁰ She also wrote an autobiographical sketch to correct the inaccuracies in a brochure that she pasted into her journal. After dealing with her early life, she summarized her work and, in the process, gave her perspective on the liberal theological trends of the day: "And I went, worked hard, learned to pray again and did not give a message like this, 'You must be repent *as it were,*

6. Ibid., June 1–19, 1926, 37.

7. Ibid., November 20, 1927, 75.

8. Crawford to Westfall, December 8, 1926, Isabel Crawford Correspondence, Katherine S. Westfall Files.

9. Crawford to Westfall, December 24, 1926, Isabel Crawford Correspondence, Katherine S. Westfall Files.

10. Journal 1926–27, 94.

and be converted, *in a measure*, or you will be damned *to a certain extent*! I gave the old fashioned gospel mixed with common sense and I remained long enough to see practically the whole settlement won to Christ!"[11]

Crawford continued to wait restlessly to learn of the society's decision. She heard that she would be permitted to have a settled dwelling, but where should it be? Crawford wrote, "I want to go to California. Mrs. Westfall says it is too far one side. Friends in Calif. say it isn't any more at one side than New York, suggested by Mrs. W."[12] No solution was obvious, so Crawford was to continue deputation work until the time of the annual meetings.

At the end of May, Crawford went to Chicago for the Northern Baptist Convention, with James Whitcomb Brougher presiding. It was a time of contention between Fundamentalists and Modernists, but Brougher exhorted the convention to maintain unity: the church should not dissipate its energies by arguing. Harry Emerson Fosdick, a leading Baptist liberal, was pastor of the Park Avenue Baptist Church. Crawford wrote, "Dr. Brougher was a wonder! His good nature & ever ready wit carried the convention . . . Park Ave Church remains in 'Good standing' whether some can stand it or not and any Baptist Church can be a Baptist Church just as long as it says so & sticks to it."[13] While she was in Chicago, Crawford visited its Art Institute three times. She observed, "Poetry pictures & pep are my hobbies!" and she reflected, "When I get old I would like to live near good pictures & books. They breathe of the heavenlies."[14]

Crawford anticipated a conference about her future while she was at the convention but, to her surprise, there was none. She was simply told to go to Ohio for two months and then to Iowa in the fall. From the convention she went to Cincinnati and visited Harriet Rychen. During the winter Crawford had learned that, in effecting a change in her position, the Woman's American Baptist Home Mission Society planned to place her on an allowance of $600 a year and then, in addition, pay her expenses when she did deputation work. She shared this with Rychen, who had worked for years in her father's ink manufacturing company. Rychen was indignant at what amounted to a reduction from eighty to fifty dollars a month, and without Crawford's knowledge, she wrote to Katherine Westfall of the women's

---

11. Ibid., 97.

12. Ibid., January 13, 1927, 103.

13. Ibid., 127. Fosdick's book *The Challenge of the Present Crisis* was on her list of books read in Crawford's 1926–27 journal.

14. Journal 1926–27, 131.

mission board, asking, "is there not something for her to do that will give her a living wage?"[15]

Westfall replied that in January, Crawford had expressed her pleasure at the plan. Then Westfall wrote to Crawford, expressing concern about the letters she had received from Rychen and also from Rychen's pastor. She said, "I am sure our Board regrets that we cannot be more generous with all our workers, and we are very sorry that these special friends of yours feel that you have not been treated fairly. I am sure you have no such feeling."[16]

Crawford, however, expressed her feelings in her prompt reply:

> With the friends who know me best I have ever been counted "soft," and "an easy mark." In the early days among the Indians when conditions became intolerable and I refused to complain, my brother, a very quiet man, took me to the train en route to my vacation & kissing me good bye dropped the following note in my lap: "If certain changes are not made I will consider it my duty to come & lock up your rooms and take you out of that."
>
> Years later my sister & brother-in law visited me. I made no complaints, yet they wrote to Chicago and said that unless other changes were made they would be compelled to take me home. Then they wrote to me "If a missionary under *our Board* [in Canada] were to 'keep still' under such circumstances we would *recall her*, for not being faithful to the Board or to the work." . . .
>
> Then came the final crash, when no one could save me, and I was crushed in the denominational machinery and God's plan for my life completely wrecked! Every personal friend I had, who could find out about it, was indignant and I was urged to expose the whole plot.
>
> "The Lord shall fight for you & ye shall hold your peace," was pasted in my book of devotions, & I quit the work and wrote "Kiowa" without making a single reference to the tragedy.[17]

Crawford went on to say that, when she wrote in January, she was so "delighted over the prospect of a settled abode," that she did not think of the financial aspects of the arrangement. She also reminded Westfall that the only time in thirty-three years that she had complained about her salary was when she asked to have it *reduced* following a salary increase.

15. Rychen to Westfall, June 14, 1927, Isabel Crawford Correspondence, Katherine S. Westfall Files.

16. Westfall to Crawford, June 21, 1927, Isabel Crawford Correspondence, Katherine S. Westfall Files.

17. Crawford to Westfall, June 23–27, 1927, Isabel Crawford Correspondence, Katherine S. Westfall Files.

In Westfall's next letter to Crawford, she stated that "the Board did not consider this as a reduced salary but a readjustment of relationship to meet present conditions."[18] Crawford replied dramatically: "To say that I am humiliated beyond expression over my own down right stupidity but mildly expresses my feelings. Will you believe me when I tell you that, notwithstanding the abundant evidence given, it never dawned on my poor little brain till I left Chicago and the N.B.C. that it was the wish of those most in authority that I 'move on' and off, for the good of the cause!"[19] After listing the hints she should have recognized, she continued, "Of course, like a goose, thinking you were making a wonderful all-round plan, including some kind of living arrangements for me I wrote that I was 'delighted,' never once suspecting that I was being gently dropped from the work!"

In response, Westfall thanked Crawford for writing "so fully."[20] She protested, that "there has been no severing in relationships between our Board and you" and explained that the board intended to give Crawford the freedom to choose how much deputation work she did and thus "to be relieved from the strain of constant travel."

Crawford's itinerary took her next to Wisconsin. Throughout her career, she had disliked people's remarks or questions regarding her lack of hearing, but in public she felt the need to remain polite. She could, however, express herself in her journal. The pastor in Sheboygan introduced her by saying "Miss C. has the misfortune of being very deaf but she has done a wonderful work." Crawford wrote, "I saw what he said & wanted to say *but didn't*: Rev. P. has the craziest legs I ever saw on a preacher but he has done wonderful work with them!"[21]

Next Crawford headed for Kansas City. Told that the mission society could not employ her full time, she had arranged to spend three months at the Kansas City Baptist Theological Seminary; she would be "fitting myself for better service."[22] She reached the seminary on December 17, and on December 19, 1927, she left for Saddle Mountain. She had turned over to that church five hundred dollars that she had been given for her trip abroad, "to repair it & save it from premature destruction," so she was not surprised

---

18. Westfall to Crawford, June 30, 1927, Isabel Crawford Correspondence, Katherine S. Westfall Files.

19. Crawford to Westfall, July 11, 1927, Isabel Crawford Correspondence, Katherine S. Westfall Files.

20. Westfall to Crawford, July 14, 1927, Isabel Crawford Correspondence, Katherine S. Westfall Files.

21. Journal 1927–28, November 28, 1927, 24.

22. Ibid., December 5, 1927, 25.

to see that its exterior was white and clean.[23] But she was dismayed when she went inside: "The old stove was moved into a corner and the new one never saw stove polish. A mamouth [sic] implement calendar—about a yard square—picturing the *Declaration of Independence*—struck the eye at once on entering & the book case was full of junk. Old missionaries returning to their former fields of labor shouldn't say 'boo' but they can't become blind!"

The people of Saddle Mountain welcomed her as warmly as ever. She held meetings in the church and, at the Indians' request, told about her trip to Palestine. "It was not easy to make the talks spiritual," she wrote, "because the description took so much time but the Indians got the message for Jesus was the center of every talk."[24]

Yet beneath these routine activities, there was a current that made Crawford uneasy. The pioneering missionary George Hicks was now the pastor at Saddle Mountain, and he was planning to retire. Some church members asked whether they could have a council with Crawford—without Hicks. Crawford declined, explaining that the pastor should be present at all councils. But the following day, when she was sent for, Crawford went, not knowing there was to be a council without Hicks. There the Kiowas expressed their hope that the church could be returned to the care of the woman's mission society. They also hoped that Sherman Chaddlesone, from the Saddle Mountain Church, could become their next pastor. Since Hicks had been excluded from the council, Crawford shared with him her notes, and Hicks agreed that it would be good if Chaddlesone became the minister. When Crawford met again with the church members, she told them what Hicks had said and asked them to pray about the matter. Then, after a brief visit with her brother and his family, Crawford returned to Kansas City.

Crawford wrote to Katherine Westfall, reporting the "talks" made by the Kiowas and suggesting that the woman's society grant their request. In her reply, Westfall chided Crawford for participating in discussions without the presence of the pastor. She also explained that the selection and support of any pastor would have to be done by the denominational mission society; the women's executive committee would take no action. The situation remained unchanged, but Crawford's interest in Saddle Mountain had been heightened by her visit.[25]

---

23. Ibid., December 20, 1927, 31.

24. Ibid., December 22–23, 1927, 39.

25. Crawford to Westfall, January 18, 1928; Westfall to Crawford, February 3, 1928; Crawford to Westfall, February 13, 1928; Westfall to Crawford, February 20, 1928; and Westfall to Crawford, June 30, 1927, Isabel Crawford Correspondence, Katherine S. Westfall Files.

Crawford settled comfortably into life at the seminary, remaining for three months. Toward the end of her stay, she received an invitation to visit the Baptist college for Indians at Bacone, near Muskogee, Oklahoma. There she enjoyed a visit with Mary Jayne and Maggie Topping, both of whom she had known on the mission field in Oklahoma. When she learned that Jayne had in her possession the minutes of the Indian Association, Crawford carefully copied down the fateful resolution and reflected in her journal on the circumstances. Then she wrote, "I retired not because I was wrong but out of harmony with the ministry on the field. But," she concluded, "this is past History."[26] Yet her acute interest in the events more than twenty years earlier belied her disavowal.

The highlight of Crawford's visit to Bacone occurred when she was taken to Atoka to see Joseph Samuel Murrow, the pioneering missionary who had been Crawford's strong supporter throughout her difficulties. He was now ninety-seven, but his "mind seemed clear," and he was delighted to see her. He said, "Why you are beautiful. You did good work among the Indians. You taught the *truth*."[27] Her entire visit immersed her once again in the experience of Indian missions, and when she boarded the train to head back to Kansas City, she wondered whether she "had done right in leaving the Indians *for conscience sake*."[28]

She remained at the seminary for a little more than a week, and then she began a new itinerary of speaking engagements, first in Kansas and then in South and North Dakota. In June of 1928, she went to Minneapolis to rest, to visit with the Ganssles whom she had known in North Dakota, and to await her next itinerary. Not wanting to outstay her welcome, she moved on to Milwaukee, to visit another friend, Grace Corwin. When she received word that there was no work for her in July, she was dismayed, for she had understood that she would have work until August. Corwin, however, made her welcome, and Crawford worked on her hostess's clothes while Corwin went about her duties as a parish worker. On July 19, Crawford left for Salamanca, arriving early the following morning. She learned that there was space for her at Chautauqua, and off she went the next day.

Crawford quickly settled in at Chautauqua, but on her second day she received an alarming phone call from her sister in Grimsby Beach. Harriet Rychen was vacationing there, and she had become ill. Rychen wanted her friend to come. Crawford quickly put back into her suitcase what she had stuffed into drawers, and the next day she arrived at Grimsby Beach. A few

26. Journal 1927–28, March 23, 1928, 64–65.
27. Ibid., March 26, 1928, 66.
28. Ibid., March 27, 1928, 67.

days later Rychen "passed on happy & glad to go 'this time.'"[29] Crawford traveled to Cincinnati with the casket and attended the funeral. When she returned to Grimsby Beach, she tried to sew and to rest "but couldnt do either satisfactorily" while she mourned the death of her dear friend.[30]

Near the end of August, Crawford was nudged back into more active life when John Kelley arrived unannounced and insisted that she return with him to Woodstock and speak the following Sunday at the East End Mission where Crawford had become a Sunday school teacher at the age of eleven. She spent a week viewing old scenes and renewing old friendships. Her September itinerary took her to Ohio. Crawford's October itinerary was in New York, and it turned out to be one of the most difficult ever. It was not as tightly packed with appointments as some; the problem was that it did not provide enough travel information and local addresses. In November she moved on to Ohio.

After Thanksgiving, she went to Kansas City. When she had left the previous March, the seminary president and students hoped that she would "fix it" so she could return the next winter, and she had.[31] After a week at the seminary, she made a trip to Oklahoma, going first to Bacone. Then she went to Elk Creek, now called Hobart, and had a "glad reunion" there.[32] At Saddle Mountain, George Hicks had retired, and Crawford met the new, young pastor, Perry Jackson. Influenza struck soon after Crawford's arrival, but she was not afflicted, so she cared for Jackson and his wife and others who were ill.

At one gathering during her visit, John Onko said, "We have heard that when you pass on you have arranged to bury yourself here with the Indians. We would like these words put on your tombstone. 'I dwell among mine own people.'"[33] And so it was agreed.

It was also Onko who remarked "When the Saddle Mt. Church made the mistake" of having Lucius Aitsan administer the Lord's Supper by vote of the congregation before he was ordained.[34] Jackson replied, "Why that was all right. I did the same thing before I was ordained." That started things moving. Jackson studied the records and called a meeting of the deacons. After she returned to Kansas City, Crawford learned that the church subsequently voted unanimously to bring the matter up at the next meeting of

29. Ibid., 84.
30. Ibid., August 15, 1928, 85.
31. Ibid., March 30, 1927, 69.
32. Journal 1929, 4.
33. Ibid., 12.
34. Ibid., January 2, 1929, 16.

the association. In her journal she wrote, "'Truth crushed to the earth will rise again' is all I have to say but more than truth was crushed this time."[35]

Perry Jackson with his wife and child. Courtesy of Barbara Cross McKinnon.

Crawford remained in Kansas City through March, and then she began work in Illinois and Indiana. Next she traveled to West Virginia, New Jersey, and Pennsylvania. Early in July, she returned to Chautauqua.

While Isabel Crawford carried on her work and enjoyed her vacation, the consequences of what had begun during her December visit to Saddle Mountain were rippling through the two home mission boards. On April 18, 1929, Bruce Kinney, director of Indian missions for the American Baptist Home Mission Society, wrote about the situation at Saddle Mountain to Frank Smith, secretary of missions for that society. On Crawford's recent visit she had "started something as she always does when there."[36] He summarized the history of Aitsan and the Lord's Supper and then said, "This church had been organized only two years at that time and none of its members was more than a few years out of heathenism. Perhaps senti-

35. Ibid., 18–19.

36. Kinney to Smith, April 18, 1929, Isabel Crawford Correspondence, Katherine S. Westfall Files.

ment in some places is more liberal now but at that time the Southern supported churches were members of the Indian Association. Despite the very moderate wording of the resolution, Miss Crawford declared she would not work there until it was rescinded." Kinney went on to explain: "Now they are incited to demand that the resolution be rescinded at the coming meeting of the Association. If that is done there will be some hot time." His opinion was strong: "If I had final authority to do so I would say to the Woman's Society that they MUST keep Miss Crawford away from that field and prevent her from interfering there or we would entirely withdraw and they would be obliged to take over that work or abandon it."

As Crawford and the Saddle Mountain Christians hoped, the "black mark" was removed on August 9, 1929, at the meeting of the Western Oklahoma Indian Baptist Association. Later that month, Jackson and five members of the congregation wrote to the woman's mission society requesting that Crawford return to Saddle Mountain "to stay as long as she lives," and also that "she be given land on which to build a house."[37] In a letter written by Jackson alone at the same time, he said, "I realize that it is not customary for the Women's Society to retire their workers on the field in which they labored. But in this case where there has been so much heart ache and hard feeling caused by the Resolution of 1905 it seems to me that possibly an exception could be made to the rule in order to make the church and its former Missionary feel good now that that Resolution is out of the way."[38] Although the surviving correspondence does not indicate that Isabel Crawford herself was part of this conversation, Jackson worked with her knowledge and approval. Now her long-held dream seemed possible: she might return to her beloved Saddle Mountain, the one place where she had experienced unqualified success and satisfaction, and she might again do some useful work. But not everyone approved of her dream.

On September 1, 1929, Kinney expressed his opinion to Katherine Westfall. Though he would not oppose the action, he felt that it would be a dangerous move. Then on September 19, Frank Smith also wrote to Westfall, expressing his view that it would be unwise for Crawford to return. Smith also wrote to Perry Jackson, asking for his feelings. In a letter to Crawford, Jackson summarized his reply: "First, on account of your suffering through the years, I felt that now it was time for the two societies to send you back to Saddle Mtn. Second, I felt that here was an opportunity for the two societies to cooperate & further His Kingdom's work. Third, because the church

---

37. Jackson et al. to Woman's American Baptist Home Mission Society, August 18, 1929, Isabel Crawford Correspondence, Katherine S. Westfall Files.

38. Jackson to Woman's American Baptist Home Mission Society, August 18, 1929, Isabel Crawford Correspondence, Katherine S. Westfall Files.

wanted you & loved you and because your return would help on the work. and fourth because we are friends and understand and admire each other and feel that we can do more working together than apart."[39]

Following her vacation at Chautauqua, Crawford visited Grimsby Beach, and then in September, she returned to work in New York. While she was attending an association meeting, she spent an evening with old friends, Marcia and Alicia Taber, and their niece, Mary Taber. Crawford read the "Jolly Journal" that she had been writing for her own entertainment. Mary "sat with her eyes transfixed & listening most intently to every incident."[40] When Crawford finished, Mary explained that she was a magazine writer, and she urged Crawford to publish her journal, promising help in finding a publisher. Crawford recorded in her personal journal that the "Jolly Journal was not written for publication but 'for fun' to keep me from thinking too much & to give pleasure to old friends scattered from ocean to ocean." Yet the professional's compliments pleased her.

The next day, at the meeting, she met Coe Hayne, assistant secretary of the American Baptist Home Mission Society. She knew of his work, visiting missions and writing about them. Mary Taber arranged for him to hear some of the "Jolly Journal," and Crawford wrote that Hayne "laughed so hard he found it hard to 'sober up' & then almost demanded the M. S. S. he would take it to the office & have it all typewritten for me—it ought to be published!"[41]

As mission society officials contemplated the question of Crawford's return to Saddle Mountain, this recent acclaim by respected professionals gave her confidence. A month later she wrote to Clara Norcutt of the woman's society expressing her belief that it was God's will for her to return to Oklahoma. But, she wrote,

> Should it be decreed that I am to be consigned to oblivion as far as the Baptist denomination is concerned my resignation will go in written on better paper than this. A friend of my child hood days stands ready to pick me up, in case I become a raving lunatic, & carry me home to Florida at her expense for the winter and until I get plans made for the new future which I have partly worked out.
>
> The Chautauqua platform & magazine writing beckon me on. I have had one Chautauqua offer & arrangements have been made by friends of influence to get me noticed by magazine

39. Jackson to Crawford, October 4, 1929, Isabel Crawford Correspondence, Katherine S. Westfall Files.

40. Journal 1929, September 11, 1929, 53.

41. Ibid., September 12, 1929, 53.

officials. . . . Believe me it is not on my programme to disappear in the darkness & suck my thumb till heaven opens. I mean to "sail on, sail on, sail on" & seek to forget the ugly past once I get settled.[42]

On the day after Crawford wrote this to Norcutt, Bruce Kinney wrote an angry letter to Perry Jackson, sending a copy to Norcutt. Kinney warned the young missionary, "You think you could get along with Miss Crawford. Then you could do something that no one else has EVER been able to do—man or woman."[43] Four days later, Jackson wrote to Norcutt, "suggesting a way out of the impending storm."[44] He proposed that Crawford be granted permission to come as a retired worker, not as a paid missionary. "Such an action would avoid a direct conflict and would enable her to return sometime in the years to come if she so desired." Jackson sent copies of the letter to Smith, Kinney, and Crawford. With the one to Crawford, he sent a cover letter, explaining that he had learned that they could not both receive support: "If you came now my Salary would stop immediately."[45] Crawford was indignant at the threat to Jackson's livelihood. She wrote to Norcutt and asked outright, "Is there any rule to prohibit my retiring to Saddle Mt?"[46] To Jackson, she replied that she had just offered herself to the women's society as a "'a living sacrifice' without salary or appointment of any kind in order to save the situation, if it can be done."[47]

While the proposals and accusations sped back and forth, Crawford continued her work, moving on to North Dakota. Next she went to Kansas City and the seminary, where she prepared for her Iowa itinerary. She was at the seminary when she received a letter written on October 29 by Jessie Brooks, secretary to Clara Norcutt. After explaining that Norcutt had gone to care for her aged parents, Brooks wrote, "As a board we appreciate the desire of the Indians to have you return to Saddle Mountain after your retirement, but in view of the whole situation it does seem that it would not

---

42. Crawford to Norcutt, October 11, 1929, Isabel Crawford Correspondence, Katherine S. Westfall Files.

43. Kinney to Jackson, October 12, 1929, Isabel Crawford Correspondence, Katherine S. Westfall Files.

44. Jackson to Norcutt, October 16, 1929, Isabel Crawford Correspondence, Katherine S. Westfall Files.

45. Jackson to Crawford, October 16, 1929, Isabel Crawford Correspondence, Katherine S. Westfall Files.

46. Crawford to Norcutt, undated, Isabel Crawford Correspondence, Katherine S. Westfall Files.

47. Crawford to Jackson, October 23, 1929, Isabel Crawford Correspondence, Katherine S. Westfall Files.

be wise for you to go back to the field, unless it be for an occasional visit. We therefore feel that we cannot give our approval of such a plan."[48]

Two weeks before Brooks announced the board's decision, Crawford had written to Norcutt, "I'm as happy as a clam & will be no matter what comes. I'm prepared for the best & the worst."[49] Her cheerful nature crumpled, however, when her hopes were dashed. On November 2, 1929, Isabel Crawford wrote bitterly, "Believing, *without the shadow of a doubt*, that God's plan for my life has been wrecked *the second time*, because of the non-co-operation of our two Home Mission Boards, I herewith present my resignation to 'The Woman's American American [*sic*] Baptist Home Mission Society, to take effect some time during the year 1930. Respectfully Isabel Crawford"[50]

A few days before Christmas, Crawford headed back to Oklahoma, to spend her third consecutive Christmas at Saddle Mountain. Although the Indians were in camp, they did not rush in to see her. When Lucius Aitsan's elderly father, Mokeen, came to call on Christmas morning, he asked, "Why do they not let you walk on the land and shut you out of our church?"[51] Crawford replied, "I do not know." Before the end of her visit, she learned that others, too, were resentful of the demands and controls of the denominational society, "the men's society," and wished they could revert to the old arrangement. But that was not possible much as they—and Crawford—might wish.

After paying a brief visit to her brother and his family, Crawford left Oklahoma to spend two weeks in her Kansas City sanctuary. In October, she had told Clara Norcutt with bravado that, if plans did not work out for her to return to Saddle Mountain, she had a friend who would pick her up and carry her to her home in Florida where Crawford would make plans for the future. Now the brave front was gone and a more sober Crawford left on January 13, 1930, for Florida to ponder her next steps.

---

48. Brooks to Crawford, October 29, 1929, Isabel Crawford Correspondence, Katherine S. Westfall Files.

49. Crawford to Norcutt, October 15, 1929, Isabel Crawford Correspondence, Katherine S. Westfall Files.

50. Crawford to Woman's American Baptist Home Mission Society, November 2, 1929, Isabel Crawford Correspondence, Katherine S. Westfall Files.

51. Journal 1929, December 25, 1929, 76.

12

Transition: Retirement

IN THE MIDDLE OF January 1930, Isabel Crawford arrived in Florida, where she was met by her friend Jean Hendrie, "with a smile on her face a mile long!"[1] Jean Hendrie's mother had been on the staff of the Canadian Literary Institute at the time that Isabel Crawford's father taught there, so the friendship between Isabel and Jean went back many decades. Hendrie welcomed Crawford to her winter home in Mount Dora. Crawford and Hendrie attended church regularly, and one Sunday, Crawford was able to observe former President Calvin Coolidge and his wife during the service. Grace Coolidge took an active part in the service while her husband "sat like a graven image . . . a dead look in his two eyes. He responded to nothing except the collection plate into which he cast in a V bill. He supplied the cash, she the interest in the service." Crawford continued, "He is Silent Cal, all right."[2] Then at the end of March, after two and a half months of sightseeing, reading, and relaxation, she returned to New York City and to work. On April 14, however, her plans were rudely shattered.

At noontime, Crawford waited to cross at Fifth Avenue at 33rd Street. As the signal was given and she rushed with the others, her ankle turned and she fell. She "felt something scrunch" but walked nearly to Sixth Avenue before she "crumpled" and took a taxi to her hotel.[3] When a doctor arrived he asked, "Were you born with one leg shorter than the other?"[4] She replied

1. Journal 1929, January 16, 1930, 86.
2. Ibid., February 9, 1930, 2–3.
3. Ibid., April 14, 1930, 25.
4. Ibid., 26.

that she was not, and he pointed out, "Well look! one of your legs is shorter than the other. You better go to the hospital." And so Crawford, in great pain, was taken to the Post Graduate Hospital on 20th Street. A hypodermic injection relieved her pain, and she slept until morning.

The next day, John J. Moorhead examined Crawford. The bone specialist and professor of surgery proclaimed, "*It is not a serious fracture.* We will try not to put you in a cast."[5] And so a framework was set up around Crawford's bed, with pulleys attached. Another physician, W. D. Ludlum, bandaged her injured leg; then they attached it to the apparatus. It pulled painfully on her ankle, but her complaints were to no avail. Eventually she "gave up & just lay & suffered from pain & cold till the tears came."[6]

The next weeks sorely tested Crawford's normally sunny disposition. The greatest problem was with the pulley arrangement. One day the weight fell off and her leg was jarred. When a doctor fixed it, it held for only an hour and twenty minutes. This happened repeatedly, and on May 16, a little more than a month after her fall, she told the nurse she could stand it no longer. An intern tried to fix the apparatus—while flirting with the nurse—and the weight crashed to the floor. Crawford screamed with pain! She wrote, "all the healing that had been done was undone for I felt everything let go."[7] The next day, Ludlum rebandaged her leg and then hooked her up to the apparatus once more. She asked whether he had allowed for the slippage, for her foot always went out of position an hour and twenty minutes after it was strung up. He said he had. The connection lasted an hour and twenty-five minutes before it slipped again.

An x-ray revealed that the bones were not knitting; they would have to apply a cast after all. The operation was performed on May 22. On July 6, the doctor cut off the cast. On July 26, Crawford received her first lesson in walking, but even with brace and crutches she was very weak. Gradually her walking improved, and on August 14 she left Post Graduate Hospital, having read fifty-two books during her four months as an impatient patient there. She went to Nanuet, New York, to stay with her friends Harry and Ina Bailey. There she reflected on her experience; she did not believe "the Lord knocked me down to give me rest—as some friends write. . . . The Lord *permitted it* but the devil *did it*, for he has the power to hinder the Lords work but not to *stop it!* That is what I think anyway."[8]

On August 20, 1930, Isabel Crawford faced the reality of her situation and wrote to Katherine Westfall of the women's mission society, retiring from

5. Ibid., 27.
6. Ibid., April 16, 1930, 29.
7. Ibid., May 16, 1930, 34.
8. Ibid., August 18, 1930, 69.

her work as a missionary. She had expected to remain with the Baileys only a couple of weeks, but it was not until October 25 that she felt able to move on. The Baileys put her on a train for Buffalo, where her nephew Gordon Cline met her and took her to Grimsby Beach to visit her family. Then on November 1, she headed for Salamanca, where the Walquists had arranged a bed for her in the parlor. Again Crawford went through the routine of examining the possessions she had stored there, sorting, and repacking. One afternoon they drove to Red House. Crawford visited old friends who assured her that "they were doing the best they could keeping on with the Jesus Road."[9]

Isabel Crawford's retirement photo. Courtesy of Barbara Cross McKinnon.

Crawford next headed for Kansas City. She arrived at the seminary on the morning of November 13. When two students escorted her to supper—for she never walked alone—she was surprised to find a banquet celebrating

9. Journal 1930–31 [–32], November 9, 1930, 8.

her return. Speakers extolled her, and the Indian tepee table decoration at Crawford's place contained seventeen handkerchiefs and a roll of dollar bills. She wrote in her journal, "If some body else had been the center of attraction I would have enjoyed it more for the programme was fitter for a bigger light."[10]

Crawford had intended to travel directly from Kansas City to California, thinking she might settle there. However she received a copy of a talk made by Sherman Chaddlesone at Saddle Mountain. He expressed the people's fear that if she went to California, they would never see her again. So after six comfortable weeks at the seminary, Crawford left to spend another Christmas at Saddle Mountain. She was moved when, as the Indians made their Christmas offerings, they divided them between large gifts for Jesus and smaller gifts for her. She regarded it "a compliment born of the Holy Spirit"—and she sent the gift to the "Jesus Women's Society."[11]

Isabel Crawford with Mrs. Lone Wolf. Courtesy of Barbara Cross McKinnon.

10. Ibid., November 13, 1930, 12.
11. Ibid., 25.

At the end of the year, Crawford went to Clinton to see her brother. Then she traveled to San Diego, where she stayed again with George and Ida Kermott, from St. Thomas, North Dakota. Frustrated by her lack of mobility, in April Crawford went to nearby National City, to Paradise Valley Sanitarium, to have her leg x-rayed once more.[12] Crawford was shocked when she saw the x-ray: it showed a crack an inch wide between the broken bones. She asked what was to be done, and the doctor replied, "Nothing." "Then I'll have to go on crutches to the end of my days?" she asked. He replied "Yes." Her hand shook as she signed her name to the check to pay for the visit, but she wrote in her journal, "I won't shed a tear if I can help it."[13]

Bitter with the thought that her fall would never have happened if she had been permitted to follow what she saw as God's plan for her life, Crawford wrote to Bruce Kinney of the denominational home mission society. She closed her letter, "Sorry as I am for myself I cant help feeling for the missionary society that 'did not approve' of my responding to the clear call of the Master to return to Saddle Mt. May we all learn from this tragedy the lessons the Eternal wants us to learn."[14] Kinney harbored his own resentment. He replied,

> I cannot tell you how sorry I am that you are in the situation you describe. But it might be a lot worse. If you had gone to Saddle Mountain to live you might have broken your leg and have been so far from efficient care that blood poison would have ended your life. You have always been so philosophical and triumphant that I am sure you will find a real reason for thanking God that there ARE crutches and that you can walk with those. I know that one who has been so active will miss that activity but again, there might be something worse. You can still read.[15]

Crawford sent her x-ray to the Mayo Clinic, and she received a reply from Melvin Henderson, an orthopedic surgeon there. He ventured the opinion that "if you are in good general health I believe that something can be done to give you bony stability."[16] Thus Crawford headed for Rochester, arriving on June 22, 1931. She registered at the renowned clinic, and two days later Crawford's leg was x-rayed. On the following day she met with Henderson. He decided that it would be best to see first whether her leg

---

12. Crawford wrote "Pleasant Valley Sanitarium," but the National City facility was Paradise Valley Sanitarium (Ibid., April 23, 1931, 42).

13. Ibid., 42–43.

14. Ibid., April 27, 1931, 46.

15. Ibid., attached to 46.

16. Ibid., June 16, 1931, 52.

could be improved by treatments alone, but after a week he gave his verdict: the treatments were not helping, and she needed surgery. When she first began her rehabilitation following the surgery, she trembled and felt seasick. Gradually, however, she improved, and on September 23, Henderson pronounced her ready to leave. When she was wheeled to the business office, she was pleasantly surprised to see that her bill was not $360 but $180. It was the clinic's policy to charge missionaries only half the usual fee.

On September 25, 1931, Crawford left for Kansas City, and once more she was warmly received at the seminary. She spent her mornings writing, and by the first of December she had edited and added to her "Jolly Journal" so that now she was able to proclaim, "Book Finished!"[17] Again she received an invitation to spend Christmas at Saddle Mountain, but before she left for Oklahoma, the students held a surprise banquet in her honor. They took delight in the fact that they had planned the entire event in her presence, but because of her lack of hearing, she had not realized what they were discussing: "They talked & planned at every meal & when any of them laughed I laughed too without the least idea of what I was laughing at."[18] Afterwards she reflected, "Everybody had such a good time that I didnt mind being the center of attraction for once."[19]

Isabel Crawford at the Kansas City Baptist Theological Seminary. Courtesy of Barbara Cross McKinnon.

17. Ibid., December 1, 1931, 85.
18. Ibid., December 18, 1931, 87.
19. Ibid., 89.

Crawford left for Clinton on the evening of December 21. From there she went to Elk Creek, Mountain View, and Saddle Mountain, where she settled herself as best she could in the Jacksons' home while life rushed on around her. Many Indians were encamped nearby, yet attendance at the Sunday service was poor. Crawford was puzzled: "Why, I signed. Jesus didn't leave you!" The reply came to her, "It is true, but your laugh that was kind, did."[20]

On Monday the Indians broke camp, and on Tuesday the missionaries of the Indian association arrived and enjoyed a banquet. Bruce Kinney spoke somberly about how hard it was to raise missionary money in these depressed times. Crawford found this an inappropriate message to give to a group of missionaries exhausted from the Christmas season. When at last he finished, he said to her, "Now you tell them something funny."[21] She did and "had the satisfaction of seeing the missionaries laugh hard & long & ask for more." Early in January, Crawford traveled to Florida, where again Jean Hendrie welcomed her.

Crawford had sent the manuscript of *Jolly Journal* to Fleming H. Revell Company, which had published her *Kiowa*. Fleming Revell Sr., her supporter and friend, had retired in 1929 and died two years later. Now his son, Fleming Revell Jr. was in charge. In March of 1932, she received the proof of *Jolly Journal*, and by the time she had read half of it, she was furious. She wrote, "It was not my intention to write a book in encyclopaedia diction but in the free & easy language of the average educated people. My mother taught me to use always, small words instead of large, short crispy sentences in place of long labored ones and to leave some words & thoughts to the imagination of the readers. The corrections your proof carries violates all these rules, makes father speak English foreign to his mode of expression, and mother use slang, a thing she abhorred. My own individuality is lost entirely."[22]

When Crawford received an air mail reply from Revell, she wrote in her journal, "Worse & worse and more of it."[23] She sent examples of incompetent editing, and she wrote, "The publication is off unless some of us can think up a way out."[24] By telegram Revell instructed her to "[m]ake such corrections as you think advisable," but there was a further problem: Crawford did not have a copy of the original, and the proof allowed no room for

20. Ibid., December 27, 1931, 92–93.
21. Ibid., December 29, 1931, 96.
22. Ibid., March 16, 1932, 116.
23. Ibid., March 19, 1932, 118.
24. Ibid., 119.

corrections. Eventually Crawford and Revell found "a way out," and when the proof of her final version reached Crawford at 3:00 in the afternoon of the April 2, she was able to correct it and mail it back by 7:30 that same day.

While Crawford struggled with the proof of her book, she was considering making a permanent move to Florida. On May 13, she attended an auction in Mount Dora. She purchased a building lot, and although it had no house, the decision motivated her to send for her possessions. On May 4, 1932, she moved into an apartment in Tremain Court. Yet despite her move, Crawford felt strangely unsettled. She moved again in October, and when she took up her journal in November, she remarked that she had not written in it since May: "Can't explain it. Don't want to think, write, use my heart or head. They all feel as if they had had a stroke."[25] In the interim, she had taught a Sunday school class in the Congregational church near her Tremain Court apartment, and she had read a great number of books, "some good, some no good & one bad."

As soon as she made her October move, she began attending the Baptist church in Mount Dora, and soon she transferred her membership to there from Saddle Mountain. Soon, too, she began teaching Sunday school. It was, however, a class of "big girls," and she had strong memories of the classes of boys with whom she had enjoyed such success in the past; she wrote "I'll never be satisfied till I have big boys."[26] In January, she got her wish. If Crawford had been depressed, she became increasingly comfortable and happy in her new quarters. She enjoyed being able to do what she pleased and eat what she liked. She wrote, "For once in my life I can think of my own comfort & not feel guilty. The spiritual in me is somewhat paralyzed but by not worrying about it, I can trust the Master for a quiet cure."[27]

At the end of May, 1933, Crawford embarked on a car trip with Jean Hendrie and two other friends. They went to Atlanta, to Chattanooga, and on to Louisville. After visiting Churchill Downs, Crawford wrote, "Horse racing is not wicked in itself. Horses like to run & play. Like baseball & other 'plays' the sin is in the betting & drinking & tough company attracted. The devil spoils everything he touches."[28] From there they drove to Chicago and visited the 1933 Century of Progress. To Crawford's eyes, this world's fair compared unfavorably with the Columbian Exposition of 1893: in contrast to that event's "Great White City," most of the buildings had "gaudy outsides"

---

25. Journal 1932–33, November 17, 1932, 1.
26. Ibid., November 20, 1932, 7.
27. Ibid., 8.
28. Ibid, June 3, 1933, 71.

that gave them a "jazzy look."[29] The group also visited the Art Institute, the aquarium, and the planetarium. Then, feeling that they had enough of culture, Crawford treated her companions to something different. Wishing to demonstrate "that the Irish not the Scotch predominated in my make up," she took them to William Heckler's flea circus. Crawford and her friends watched the remarkable performance of the fleas; she commented in her journal, "Think of any sane man giving *his life to such crazyness* [sic]!!"[30]

When Crawford's friends departed, she stayed on to attend the graduation exercises at the Baptist Missionary Training School. She reflected: "If I were living my life over again would I follow the same course? Yes & No. I would give my life in missionary service, in response to the call of the Master, but it would be under *Canadian supervision* . . . Friction between the two boards, the reason."[31]

From Chicago, Crawford took the train for Rochester and the Mayo Clinic. There, on June 14, she was x-rayed and then examined by her doctor, Melvin Henderson. She was also examined by Henry William Meyerding, whom she had not seen on her previous visit. Meyerding recommended surgery although he could not guarantee that it would bring about an improvement. Crawford replied, "Operate. I'm determined to walk."[32] Following the surgery, she awoke from the anesthetic "as spry as a cricket but with both legs in casts."[33] When they removed the cast, she was happy to discover that her leg worked and she had no pain. On August 14 she was discharged from the clinic. Meyerding assured her that her leg would improve but warned that it would never be as strong as the other. Two days later, Crawford left for Florida. She returned to her Tremain Court apartment and to teaching her Sunday school class.

On Isabel Crawford's birthday in May of 1934, a celebration was held in her honor. The young men of her Bible class stood in a row and, to her astonishment, signed in Plains Indian sign language, "We will love you forever."[34] The cake, she noticed, said 1865–1934, and she pointed out to the group that she was not dead yet. There should have been a dash after "1934."

In June, Crawford found in Orlando an apartment that she liked. It was a downstairs flat in the home of a druggist, William Emrich, and his wife, Alice. Crawford moved to Orlando and then, early in July, she headed

29. Ibid., June 6, 1933, 79.
30. Ibid., 100–101.
31. Ibid., 108.
32. Ibid., June 27, 1933, 110.
33. Ibid., June 30, 1933, 112.
34. Journal 1934, May 25, 1934, 11.

north to stay with a friend in the Boston area. Again she sought medical advice, this time from Robert H. Morris. Examining x-rays of Crawford's leg, he observed that the results of the previous summer's surgery in Minnesota were good. Thus he believed he could help her, and Crawford settled in to a routine of treatments every other morning. As usual, she took advantage of nearby cultural opportunities, seeking out various works of art. But what she most wanted to see had nothing to do with higher culture: she wished to visit Jumbo the elephant. The Crawford children had heard from their mother about Jumbo, the elephant, who had been a great favorite in the London zoo. P. T. Barnum bought him and brought him to North America years ago, and Crawford had gone to see Jumbo in Toronto with her sister Fanny and Fanny's husband. Within a week, Jumbo was struck by a train and killed in St. Thomas, Ontario. Now she wanted to see his stuffed hide, which stood in the Barnum Museum of Natural History at Tufts College. She wrote, "Not a hair was on him but his hide seemed perfect & perhaps dyed a bit darker than his hair had been. I patted his trunk for I knew how he had loved little children & swung them back & forth in London where the whole of England loved him & mourned deeply when he was killed."[35]

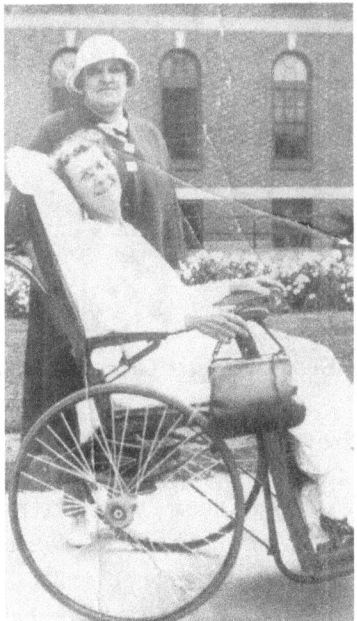

Isabel Crawford with a friend at the Mayo Clinic. Courtesy of Barbara Cross McKinnon.

35. Ibid., August 15, 1934, 33–34. In 1975, fire destroyed the building and with it Jumbo's remains.

In September, Isabel Crawford returned to her home in Orlando. Not satisfied with the arrangement of her apartment, she engaged a local handyman. With his help, she reversed the uses of the rooms. Over the years, Crawford had been given many things made by Indians and she had purchased others in the course of her travels. They were interesting in themselves, and they reminded her of both the people and the work she had loved. Carefully she arranged them in one room until she could say that it was "all Indian & everything fits in to perfection & looks *museumy* & artistic."[36]

Isabel Crawford at her Florida apartment. Courtesy of Barbara Cross McKinnon.

During the winter and early spring, Crawford attended various meetings and services, but she felt a nagging discontent. She wrote, "I seem paralyzed since I gave up my missionary work. I feel physicaly [sic] alive but spirtually [sic] dead."[37] On April 14, she reflected on the five years since her fall in New York City. When she was released from the hospital, she had said to herself, "'If I don't walk *in five* years I'll give up—but I wont till then.' The five years is *up* today & I'm as far from giving up as I was five years ago so I'll

36. Ibid., November 21, 1934, 89.
37. Journal 1935–36, 15.

extend the time. If I don't walk five years from now—'I'll never give up.'"[38] The following month she observed, "Some one wrote & asked me piously 'if I was able to kiss the crutch'? Not much! You may be forced into partnership with a crook but you don't have to be affectionate."[39]

The previous autumn, Crawford had turned down an invitation to join the Baptists of North Dakota for a celebration of their fiftieth anniversary. She had sent them her greetings and also her father's scrapbook. Now, by the time of her birthday in May of 1936, the North Dakota Baptists had sent Crawford a check for $75 for a radio. Although her hearing was severely impaired, this was something she could enjoy. She wrote, "I'm revelling in the noises! I haven't heard any for over 25 years & even when people laugh they take down my phone if they are using it. Now I can lie on my back, reach over & turn a knob & get all the noise I want."[40]

In July, Isabel Crawford embarked on another trip. After visiting friends in several locations, she arrived back at the Mayo Clinic in Rochester. She wrote, "Blessed are those who expect nothing for they shall not be disappointed."[41] The news was disappointing indeed, for her surgeon, Melvin Henderson, told her, "they had done their best & could do no more."[42] She replied, "Cheer up! Don't cry! It is tough to tell people they wont be any better but you needst groan over me." In her journal she continued, "Thus ends that chapter in my life! I accept the crutch glad it isn't a cross!" Crawford arrived back in Orlando on August 14, 1936.

During the past several years, Crawford had written less often than previously in her current journal, but she was rereading the past volumes carefully. She had usually written them in haste, so she found mistakes that she corrected as she read. In March of 1937, she made an extra push toward finishing: she cut down her activities to eliminate almost everything except attending church services. Finally, on March 27, she declared triumphantly that she had completed the task. She had kept a list of misspelled words and was pleased to find that there were only forty-eight, "& most of them were hurried slips."[43]

On June 21, 1937, Isabel Crawford left Florida to make a bus trip to Canada. Her first stop was Cincinnati. Although it had been almost nine

38. Ibid., April 14, 1935, 23.
39. Ibid., 25.
40. Ibid., June 25, 1936, 32.
41. Ibid., July 29, 1936, 88.
42. Ibid., 89.
43. Journal 1937–38, March 27, 1927, 38. In her 1947–48 journal, she listed forty-four words she had misspelled (13). It is not surprising that she failed to notice other misspelled words since they looked correct to her.

years since the death of her friend Harriet Rychen, Crawford had retained contact with Harriet's niece, Clair Paddack, and with other friends there. Paddack met Crawford and took her to a lawyer's office. Crawford had made her will, and the lawyer wanted her to sign it without understanding the unfamiliar legal terms that seemed necessary to put it into proper form. Crawford resisted, requiring him to explain everything "in plain English" before she signed.[44] Only then did Crawford begin the visits that brought back many memories.

Crawford arrived at Grimsby Beach on June 27. Cherries were in season, then raspberries, then gooseberries and currants. At home with biblical language, Crawford wrote, "I ate so much I almost became a fruitful vine."[45] She visited with family and also spent a weekend in Woodstock where she enjoyed seeing old friends and sharing stories of bygone days.

Much as she liked reconnecting with friends and family, she had one more activity on her agenda. In May of 1934, quintuplets had been born to Elzire and Oliva Dionne near Callander, Ontario. The tiny girls were the first quintuples known to have survived infancy, and they had become a major tourist attraction. Crawford wrote, "I had informed my friends & relations that I was going to see 'The Quintuplets' before I left Canada if I had to walk! Bus fare was $13.00 for return trip. A neighbor offered to take a party of 5 for $11.00 each. It looked as if I'd have to walk."[46] When she returned from Woodstock, however, she discovered that a friend, Miss Brill, would be ready to take them in her car, departing at five o'clock the next morning.

The group reached Callander at about one in the afternoon and saw what "looked like a country fair with people parking & unparking, running & walking, eating drinking, holding ice cream cones & babies."[47] Crawford and the others stood in line with the mob. Eventually their turn came. She wrote, "A whole row of cheap windows lined a corridor facing the children's play ground. And there they were all looking exactly alike in dresses & bonnets of every-day material. . . . They didn't know they were being watched as the mobs of 80 peered through the windows marching as to war."[48] After their visit, the group stayed at a tourist camp, and the next day they reached Grimsby Beach at about sunset: "The 5 of us paid all expenses & $4.00 a

---

44. Journal 1937–38, June 23–26, 1937, 50.
45. Ibid., June 27, 1937, 52.
46. Ibid., 57.
47. Ibid., 58.
48. Ibid., 61–62.

piece more than paid the bill with some over for a gift for Miss Brill! And I didn't have to walk."⁴⁹

On the evening of July 30, as Isabel Crawford was getting into bed, she received alarming news: her sister Emily had been struck by a car. Emily had gone to the fruit stand across the highway from their home; her eyesight had been deteriorating, and as she started back, she had run into the side of an auto. Very soon she was taken by ambulance to Hamilton. Later, when a woman from across the street offered Isabel some brandy, she replied, "I won't take the dirty horrid stuff. I'm not going to go to pieces. Is my sister dead?" "Yes," replied the neighbor, "she died on the operating table without regaining consciousness."⁵⁰ Emily Crawford Cline was buried beside her husband in Queens Lawn Cemetery, Grimsby, on August 2, 1937.

Isabel had arranged to go to Chautauqua on August 4. She was all packed, and so she went. But it rained constantly, and Crawford discovered that she didn't know any of the other missionaries in the Baptist house. For five days she took in a few of the offerings, but most of the time she just "went limp." She wrote, "I had made up my mind to stand the shock of my sister's death like a Christian but the physical gave way & I left for Salamanca Tuesday Aug. 10."⁵¹ She remained with her friends the Walquists ten days, glad for solitude and for mending to do. Then she headed south, arriving in Orlando on August 25.

As Christmas approached, Crawford realized that she was going to feel deeply the loss of her sister, but she was determined not to let it weigh her down. She wrote, "I didn't pray about it for I was ashamed of missing my sister when He was giving her the best one she ever had, so I just made up my scotch mind to not think & try to be glad."⁵² In the afternoon of Christmas Eve she fell asleep. It was dusk when she awakened, but the room was blazing with light. Her landlady and friend, Alice Emrich, had supplied her table with a Christmas tree and had turned on its electric lights. Although Crawford had provided Christmas trees for Sunday school and church celebrations, it was the first time in her seventy-two years that she herself had enjoyed one in her home. The next evening she wrote, "Xmas 1937 that threatened sadness had passed without a tear or a sigh. Not because I had determined it should be so but because friends on earth and The Friend in Heaven had co-operated in not letting me fight the battle alone."⁵³

49. Ibid., 65.
50. Ibid., 75.
51. Ibid., August 10, 1937, 77.
52. Ibid., 89.
53. Ibid., 91.

In February of 1938, Crawford mentioned in her journal for the first time a friend, A. Girouard, to whom she later referred as Dr. Girouard. He took her in his car to Winter Park to hear George Washington Carver, the African-American botanist and inventor. Crawford appreciated his kindly eyes and his attitude: "Dr Carver proved himself a genius but gave the Creator all the credit for his discoveries. Like the great artists he prayed & the results were Gods."[54] Later Girouard also took her to hear the deaf and blind Helen Keller. Crawford wrote, "Poor woman! She surely is an overcomer! She was amazing yet pathetic & though intensely interested I felt like crying the whole time."[55]

In March, Isabel Crawford made a decision. She had felt listless in Florida even before her sister's death, and now she knew she needed a change. She decided to go to California and stay if she liked it, return if she did not. She would travel by way of the Panama Canal. On March 22, 1938, she sailed from Miami to Havana, where she transferred to a ship bound for Los Angeles. Crawford reflected that the eight-hour trip through the canal "seemed to me like the journey of life with its ups & downs."[56]

On April 2, the ship reached Los Angeles, and a friend, Sophia Cain, met Crawford and took her to see to what might become her new residence, the Pacific Home for the Aged. At Crawford's request, Cain had visited the home earlier and sent a glowing report. Crawford spoke with the superintendent, who was about to leave for ten days. He agreed that she could spend that time making her decision before signing the papers and paying the required $4,600. Then an attendant took her to her room. Cain had described it enthusiastically. What she had failed to report was that the bathroom was equipped not with a tub but with a shower, a potential hazard since Crawford used crutches and could not safely stand without them. Crawford decided to try the accommodation anyway, but soon she discovered that there was no church close enough for her to walk to, and her two experiences in the shower frightened her. She left the home but remained in California until June. Then she began her bus trip back to Florida, where the Emriches were holding her apartment "hoping the prodigal will return!"[57]

On June 30, Crawford arrived in Clinton, Oklahoma, and for three weeks she visited at her brother's home. Then she went on to see her Kiowa friends. She was saddened by the changes she observed: "Saddle Mt Mission is not the Saddle Mt I left. The Indians surely have melted away. Some lie in

54. Ibid., 96.
55. Ibid., February 26, 1938, 98.
56. Journal 1938–39, March 25, 1938, 13.
57. Ibid., May 6, 1938, 20.

the little cemetery back of the church, some have turned Methodists & have become M. E. preachers to their people & others have joined 'The Church of God.' The splendid buildings are too many & too large now for the few who are left. Reverence has also departed, with Sabbath observance."[58] As she had done so often when she was a visitor, she mended and sewed as much as she could, to help out the Jackson family. Traveling on, Crawford visited Bacone College near Muskogee. There she was worried by some of what she saw on the campus, for the fashionably-dressed girls reminded her all too well of the returned students she had just seen at Saddle Mountain who bought pop and ice cream, and flirted, and played ball instead of coming to the religious services.

Crawford arrived back in Orlando on August 19, and in general her life was quiet. In July of 1939, Crawford went to Grimsby Beach. Her niece Eva had taken charge of the house and fruit farm. Isabel wrote, "She'll make a go of it."[59] Early in September she left for New York City. There she judged the New York World's Fair to be "the best managed of the four World Fairs I've attended—splendid out of doors restaurants seats & garbage holders galore & polite officials."[60]

Finally, on September 18, she arrived back in Orlando and spent a quiet season knitting, sewing, and reading. She attended church services and missionary meetings, and she visited with friends. When summer brought its hot weather, she headed north, making stops along the way as usual. Canada had entered the war the previous September, and Crawford reported, "At Niagara Falls Canada I had to leave the bus to be examined or questioned as if I were a German spy. I expected it, but not as much of it. I had credentials from Chicago but had to answer 101 questions beside. The official asked me everything except to be his wife."[61] Once more at Grimsby Beach she enjoyed the abundant fruit, and again she made herself useful by mending.

Crawford had long wanted to visit an Indian reservation in Canada, and at last her wish was granted, as she attended the one hundredth anniversary of the organization of the Indian Baptist church at Ohsweken on September 8. These Indians on the Six Nations Reserve were historically related to those among whom Crawford had worked in western New York, but her heart remained with the Kiowas of Oklahoma. She observed, "The Indians didn't look like mine. There were no artistic costumes on the men

58. Ibid., August 3, 1938, 41.
59. Ibid., July 8 1939, 67.
60. Ibid., 81.
61. Journal 1940–41, July 10, 1940, 19.

& women & the children were also in civilized garments. It seemed like a regular service with regular people at it."[62]

On October 14, thirteen family members sat around two tables at Grimsby Beach to share in their Thanksgiving dinner. The leaves were changing color, and she appreciated the beauty as never before. Then, when she looked out the window on the morning of November 7, she saw snow. She had seen snow during all the winters of her youth, but she had never observed its beauty as she did now.

She remained in Ontario for Christmas. On New Year's Day, many members of the Cline family gathered for a reunion. After that, Isabel and her niece Eva rushed to get ready for their departure, for Eva was to spend the winter with Isabel in Florida. They arrived in Orlando on January 9, 1941. The Emriches had been hard at work, and Crawford discovered a new carpet, freshly painted woodwork, a new gas stove, and much more. There was also a unique little wheelchair, made by Dr. Girouard, and Crawford was delighted with the ease with which she could maneuver. During the next weeks, Girouard took them sightseeing, allowing Isabel to share with Eva the things she had already enjoyed and also to explore places she had never seen before.

On February 8, the three left for a longer trip around Florida. For Crawford, the climax of the trip came at Okeechobee, where they met Willie King, a Baptist missionary. He made them welcome, and with him they went to a Seminole encampment. King began holding a service and then turned it over to Crawford. Girouard gave a talk and Crawford followed it "with a simple gospel message."[63] After an Indian dinner and a hearty invitation to return, the travelers left for home.

Early on the morning of Easter Sunday, April 13, Girouard arrived at Crawford's apartment, and the three headed back to the Okeechobee area. Willie King was waiting for them, and the Seminoles were ready. When the congregation was assembled, each of the three visitors spoke. Crawford wrote later, "No Indians responded but the promise of the Holy Spirit's power must follow the Word!"[64] After the service they ate dinner, and then Girouard, Crawford, and Cline drove back to Orlando. Crawford wrote, "It was a long drive but if one poor Seminole finds the resurrection light we felt it was worth while." On the day after Easter, Eva Cline left to return to Grimsby Beach.

---

62. Ibid., September 8, 1940, 27.
63. Ibid., February 16, 1940, 58.
64. Ibid., April 13, 1940, 68.

Crawford had received an invitation to attend the Northern Baptist Convention to be held in Wichita, Kansas, May twentieth through twenty-fifth of 1941. She left for the meeting by bus on May 10. Once more she demonstrated how she had kept in touch with a vast network of friends throughout the years, for she paid visits in Memphis, Little Rock, and Tulsa, before arriving in Wichita on May 19. One evening the program was a pageant, "Baptists Come to the Plains," and in it, Crawford was to present the Twenty-third Psalm. The platform held a tepee and some Indians—and a microphone. Crawford wrote, "When I started giving the Psalm the older Indians mixed up a bit & stared with all their eyes until I forgot the mike till an Indian moved it closer to me. I was more interested in giving the poor old Indians God's message than in interesting the audience."[65] The next day a woman said to Crawford's hostess, "I heard Miss Crawford give that Psalm years ago, when I was a girl & I never forgot her or it. The proxy was perfect even the voice sounded natural." When the hostess explained that she had just seen Crawford herself, the woman exclaimed, "Why I thought Miss Crawford passed away years ago." Crawford was in the memories of many, and they were delighted to see her in person. Afterwards she remarked, "There were 4570 delegates & I think 4500 shook my hand, squeezed one or patted me on the back."[66]

Crawford arrived in Clinton, Oklahoma, on May 26, in time to celebrate her seventy-sixth birthday and also, two days late, her brother's eightieth. She spent six weeks visiting with Hugh and his family. One day they went out to see Isabel's farm. To her horror, there was a large liquor advertisement nailed up on one of the posts. Hugh's son, Gordon, "smashed it into smithereens" at her command.[67] Next Isabel went to Saddle Mountain. She was warmly welcomed as usual, and she mended and sewed as usual, but some things had changed. She saw washing machines and a Frigidaire but, she wondered, "As to the Indians: Have they improved? I cannot answer. Most of them have been to Bacone, have nice bungalows, dress well, but alas! I see more autos than ploughs & more thistles than crop!"[68]

After a week in Saddle Mountain, Crawford went with the Saddle Mountain minister, Perry Jackson, to the Indian Baptist Assembly at Watonga. There Jackson was scheduled to preach the doctrinal sermon, but he "had a cold & 'cold feet,'" and asked Crawford to do it.[69] She first refused,

---

65. Journal 1941–42, 12.
66. Ibid., May 26, 1941, 15.
67. Ibid., 16.
68. Ibid., 18.
69. Ibid., 26

but she learned that all the missionaries wished it. Then she said, "All right. I don't preach—I'm a woman—but as for the doctrines of our faith I'm sound & can speak on any of them & will likely bring them all in." Afterwards one of the ministers told her that she should preach at all the rest of the meetings, but Crawford was touched most by the response of the Indians: "Every testimony after, referred to the sermon ? [sic] 'preached by a lady.' At the night meeting . . . an old Indian said 'A lady preached the doctrin' sermon this morning. The lady was inspired by God & gave us God's own message. . . . She is a lady but she preached a good doctrin' sermon we all understood. It was like good medicine to our souls. The Holy Spirit told her what to say & she is a lady woman.'"[70]

Following her stay in Oklahoma, Crawford headed for California, arriving in San Diego on the evening of July 29, 1941. Once again she was welcomed into the Kermott home, where she settled in for a month-long visit. Whenever she went out, Crawford noticed evidence of war even though the United States had not yet entered the hostilities. Then she left for Spokane, where again she stayed with friends. She spoke in Grace Baptist Church, and afterwards she wrote, "In the morning I happened to say that our treatment of the Indians might have given Bro Hitler the idea of taking land that didnt belong to him & conquering the natives & subduing them etc A woman near the front gasped to her neighbour 'Brother Hitler'! Reading her lips I said: 'Well isn't he a brother man?' The woman gasped again & at the close of the service came up to shake hands & ask how I knew what she said."[71]

From Spokane, Crawford went to Calgary, where she stayed in the home of Addie Clark and her daughter. Addie had been a student in Woodstock and her late husband a professor at the Canadian Literary Institute, so they pored over old albums and shared old memories. Now when Crawford went out, she was strongly aware that she was no longer in the United States, for everywhere she saw V for Victory: this was a country at war. Crawford went on to Brandon, Manitoba. There she made a trip to Rapid City and saw where Prairie College had once stood. There was nothing left but piles of stones; the building had been struck by lightning years before. Afterwards Crawford reflected, "I looked at the wreck, thought of father but did not cry. His broken heart & my deafened ears were hidden beneath the stones but the foundation stood & the uncompleted spire reached to Heaven."[72]

Crawford crossed back in to the Unites States and went once more to Rochester and the Mayo Clinic. She wrote that after a week's examination

---

70. Ibid., 30.
71. Ibid., 40.
72. Ibid., 55.

and treatment, she was declared "too healthy or tough to be cured."[73] Finally, after a visit with her nieces in Grimsby Beach and a meeting in Washington, Crawford headed to Orlando. On October 28, Alice Emrich and Dr. Girouard met her and took her to her apartment. For the next month, Crawford rested, caught up on her correspondence, and wrote of her trip.

On December 7, 1941, when Crawford learned the terrible news of the attack on Pearl Harbor, she wrote in her journal, "War! War! War! Why does the Heavenly Father allow it? Why does He deafen my ears & make me walk on crutches? I'm sure I could serve Him better unhindered yet He wills it otherwise so I'll just hobble along, grinning every chance I get, without hearing walking, or doubts. We must trust in His management no matter what happens."[74] In the weeks to come, she sent money to war relief rather than buying Christmas presents: "My trunk & my walls delivered up all the gifts I needed."[75]

Late in the winter, Crawford experienced her first wartime blackout. She wrote, "When the hour came I was comfortably in bed in the dark listening to the radio when a policeman tapped on the window. Light from the back of the radio was shining on the street! And the fine was to be $300 or 60 days imprisonment! I shut off the radio & thought out what things I'd take to the jail. I was delighted, for ever since I've been in Orlando I've wanted to teach a Bible Class. In jail I'll have one every day if I can. Good!"[76] They neither fined nor imprisoned her, however, and Crawford claimed that she was disappointed.

Orlando had more blackouts, and drunken and disorderly servicemen became common sights. Florida was "becoming a fort," and Crawford decided to "move on."[77] She would return to Ontario. Although she disliked the changes she was witnessing in Florida, she had an additional reason for her decision: "I simply can't be happy without friends & church work! I've lived here for 10 years & have found neither."[78] She was no longer able to walk the three blocks to church and then climb the many steps to the auditorium, and since Girouard had been stationed at Tampa, she felt increasingly isolated. Gradually she packed. Before her departure, she had a brief visit with her friend Jean Hendrie, who drove her past the building lot

73. Ibid., 62.
74. Journal 1940–41, December 7 1941, 74.
75. Ibid., December 21, 1941, 74.
76. Ibid., 81.
77. Ibid., April 5, 1942, 82.
78. Ibid., April 19, 1942, 97.

that Crawford had owned and sold. On April 19, 1942, Isabel Crawford left on another bus trip, this time to Grimsby Beach, to remain there.

13

At Home in Ontario

ISABEL CRAWFORD REACHED GRIMSBY Beach on April 28, 1942, to take up residence in the country of her birth. The five children of her sister Emily and her husband had inherited their parent's house, Elmcroft, with its three-acre fruit farm on the Niagara Peninsula. The two unmarried daughters, Eva and Miriam, bought out their brothers' and sister's interests. Eva gave up her job and took over management of the fruit ranch, and now Miriam had ended her work as a missionary and joined Eva at Elmcroft. Isabel came to live with them less than a month before her seventy-seventh birthday. Her possessions arrived early in June, to be stored until the house had proper space for its new occupant.

Elmcroft, Grimsby Beach, Ontario. Courtesy of Barbara Cross McKinnon.

The house was large, but it had two stories and Crawford could not easily climb the stairs, so builders were hired to construct a three-room addition to the lower level. They agreed that Crawford's word was as good as her signature, and no contract was signed. With war going on, it was difficult to obtain the necessary materials, but gradually the builders gathered the supplies and went to work. Three days after Christmas, the addition was ready, and Crawford moved into her new apartment. As she had done in Orlando, she set her large collection of Indian artifacts on display in her parlor.

Crawford enjoyed a peaceful spring and summer. She prepared the participants for an Indian pageant that was held in September on their Grimsby Beach lawn, and she went to Woodstock for the dedication of a new Sunday school building at the East End Mission where she had begun her Sunday-school-teaching career. A few nights later, she spoke at a meeting there, and the costumed pageant was included in the program. She concluded the pageant by presenting, once again, the Twenty-third Psalm in sign language.

On October 14, 1943, Isabel and Miriam went to Ottawa by train. There they were welcomed by Miriam's sister Helen and Helen's husband, Ewart Cross. Back in Toronto, they visited in the elegant home of Isabel's nephew Harold Firstbrook and his wife, with the nearby relatives joining them for an enjoyable evening. Miriam and Isabel returned to Grimsby Beach on October 27. This Christmas there was no family gathering, but Elmcroft entertained a few friends, and they celebrated with "gifts feasting fun and spiritual remembrances of the past."[1]

Isabel Crawford's life at Grimsby Beach was quiet, and by September of 1944 she described herself as "almost a shut in."[2] As her activities decreased, she recorded fewer events in her journal, but there were highlights. On July 1, 1944, she celebrated Canada's Dominion Day, and Miriam and Eva took her out in her new outdoors wheelchair. Elmcroft took in a few paying guests, and one of them invited Crawford to visit her in Toronto. Crawford enjoyed seeing "the sights," and her nephew Harold Firstbrook took her to Park Road Baptist Church, where she saw the window that was a memorial to Isabel's sister Fanny. They also went to Mount Pleasant Cemetery, which held the graves of her parents, her sister, and her brother-in-law. And Crawford and her nieces went to Woodstock. Crawford spoke at the East End Mission and attended a service at First Baptist Church, where she had been baptized.

---

1. Journal 1942–43, December 25, 1943, 38.
2. Journal 1944–46, 32.

On November 22, Dr. Girouard arrived in Grimsby Beach to assist Crawford as she went to Florida for the winter, for she no longer felt able to travel alone on crutches. In Orlando, Crawford visited the Emriches; then she went on to St. Petersburg. Crawford's doctor at the Mayo Clinic had suggested that the sunshine of the city would help her legs, but alas, in St. Petersburg the weather was damp, cloudy, and foggy. She had consolation, however, as she read about the deep snow blanketing the Grimsby area. In May, Crawford headed back to Grimsby Beach. On her birthday on May 26, 1945, she received gifts of stationery. She wrote, "will take the hint and 'stay put.'"[3]

Bookcase in Elmcroft, with Isabel Crawford's journals. Courtesy of Barbara Cross McKinnon.

3. Ibid., May 26, 1945, 67.

During the next months, Crawford ventured out from time to time, but for the most part she stayed in her comfortable apartment and worked on her journals. In September she went to Toronto for a medical appointment. The doctor's report said, "Bones in hip shrinking moving round in socket causing the pain. Nothing can be done." In her journal Crawford wrote, "I took the dose as if it had been a drink of water for I expected it. I will never walk again but my stockings will run."[4]

Crawford was eighty, and although her physical abilities were diminished, her curiosity and interest in the world remained as strong as ever. Like so many Canadian children, she had skated "just for fun" when she was a girl, but she wanted to see "real skating professionally demonstrated."[5] In February of 1946, Miriam was to go to Toronto on "Baptist business," and Eva and Isabel decided to take the bus with her, get a room at the YWCA, and attend a performance of the Ice Follies at Maple Leaf Gardens. Although they found obstacles along the way, they got to the show. There Crawford was unprepared for what she saw: "[T]he whole performance was a mixture of theatre, movie & anything but skating as I knew it. . . . Running jumping whirling on one foot made me gasp at first but as the programme continued I became accustomed to the dare-devil stunts & felt sure the ice wouldnt break and let anyone drown with a broken leg back or skull."[6] She did not get to bed until after midnight, but to her surprise, she "wasn't a bit tired though 'up & at it' all day."[7]

They returned to Grimsby Beach the next day. The outing had cost Isabel $21.55, for she had "treated" Eva. She wrote, "I had missed all 'funnies' the 37 years of my missionary career & won't likely be able to take in another so feel no uneasiness of conscience over the outlay."[8] Yet her reflection was an exaggeration, for her trip to the Ice Follies only continued (and in her mind concluded) a long-standing pattern of enjoying popular entertainment whenever she had the opportunity.

On May 25, 1946—one day early because her birthday fell on Sunday—Crawford celebrated her birthday with her two nieces, one nephew and his wife, and a few friends, and she gave gifts to all of them. Summer brought the usual procession of visitors to Elmcroft, and as soon as the fruit season ended, the church season began. In addition to bringing in the last of the crops and canning, Isabel's nieces attended choir practice and various

---

4. Ibid., September 24, 1945, 74.
5. Ibid., February 5, 1946, 83.
6. Ibid., 84–85.
7. Ibid., 86.
8. Ibid., 87.

meetings. Crawford was glad to be living a quieter life. She had given up teaching her Bible class, and on Sunday mornings she stayed in bed. She did not, however, fail to observe the day: she studied the Sunday school lesson and listened to church services on her radio. One week the preacher prayed "for all confined to their room from sickness or old age." The eighty-one-year old Isabel wrote, "Not me! I'm neither sick nor old. I can't walk, that's all. The legs are not me. They are only hangers on. I live above them."[9]

On New Year's Day of 1947, Isabel Crawford began a new journal. She recorded the visit of her nephew Gordon Cline and his wife on that day and the visit of her Bible class on January 12. After that, she wrote little more in her journal, but she did not set it aside. Into it she pasted some photos and many clippings reflecting her varied interests and also her literary tastes. As usual, she read: the journal contains long lists of her reading during 1947 and 1948, both fiction and non-fiction. And other things occupied Crawford. She and her nieces decided to sell the fruit farm and build a house in the town of Grimsby. The new home was specifically designed with wide doorways to accommodate Crawford's wheelchair, and when they moved to 26 Nelles Boulevard in 1948, she continued to have her own separate but connecting accommodation. Eva and Miriam no longer had the responsibilities of running the fruit farm and hosting summertime guests, and they were close to their church so they could easily attend their activities there.

Home on Nelles Boulevard, Grimsby, Ontario. Courtesy of Barbara Cross McKinnon.

9. Ibid., November 3, 1946, 95.

Crawford retained an interest in Baptist affairs, and she continued to reflect upon the past. In May of 1948, she wrote a letter to the editor of the American Baptist paper, the *Watchman Examiner*. After decades of silence, she felt that she should finally "let it be known publicly" why she had left Saddle Mountain.[10] She told the full story and ended with a plea that the church might revive what had become an "almost lost cause." She left it to the editor to decide whether to publish her account, and Crawford's collection retained only a carbon copy of her letter, not a clipping. The letter was not published, and so the world did not learn that Isabel Crawford had finally chosen to break her silence.

Also reflecting on the past, Crawford decided to write another book. She perused her journals; she obtained permission from the publisher to include excerpts from *Kiowa* and *Jolly Journal*; and she added experiences about which she had not previously written. In 1951, *Joyful Journey: Highlights on the High Way* was published by Judson Press which, in earlier years, had been the American Baptist Publication Society. In its final chapter, "Toward the End of the Trail," she wrote of the convenience of life in her present accommodations. Furthermore she explained, "I am able to 'hold up my head with the rest,' paying my share of the living expenses and contributing to the local church, not forgetting the Training School and the beloved Saddle Mountain Indian Church."[11]

Crawford had carefully retained and corrected her bulky set of journals, and she ensured that they would be preserved for posterity. To that end, she sent them to Chicago, to the Training School.[12] Not only would her legacy live in her three autobiographical writings: much more would be available in her journals, scrapbooks and notebooks. Despite her long silence, Crawford's side of the story of Saddle Mountain would be available for future readers.

In June of 1951, Crawford went with her nieces to the Northern Baptist Convention in Buffalo, the same city where she had attended the 1920 convention. Returning to Grimsby, she wrote a letter to the *Watchman Examiner* in which she commented on a pageant she had just seen: "I was especially pleased to see 'Dr. Morehouse.' A lot of us thought he should have married Miss Burdette, thus drawing the two Home Mission Societies closer together, but the only move they made was to sing, 'Blest be the tie that

---

10. May 1948 letter pasted inside the back cover of Isabel Crawford's copy of her *Jolly Journal*, Barbara Cross McKinnon collection.

11. Crawford, *Joyful Journey*, 173–74.

12. At the start of her 1947–48 Journal she wrote, "This journal is a continuation of the others in Chicago after the others were sent." She did not give the date, nor did she record when she did the preparation of her *Joyful Journey* manuscript.

binds,' on the same platform from different books. He used to say to her: 'You women raise all the money you can, give it to us, and we will spend it.' And she would reply: 'We can raise more money if we don't.'"[13]

Crawford's eyesight had deteriorated, and on October 4, 1951, she went to Toronto expecting to have a cataract removed from her one good eye. The specialist who examined her, however, discovered that a hemorrhage had taken place, so removing the cataract would have no benefit. In her journal she wrote, "It was a surprise & should have been a shock to me but as soon as I heard the verdict I said to myself, 'It wont beat me—deafness & the broken leg didn't & neither will this.'"[14]

Isabel Crawford in her room in Grimsby, Ontario. Courtesy of Barbara Cross McKinnon.

In August of 1952, she returned to Oklahoma for the sixtieth anniversary celebration of Rainy Mountain mission. She was in a wheelchair, and her vision was limited, but she addressed the group for more than an hour, recalling the humorous as well as the serious aspects of her life as a missionary in the early days.

Crawford also went to Chicago one more time. In June, 1953, the Baptist Missionary Training School was observing the sixtieth anniversary of the class of 1893, and Crawford was one of two surviving members. Her

13. Undated clipping in Journal 15 [1951], Barbara Cross McKinnon collection.
14. Ibid., October 4, 1951, Barbara Cross McKinnon collection.

niece Miriam accompanied Isabel to Chicago. Because of Crawford's very poor eyesight, the railroad gave Miriam a ticket at a much reduced rate. The missionary training school charged nothing for their six-day stay in a comfortable apartment, and Crawford was pleased with the economy of the trip. She spoke at two receptions, and Robert Beaven, president of the school, drove the two women to Wilmette, on the north side of Chicago, to see the Baha'i House of Worship there. The building had been completed in the year only a few months earlier, and Crawford pronounced it "the most artistic beautiful building my eyes have ever seen."[15]

During the next years, Eva Cline was diagnosed with cancer. As her condition worsened, she organized her possessions and her affairs in order to make things as easy as possible for her sister. She died on April 8, 1960, and was buried in Queen's Lawn Cemetery, Grimsby, beside her parents.

Isabel Crawford had drawn up a new will in August of 1954, making bequests to Miriam and Eva, and to both the Woman's American Baptist Home Mission Society and the Ministers and Missionaries Benefit Board of the American Baptist Convention. She revised it in May of 1956, leaving $30,000 to the Baptist groups and dividing the rest among the five Cline children. Then, after Eva Cline's death, Isabel directed that the residue of the estate go to her niece Miriam. The will requested that her remains be interred in the Indian cemetery at Saddle Mountain, with a simple marker giving the years of her birth and death, and with the statement "I Dwell Among Mine Own People." She was ready.

Eventually Isabel needed more care than Miriam could provide, and she moved into the Loch Sloy Nursing Home in Winona, a few miles from Grimsby. Miriam, too, left the Nelles Boulevard home, and she went to live with her sister, Helen Cross, in Port Credit, Ontario. Isabel Crawford died on November 18, 1861, at the age of ninety-six. She kept the promise she had made long years before to the Christians of Saddle Mountain: her body was returned to Saddle Mountain, with her niece Miriam accompanying her. There Isabel was buried among her "own people" near the graves of her first converts. The Baptist missionary James Treat officiated. The service was conducted primarily in English, but it included hymns in Kiowa. Isabel Crawford had worked to help the Kiowas of Saddle Mountain make Christianity their own faith; now in their own way they welcomed her back among her own people.

---

15. Notebook untitled [Miscellaneous 1950–53], June 17, 1953.

Epilogue

THE SADDLE MOUNTAIN BAPTIST Church closed later in 1961, the year of Isabel Crawford's death, but her memory lived on. In his introduction to the 1996 re-publication of Crawford's *Kiowa*, Clyde Ellis raised the question of why Crawford and her memoir "matter." They matter, he stated, "because of their place in the Kiowa community today. What she and the Saddle Mountain Kiowas did has become an integral part of Kiowa history that continues to be told and retold as part of a community-wide narrative."[1] When he conducted oral history interviews during the 1980s and 1990s, Ellis found many people who retained memories of Crawford and the history of the church. This was clear in a number of interviews done earlier, between 1967 and 1972,[2] and in his more recent visits to the area, Paul R. Dekar reported that the memory has persisted into the twenty-first century.[3]

In accounting for Isabel Crawford's unique relationship to the Kiowas, Linda Williams Reese observed that the Kiowas "clung to traditional patterns. They incorporated new ideas that they found valuable and discarded the rest."[4] Crawford had not separated herself from the Kiowas but had entered into their lives. From her they learned new ideas. Some they "found valuable," and they "discarded the rest." Thus, committed as she was to bringing "civilization" to the Kiowas, she also helped them to negotiate a difficult period in their history.

On Thanksgiving Day in 2004, I visited the Saddle Mountain cemetery and took a few pictures. Later I posted one on a web site and mapped its location. In October of 2008, I received a comment on the photograph by someone who lived nearby and had learned through conversation on my

1. *Kiowa*, xv–xvi.

2. The typescripts of these interviews are available in the Doris Duke Collection of American Indian Oral History, University of Oklahoma.

3. Interview with the author, June 2, 2008.

4. Reese, Women of Oklahoma, 141.

photo's page of my interest in Crawford. He closed his comment by stating "A great lady . . . so much of our history."⁵ Thus 102 years after she had left Saddle Mountain, I received simple but eloquent testimony to the place Isabel Crawford retained in the memory of her "own people."

---

5. Comment to the author, October 8, 2008. Ellipsis original.

Bibliography

ARCHIVAL SOURCES

Barbara Cross McKinnon collection, privately held, Guelph, ON.
Canadian Literary Institute Fonds, Box 701. Canadian Baptist Archives, McMaster Divinity College, Hamilton, ON.
Census Returns for 1861, Roll: C-1063. Library and Archives Canada; Ottawa, ON.
Crawford, Isabel Alice Hartley. Biographical Files. Board of International Ministries, American Baptist Historical Society, Atlanta, Georgia.
———. Correspondence. Katherine S. Westfall Files. American Baptist Home Mission Society & Woman's Home Mission Society. American Baptist Historical Society, Atlanta, Georgia.
———. Correspondence, Mary Burdette Files, American Baptist Home Mission Society & Woman's Home Mission Society, American Baptist Historical Society, Atlanta, Georgia.
———. Missionary, Journals and Diaries, 1891–[1954]. RG-1024, American Baptist Historical Society Manuscript Collections, Atlanta, Georgia.
Doris Duke American Indian Oral History, Western History Collections, University of Oklahoma, http://digital.libraries.ou.edu/whc/duke/browse.asp?sid=5.
Hilon A. Parker family papers, 1825–1953. William L. Clements Library, University of Michigan.
Minutes of the Workers' Conference and Oklahoma Baptist Indian Association, RG 252–27. American Baptist Home Mission Society. American Baptist Historical Society.

PUBLISHED WORKS

Adams, Samuel Hawley. *Life of Henry Foster, M.D.* Canandaigua, NY: Humphrey, 1921.
The Baptist Missionary Training School, 1881–1893. Donnelley & Sons, 1897.
Beaver, R. Pierce. *Church, State, and the American Indians.* St. Louis: Concordia, 1966.
Berkhofer, Robert F. Jr. *Salvation and the Savage: An Analysis of Protestant Missions and American Indian Response, 1787–1862.* New York: Atheneum, 1976.

BIBLIOGRAPHY

Berton, Pierre. *The Last Spike: The Great Railway 1881–1885*. Toronto: McClelland & Stewart, 1971.

Bowden, Henry Warner. *American Indians and Christian Missions: Studies in Cultural Conflict*. Chicago: University of Chicago Press, 1981.

Briggs, J. H. Y. *The English Baptists of the Nineteenth Century*. Didcot, UK: Baptist Historical Society, 1994.

Burdette, Mary G. *The Heroine of Saddle Mountain*. Chicago: R.R. Donnelley, 1903.

———. *Young Women among Blanket Indians: The Trio at Rainy Mountain 1892–1898*. Chicago: Woman's American Baptist Home Missions Society, [1910].

Clark, Blue. *Lone Wolf v. Hitchcock: Treaty Rights and Indian Law at the End of the Nineteenth Century*. Lincoln: University of Nebraska Press, 1994.

Corwin, Hugh D. *The Kiowa Indians: Their History and Life Stories*. Lawton, OK: printed by the author, 1958.

———. "Protestant Missionary Work among the Kiowas and Comanches." *Chronicles of Oklahoma* 46 (1968) 41–67.

———. "Saddle Mountain Mission and Church." *Chronicles of Oklahoma* 36 (1958) 118–30.

Craig, Terrence L. *The Missionary Lives: A Study in Canadian Missionary Biography and Autobiography*. Leiden: Brill, 1997.

Crawford, Isabel. *A Jolly Journal*. New York: Revell, 1932.

———. *Joyful Journey: Highlights on the High Way*. Philadelphia: Judson, 1951.

———. *Kiowa: The History of a Blanket Indian Mission*. New York: Revell, 1915. Reprinted as *Kiowa: A Woman Missionary in Indian Territory*, with introduction by Clyde Ellis, Lincoln: University of Nebraska Press, 1998.

Crawford, Suzanne J., and Dennis F. Kelley, eds. *American Indian Religious Traditions: An Encyclopedia*. Santa Barbara, CA: ABC-CLIO, 2005.

Cross, Anthony R., and Philip E. Thompson, eds. *Baptist Sacramentalism*. Waynesboro, GA: Paternoster, 2003.

Davis, John Edwin. *The Life Story of a Leper: Autobiography of John E. Davis, Missionary among the Telugus*. Toronto: Toronto Canadian Baptist Foreign Mission Board, 1917[?].

DeWolfe, Barbara. "Expressions of Assimilation?" *The Quarto* 32 (2009) 8–9.

Dick, Claribel Featherngill. *The Song Goes On: The Story of Ioleta Hunt McElhaney*. Philadelphia: Judson, 1959.

Ellis, Clyde. *To Change Them Forever: Indian Education at the Rainy Mountain Boarding School, 1893–1920*. Norman: University of Oklahoma Press, 1996.

———. "The Jesus Road at the Kiowa-Comanche-Apache Reservation." In *The Jesus Road: Kiowas, Christianity, and Indian Hymns*, edited by Luke Eric Lassiter et al., 17–68. Lincoln: University of Nebraska Press, 2002.

Gagan, Rosemary R. *A Sensitive Independence: Canadian Methodist Women Missionaries in Canada and the Orient, 1881–1925*. Montreal: McGill-Queen's University Press, 1992.

Galey, Mary. *The Grand Assembly: The Story of Life at the Colorado Chautauqua*. [Boulder, CO]: First Flatiron, 1981.

Garrett, James Leo Jr. *Baptist Theology: A Four-Century Study*. Macon, GA: Mercer University Press, 2009.

Gaskin, J. M. *Baptist Milestones in Oklahoma*. Oklahoma City, OK: Messenger, 1966.

Gibson, Theo T. *Robert Alexander Fyfe: His Contemporaries and His Influence.* Burlington, ON: Welch, 1988.
Gifford, James T., and Frederick Loren Gifford. *Clifton Springs through the Years.* Geneva, NY: Geneva Printing, 2006.
Hagan, William T. "Adjusting to the Opening of the Kiowa, Comanche, and Kiowa-Apache Reservation." In *The Plains Indians of the Twentieth Century*, edited by Peter Iverson, 11–30. Norman: University of Oklahoma Press, 1985.
Haines, Francis. *The Plains Indians: Their Origins, Migrations, and Cultural Development.* New York: Crowell, 1976.
Hayne, Coe. *Kiowa Turning.* New York: Council on Finance and Promotion of the Northern Baptist Convention, 1944.
Herring, Rebecca. "Their Work Was Never Done: Women Missionaries on the Kiowa-Comanche Reservation." *Chronicles of Oklahoma* 64 (1986) 68–83.
Hertzberg, Hazel W. *The Search for an American Indian Identity: Modern Pan-Indian Movements.* [Syracuse]: Syracuse University Press, 1971.
Hoxie, Frederick E. *A Final Promise: The Campaign to Assimilate the Indians, 1880–1920.* Lincoln: University of Nebraska Press, 1984. Reprint with new preface, Lincoln: Bison Books, 2001.
Huber, Mary Taylor, and Nancy C. Lutkehaus, eds. *Gendered Missions: Women and Men in Missionary Discourse and Practice.* Ann Arbor: University of Michigan Press, 1999.
Hull, Eleanor. *Women Who Carried the Good News: The History of the Woman's American Baptist Home Mission Society.* Valley Forge, PA: Judson, 1975.
Irwin, Lee, ed. *Native American Spirituality: A Critical Reader.* Lincoln: University of Nebraska Press, 2000.
Jewett, Robert. *Mission and Menace: Four Centuries of American Religious Zeal.* Minneapolis: Fortress, 2008.
Josephson, Robi. *Mohonk Mountain House and Preserve.* Charleston, SC: Arcadia, 2002.
Kracht, Benjamin R. "The Kiowa Ghost Dance, 1894–1916: An Unheralded Revitalization Movement." *Ethnohistory* 39 (1992) 452–77.
———. "Kiowa Religion in Historical Perspective." *American Indian Quarterly* 21 (1997) 15–33.
Lassiter, Luke Eric. *The Power of Kiowa Song.* Tucson: University of Arizona Press: 1998.
Leonard, Bill J. *Baptist Ways: A History.* Valley Forge, PA: Judson, 2003.
Luck, F. A., and G. P. Gilmour. *Cheltenham Baptist Church: Centennial Anniversary, 1844–1944.* Cheltenham, Canada: s.n., 1944.
Mardock, Robert Winston. *The Reformers and the American Indian.* Columbia: University of Missouri Press, 1971.
Marriott, Alice. *Kiowa Years: A Study in Culture Impact.* Anthropology Curriculum Study Project. New York: Macmillan, 1968.
Marsden, George M. *Fundamentalism and American Culture.* 2nd ed. Oxford: Oxford University Press, 2006.
Mathes, Valerie Sherer. *Helen Hunt Jackson and Her Indian Reform Legacy.* Austin: University of Texas Press, 1990.
———. "Nineteenth Century Women and Reform: The Women's National Indian Association." *American Indian Quarterly* 14 (1990) 1–18.
Mayhall, Mildred P. *The Kiowas.* Norman: University of Oklahoma Press, 1962.

McLaurin, C. C. *Pioneering in Western Canada: A Story of the Baptists*. Calgary, Canada: printed by the author, 1939.
McLeod, Tommy, "'To Bestir Themselves:' Canadian Baptists and the Origins of Brandon College." *Manitoba History* 56 (2007) 22–31.
Meadows, William C. *Kiowa Ethnography*. Austin: University of Texas Press, 2008.
Means, Florence Crannell. *Sunlight on the Hopi Mesas: The Story of Abigail E. Johnson*. Philadelphia: Judson, 1960.
Miller, Darlis A. *Captain Jack Crawford: Buckskin Poet, Scout, and Showman*. Albuquerque: University of New Mexico Press, 1993.
Milner, Clyde A., and Floyd A. O'Neil, eds. *Churchmen and the Western Indians, 1820–1890*. Norman: University of Oklahoma Press, 1985.
Mooney, James. *Calendar History of the Kiowa Indians*. Washington, DC: Smithsonian Institution, 1979.
Mondello, Salvatore. "Isabel Crawford: The Making of a Missionary, Part I." *Foundations* 21 (1978) 322–39.
———. "Isabel Crawford and the Kiowa Indians, Part II." *Foundations* 22 (1979) 28–42.
———. "Isabel Crawford, Champion of the American Indians, Part III." *Foundations* 22 (1979) 99–115.
Morrison, Tully. "Isabel Crawford: Missionary to the Kiowa Indians." *Chronicles of Oklahoma* 40 (1962) 76–78.
Muccigrosso, Robert. *Celebrating the New World: Chicago's Columbian Exposition of 1893*. Chicago: Dee, 1993.
Nelles, Frank. *Cheltenham: A Credit Valley Mill Town*. Cheltenham, Canada: Boston Mills, 1975.
Nitchie, Edward Bartlett. *Lip Reading Made Easy*. 1902. Reprint, Port Townsend, WA: Loompanics, 1985.
Oberg, Michael Leroy. *Native America: A History*. Chichester, UK: Wiley-Blackwell, 2010.
Pattison, John W. *Museum Musings: Brief Glimpses of Wingham's Past*. [Mildmay, Canada]: n.p., 1982.
Peterson, Linda H. *Traditions of Victorian Women's Autobiography: The Poetics and Politics of Life Writing*. Charlottesville: University Press of Virginia, 1999.
Pettem, Silvia. *Chautauqua Centennial, Boulder Colorado: A Hundred Years of Programs*. Boulder, CO: Book Lode and Colorado Chautauqua Association, 1998.
Pommersheim, Frank. *Broken Landscape: Indians, Indian Tribes, and the Constitution*. Oxford: Oxford University Press, 2009.
Printup, Bryan, and Neil Patterson Jr. *Tuscarora Nation*. Charleston, SC: Arcadia, 2007.
Prucha, Francis Paul. *American Indian Policy in Crisis: Christian Reformers and the Indian, 1865–1900*. Norman: University of Oklahoma Press, 1976.
———, ed. *Americanizing the American Indians*. Cambridge: Harvard University Press, 1973.
Rand, Jacki Thompson. *Kiowa Humanity and the Invasion of the State*. Lincoln: University of Nebraska Press, 2008.
Rawlyk, George A., ed. *Canadian Baptists and Christian Higher Education*. Montreal: McGill-Queen's University Press, 1988.
Reese, Linda Williams. *Women of Oklahoma, 1890–1920*. Norman: University of Oklahoma Press, 1997.

Rieser, Andrew C. *The Chautauqua Moment: Protestants, Progressives, and the Culture of Modern Liberalism*. New York: Columbia University Press, 2003.

Robert, Dana L., "The 'Christian Home' as a Cornerstone of Anglo-American Missionary Thought and Practice." In *Converting Colonialism: Visions and Realities in Mission History, 1706–1914*, edited by Dana L. Robert, 134–65. Grand Rapids: Eerdmans, 2008.

Rubin, Joan Shelley. *Songs of Ourselves: The Uses of Poetry in America*. Cambridge: Harvard University Press, 2007.

Sawtell, R. W. *The History of the First Baptist Church, Woodstock, Ont.* [Woodstock, Canada]: Woodstock Times, 1892. Reprint, BiblioLife, 2009.

Semple, Rhonda Anne. *Missionary Women: Gender, Professionalism, and the Victorian Idea of Christian Mission*. Rochester, NY: Boydell, 2003.

Thirty-six Years among Indians. Chicago: Woman's American Baptist Home Mission Society, 1914.

Thompson, Margaret Ellis. *The Baptist Story in Western Canada*. Calgary, Canada: Baptist Union of Western Canada, [1974].

Tinker, George E. *Missionary Conquest: The Gospel and Native American Cultural Genocide*. Minneapolis: Fortress, 1993.

Trennert, Robert A. "Mary A. Eldridge: Serving God and Country on the San Juan." *New Mexico Historical Review* 77 (2002) 145–72.

Wallace, Anthony F. C. *The Death and Rebirth of the Seneca*. New York: Knopf, 1970. Reprint, New York: Vintage, 1972.

Ward, Doris Cline. *Ancestry of Emily (Crawford) Cline*. Asheville, NC: Ward, 1998.

Wells, James Edward. *Life and Labors of Robert Alex. Fyfe, D. D.* Toronto: Gage & Company.

Whiteley, Marilyn Färdig. "Prairie College, Rapid City, Manitoba: The Failed Dream of John Crawford." *Historical Papers: Canadian Society of Church History* (2013) 85–97.

———. "The Question of Women's Leadership: Tensions in the Life and Thought of Isabel Crawford," *Historical Papers: Canadian Society of Church History* (2012) 41–51.

Wright, Muriel H. "Notes on Saddle Mountain Mission Church and Miss Isabel Crawford, Missionary." *Chronicles of Oklahoma* 36 (1958) 318–19.

Index

Italicized page numbers refer to illustrations.

Addams, Jane, 117
Aitsan, Amos, 112
Aitsan, Lucius, 69–71, 73, 76–77, 84, 86, 94, 97, 126–27
   and Lord's Supper, 85–86, 91, 95–96, 99
   and ministry, 93, 95–96, 110–11, 115
Aitsan, Mabel, 71, 73, 110–11
Allegany Indian Reservation, 119–20, 121–22
   See also Red House
American Baptist Home Mission Society, 2, 77–78, 89–90, 100–101, 105, 125, 128–29, 163–64, 166
Anadarko, 55–56
Anthony, Susan B., 47–48
Armenian massacres, 146–47

Bacone College, 161, 162, 183, 185
Baha'i House of Worship, 196
Bailey, Harry and Ina, 107–8, 169–70
Baldwin, Frank, 64, 66, 67, 73, 76
Ballew, Lauretta, 85–86, 92
Baptist Missionary Convention of Manitoba and the Northwest (1883), 26
Baptist Missionary Training School, 30, 39–45, 48, 49, 76, 126, 130, 194, 195–96
Bare, Kittie, 76, 78, 82–83, 85–86, 90–91, 156

Barnes, Lemuel C., 125, 128
Barnes, Mrs. L. K., 124, 129–30
Battle Cry of Peace (film), 118
Battle Hymn of the Republic, 48
Beaven, Robert, 196
Berry-au-Bac, 149–50
Bethlehem, 146
bison, 75–76, 94–95
Blarney Castle, 152–53
Blinkey, Harley, 133
Bonney, Mary, 72, 116
Brooks, Jessie, 166–67
Broughall, H. T., 127–29
Brougher, James Whitcomb, 157
buffalo, 75–76, 94–95
Buffalo Bill's Wild West, 107–8
Burdette, Mary Gertrude, 76, 83–84, 93, 101, 194–95
   at Baptist Missionary Training School, 7, 30–31, 39–41
   death, 102
   and Hopi mission, 80
   and Isabel Crawford's assignment, 49–51, 53
   Lord's Supper controversy, 87–90, 95, 97–99
   and move to Saddle Mountain, 70–71, 72
Burton Baptist Assembly Grounds, 140

Cain, Sophia, 182

California, 75–76, 113, 139–40, 142, 156–57, 182, 186
Canadian Literary Institute, 14, 18–19, 40, 186
Carlisle Indian Industrial School, 69, 116–17
Carson, Alexander, 11, 153
Carver, George Washington, 182
Castledawson, 10, 153
Castle of Chillon, 149
Cattaraugus Association of Baptist Churches, 127, 134
Cattaraugus Indian Reservation, 111, 119–21
Cavenaugh, John, 45
Century of Progress, 175–76
Chaddlesone, Sherman, 137, 160, 171
Chautauqua Associations, 110, 165
Chautauqua Institution, 110, 111, 117, 124, 137–38, 161, 163, 181
 liberalism at, 125–26, 132, 155
Cheltenham, 13–14
Cherokee Outlet, 54
Chicago, Isabel Crawford in, 40–48, 51–52, 117–18, 157, 175–76, 195
Chicago World's Fair. *See* Century of Progress; World Columbian Exposition
Chippewa Cree, 141–42
Chivers, Elijah Eynon, 89, 100–101
Church of Jesus Christ of Latter Day Saints, 94
Chute, Elbert and Sarah, 17–18, 139
circuses, 30, 66, 123
Clark, Addie, 186
Cleveland, Grover, 46–47
Clifton Springs Sanitarium, 103–4, *104*, 108
Cline, Emily. *See* Crawford, Emily
Cline, Eva, 183, 184, 189, 192–94, 196
Cline, Gordon, 170, 193
Cline, Helen (Mrs. Ewart Cross), 190, 196
Cline, Miriam, 189, 190, 192–94, 195–96
Cline, William Henry, 29, 88, 102, 154
Clouse, Howard, 71, 85, 89–91, 93, 97, 100–101

Cody, William (Buffalo Bill), 107–8
Colorado Chautauqua, 110
Coolidge, Calvin and Grace, 168
Cooper, C. C., 82, 90–91, 156
Corwin, Grace, 161
Corwin, Hugh D., 6
Craig, Terrence L., 7–8
Crawford, Edith, 13
Crawford, Emily Augusta (Mrs. William Henry Cline), 11–12, 29, 100, 102, 124, 154
 death, 181
 marriage, 29
 Prairie College, 20, 23–24
Crawford, Frances (Mrs. John Firstbrook), 12, 29, 29, 38–39, 100, 116, 122–24
 death, 130
 wedding, 26–27
Crawford, Frances Brown (mother of John Crawford), 10
Crawford, Gordon, 185
Crawford, Hugh (father of John Crawford), 10–11, 14
Crawford, Hugh Frederick (son of John and Sarah Crawford), 13, 20, *29*, 51
 in Oklahoma, 65, 82, 111, 131, 137, 142, 182, 185
Crawford, Isabel Alice Hartley, 29, 34, 42, 86, *106, 109, 114*, 138, 147, *170, 171, 173, 177, 178*
 and art, 148–49, 157
 birth and childhood, 13, 16–18
 call of, 7, 40–41, 102, 131
 church membership, 17, 138–39, 143, 175
 citizenship, 78
 deafness, 28, 47, 69, 105–6, 107, 108, 149, 150–51, 159, 173, 179
 death and burial, 1, 162, 196
 deputations work, content of presentations, 51, 61, 66–67, 72, 81 121
 deputations work, overscheduling, 111, 115–18, 140–41
 description, 6–7, 142
 dolls, 14–15, 145–46, *147*

INDEX

education, 16, 18, 21, 30–31, 39–45, 48
and fashion, 28, 47, 66, 100, 154–55
finances, 5, 131, 147, 157–59, 192, 196
and gender roles, 8, 40–41, 47–48, 53, 64, 78, 86–87, 94, 113, 156
as General Missionary for the Inland Empire, 116
health, 27–28, 103–4, 108, 140–41, 155–56, 186–87, 190, 192, 195–96
humor, 41, 58–59, 174
independent spirit, 8–9, 67, 128, 154–55
Indian advocacy, 61, 66–67, 72, 81, 121, 124
and Indian crafts, 114–15, 178, *191*
Indians, opinions of, 25, 49–51, 55, 59, 74, 114, 122–23, 183–84
injury and treatment, 168–70, 172–73, 176, 177, 178–79
journals, 3–8, 42, 58, 60–61, 101, 110, 179, *191*, 193, 194
land claim, 65, 111, 137, 185
Lord's Supper controversy, 87–99
and movies, 118, 139, 142, 155
painting, 35–37, 102, *103*
and Plains Indian sign language, 62, 76, 105, 107–8, 112
and popular entertainment, 66, 107–8, 176, 192
reading, 15–16, 59, 79–80, 102, 141, 157, 175, 193
resignations, 92, 96, 98, 134, 167, 169–70
and Roman Catholics, 43–44, 144, 148, 150
Sabbath observance, 81, 145, 183, 192
Saddle Mountain, later visits to, 110–11, 112, 116, 137, 159–60, 162–63, 167, 171, 174, 182–83, 185
Saddle Mountain, move to, 67, 68–71
silences, 4–5, 39–40, 65, 131, 194
as Sunday school teacher, 17–18, 24–25, 33, 175, 176, 193
and women's ministry, 8, 47–48, 53, 72, 86–87, 94, 121–22, 185–86
Crawford, John, 10–14, *12*, 16, 18
death, 44–45
Prairie College, 19–21, 23–27
St. Thomas, 28–30, 33–34, 36
Toronto, 38–39
Crawford, John Wallace (Capt. Jack), 102–3, 106–7, *107*, 118, 123
Crawford, Sarah Louise Hackett, 11–12, *12*, 14–16, 22–23, 151
death, 73–74
in St. Thomas, 30–32, 36
in Toronto, 38–39, 44
Crosby, Fanny, 107
Cross, Ewart, 190
Cross, Helen. *See* Cline, Helen
Curtis, Edward, 108–9

David (Michelangelo), 148
Davis, George B., 20, 23–24
Davis, Miss (Saddle Mountain assistant), 92
Dawes Severalty Act, 59–60
Dekar, Paul R., 197
Dionne quintuplets, 180–81
Donnelley, Naomi, 95
Dumot, 67, 74, 79, 81
Duncan, William, 115

East End Mission, 17–18, 21, 162, 190
Edinburgh, 11, 153
Egypt, 145
Elk Creek mission, 55–60, 61–65, 67, 88, 112, 162
agriculture at, 63–65
Ellis, Clyde, 197
Emrich, William and Alice, 176, 181, 184, 187, 191
England
and Crawford family, 11–12
Isabel Crawford in, 150–52
English Channel, flight over, 150–51
Evans, Herbert and Elizabeth, 149–50
Everts, Hattie, 54, 57, 59, 60, 61

evolution, theory of, 33–34, 132, 139, 154

First Mesa, 112
Firstbrook, Ada, 123
Firstbrook, Frances. See Crawford, Frances
Firstbrook, Harold, 190
Firstbrook, Jack, 117–18, 122–24
Firstbrook, John, 26–27, 30, 38–39, 122–24
Firstbrook, Mary, 123
Florida, 136–37, 168, 174–79, 181–84, 187–88, 191
Fogarty, William Frederick, 11, 151
Fosdick, Harry Emerson, 157
Foster, Henry, 103–4
France, 149–50
Friends of the Indian, 109–10, 116–17
fundamentalism, 7, 132, 154, 156–57
Fyfe, Robert Alexander, 14, 18–19

General Allotment Act, 59–60
General Conference on Fundamentals, 132
Ghost Dance, 70, 72–73, 141
Gilkey, Charles, 155
Girouard, A., 182, 184, 187, 191
Given, Julia, (Mrs. George Hunt), 55, 92, 95
Goodspeed, Edgar John, 155
Grand Canyon, 113, *114*,
Granger, William Alexander, 125
Grimsby, 193, *193*, *195*
Grimsby Beach
  residence of Isabel Crawford, *189*, 189–93
  visits to, 154, 161–62, 165, 170, 180, 183–84, 187

Hackett, Inez, 151
Handsome Lake, 120
Hayne, Coe, 165
Heckler, William, 176
Henderson, Melvin, 172–73, 176, 179
Hendrie, Jean, 168, 174–76, 187–88
Henson, Poindexter Smith, 41

Hicks, George, 55–56, 59, 62–63, 160, 162
Hosman, E. R., 91
Howe, Julia Ward, 48
Hubbard, Elbert, 102–3
Hunt, George, 92, 95
Hunt, Julia. See Julia Given
Hunter, Anna, 13, 30
Hunting Horse, 137
Huntley, G. W., 4–5, 39

Ice Follies, 192
Illinois Baptist Convention (1893), 52–53
Ireland
  and Crawford family, 10–12
  Isabel Crawford in, 152–53
Italy, 148

Jackson, Fillmore, 121, 127, 133–34, 155
Jackson, Helen Hunt, 59
Jackson, Perry, 162–63, *163*, 164–65, 166, 183, 185–86
Jayne, Mary, 161
Jerome Agreement, 59–60, 77, 79
Jerusalem, 146
Jolly Journal, 2, 165, 173, 174–75
Jones, Carter Helm, 115–16
Jones, Elmer, 133–34, 143
Jones, William Arthur, 77
Joyful Journey: Highlights on the High Way, 2, 6–7, 194
Jumbo (elephant), 30, 177

Kansas City Baptist Theological Seminary, 159, 161, 162–63, 166, 170–71, 173, *173*
Keller, Helen, 182
Kelley, John, 162
Kermott, George and Ida, 139, 172, 186
King, Willie, 184
Kinney, Bruce, 163–64, 166, 172, 174
Kiowa-Comanche-Apache Reservation, 54, 60, 77
Kiowas, 54, 120
  and agriculture, 63–64

assimilation, 56–57, 70, 71
clothing, 55–57, 70
customs of, 62
questions by, 58, 63
Kiowa, Story of a Blanket Indian Mission, 2, 6, 110, 116, 117
Kokom, 95
Komalty, 56–57, 58, 62

Lake Mohonk, 109–10, 116–17
Lancaster, Mr. and Mrs. W. D., 56, 61, 62
Laws, Curtis Lee, 132
Lebanon, 146–47
liberalism, 126, 132, 154, 156–57
Little, Mrs. M. B., 148, 149
London
   and Crawford family, 11–12
   Isabel Crawford in, 151–52
Lone Wolf, Mrs., 65, *171*
Lone Wolf the Elder, 55n3
Lord's Supper controversy, 87–99, 121–22, 161, 163–64
Louvain, 150
Louvre, The, 149
Ludlum, W. D., 169

MacVicar, Malcolm, 26
Malines, 150
Mathews, Shailer, 125–26, 132
Mayo Clinic, 155–56, 172–73, 176, 179, 186–87
McDonald, Alexander, 19, 26
McKillen, George, 153
McLean, Mary, 73, 76, 78, 80, 112–13
McPherson, Aimee Semple, 139–40
Medicine Lodge Treaty, 79
Meyerding, Henry, 176
Mokeen, 69, 126–27, 167
Montana, 116, 141
Moody, Dwight, 45–46
Moorhead, John J., 169
Morehouse, Henry Lyman, 101, 105, 194–95
Mormon Church, 94
Morris, Robert H., 177
Morrison, Tully, 5–6
Mount Dora, 168, 175

Murrow, Joseph Samuel, 56, 69, 73, 84, 88, 96, 161

Nep (the Crawfords' dog), 32, *32*
New York City, 105–8, 168–69
New York World's Fair (1939), 183
Nitchie, Edward Bartlett, 105–6
Norcutt, Clara, 137, 140, 165–67
North Dakota, Isabel Crawford in, 28–37, 135
Northern Baptist Convention
   1920 (Buffalo), 132
   1927 (Chicago), 157
   1941 (Wichita), 185
   1951 (Buffalo), 194–95
Nuveen, Ida, 105

Odlepaugh, 88–89, 96,
Okeechobee, 184
Oklahoma Indian Baptist Association, 91, 93, 95–96, 98, 161, 162–64
Onko, John, 162
Orlando, 176, 178, 181, 183, 184

Pacific Home for the Aged, 182
Paddack, Clair, 179–80
Palmer, Bertha Honoré, 47
Panama, Canal, 182
Paradise Valley Sanitarium, 172
Parker, Grace Rowley, 83–84, 99, 136, 142, 145, 148, 151–52
Parker, Hilon, 80, 83–84, 99, 136
Plains Indian sign language, 62, 76, 107–8
Pledge of Allegiance, 46
Post Graduate Hospital, 169
Prairie College, 19–21, 23–28, 186
Pratt, Richard H., 116–17
Presbyterians, 10, 127–28, 155

quinine, 28, 149
Quinton, Amelia, 80, 116

Rainy Mountain mission, 5–6, 56, 64–65, 76, 84, 85, 88, 89, 112, 137, 195
Rairden, Nelson, 89–90, 97, 99, 100–101

Ramona, 59
Randlett, James, 77, 83
Rapid City, 20, 24–25, 27, 186
Red House, 121–23, 132–33, *133*, 136–38
   later visits by Isabel Crawford, 142–43, 154–55, 161, 170, 181
   problem of native pastor, 127, 133–34
   proposal to close, 127–29
Reese, Linda Williams, 197
Reeside, Marietta, 55, 85–86
Reformation Wall (Geneva), 149
Revell, Fleming H. Jr., 174–75
Robin Hood (film), 139
Robinson, Corrine Roosevelt, 130
Rocky Boy Reservation, 141–42
Roman Catholic Church, 43–44, 144, 148, 150
Roosevelt, Theodore, 130
Rosetta Stone, 151
Rychen, Harriet, 66, 94–95, 110, 142, 155, 157–58, 179–80
   at Chautauqua, 111, 137
   death, 161–62

Sabbath observance, 10, 81, 145
Saddle Mountain Baptist Church, *84*, 138–39, 159–60, 197
   baptisms, 84
   church dedication, 83–84, *83*
   church opening, 82
   departure of Isabel Crawford, 98–99
   Lord's Supper, 85–86
   Lord's Supper controversy, 87–99
   minister, 92–93, 95–96, 111, 115, 126–27, 160, 162
Saddle Mountain mission
   baptisms, 71, 73
   china painting, 75, 78
   church building, 75, 77–78, 79, 81–82
   church building fund, 72–73, 75, 80
   church opening, 82
   Lord's Supper, 85–86
   missionary society, 74
   self-reliance, 64–65, 75–77, 82–83
Salamanca. *See* Red House

San Francisco
   bison, 75–76
   missionary convention, 76
Scopes Trial, 154
Scotland
   and Crawford family, 10–11
   Isabel Crawford in, 153
Sea of Galilee, 146
Second Mesa, 80, 112–13
Seminoles, 184
Senecas, 119–20
Shaw, Anna Howard, 47
Sistine Chapel, 148
Six Nations Reserve, 183–84
Smiley, Albert, 109–10
Smith, Frank, 163–64, 166
Smith, Mrs. Charles, 115
Society of American Indians, 111
Sousa, John Philip, 46
Southern Baptist Convention, concern regarding, 89, 91, 163–64
Spurgeon, Charles, 51, 151
Stone, Lucy, 48
Stratford-upon-Avon, 152
St. Petersburg, 191
Strong, Augustus, 88, 91, 93, 96
St. Thomas, 26, 28–29, 33, 35–37, 135
Sunday, Billy, 123
Sunlight Mission, 80, 112–13
Surrat, Walter, 152
Switzerland, 148–49

Taber, Mary, 165
Ten Commandments (film), 142
Three Graces (Jean-Baptiste Regnault), 149
Tonawanda Indian Reservation, 119–20
Topping, Maggie, 110, 161
Toronto, 30–31, 38–39, 122–23, 190, 192, 195
Treat, Harry H., 111
Treat, James, 196
Tuscarora Indian Reservation, 71–72, 102, 119–20, 124, 127–28
Twenty-Third Psalm, 76, 105, *106*, 108, 112, 185

Vanishing American (film), 155
Van Ness, Martha, 61
Venus de Milo, 149

Waif's Mission (Chicago), 44
Waldo, Jennie, 34–35
Waldo, William A., 4–5, 39–40
Wallace, Anthony, 120
Walquist, Carl and Hulda, 126, 129, 136, 142, 181
Ward, Henry, 128–29
Washington (state), 116
Watchman Examiner, 132, 194
Westfall, Katherine, 115, 118, 123–24, 130, 134, 156–59, 160, 164, 169–70
Wingham, 38
Woman's American Baptist Home Mission Society, 118, 122–23, 126, 131, 156–59, 164, 166–67, 196
Women's Baptist Home Mission Society, 49–51, 61, 70–71, 77–78, 83, 94, 95, 98–99, 105
Women's National Indian Association, 72, 80, 116
Woodstock, 14, 15, 17–19, 21, 162, 180, 190
World in Cincinnati (1912), 112
World's Columbian Exposition, 46–48, 51–52, 145, 175–76
World's Congress of Representative Women, 8, 47–48
World's Parliament of Religions, 51–52
World War I, 116, 117–18, 122, 126, 149–50
World War II, 183, 186, 187
Wright, Ora Campbell, 140–41

Yosemite National Park, 114

Zotom, Paul and Mary, 67, 68, 70

www.ingramcontent.com/pod-product-compliance
Lightning Source LLC
Chambersburg PA
CBHW062026220426
43662CB00010B/1488